P9-BYV-363

OFF THE BEATEN PATH®
FLORIDA →

BRAINERD MEMORIAL LIBRARY
920 Saybrook Road
Haddam, CT 06438

Help Us Keep This Guide Up to Date

We would love to hear from you concerning your experiences with this guide and how you feel it could be improved and kept up to date. Please send your comments and suggestions to:

editorial@GlobePequot.com

Thanks for your input, and happy travels!

OFF THE BEATEN PATH® SERIES

ELEVENTH EDITION

OFF THE BEATEN PATH®
FLORIDA ➡

A GUIDE TO UNIQUE PLACES

DIANA & BILL GLEASNER

gpp®
travel

Guilford, Connecticut

To Ed and Susan Cottle—Intrepid Florida Explorers
And to our noble assistants, Bob and Carole Rowell

All the information in this guidebook is subject to change. We recommend that you call ahead to obtain current information before traveling.

To buy books in quantity for corporate use
or incentives, call **(800) 962-0973**
or e-mail **premiums@GlobePequot.com.**

Copyright © 2012 Morris Book Publishing, LLC

ALL RIGHTS RESERVED. No part of this book may be reproduced or transmitted in any form by any means, electronic or mechanical, including photocopying and recording, or by any information storage and retrieval system, except as may be expressly permitted in writing from the publisher. Requests for permission should be addressed to Globe Pequot Press, Attn: Rights and Permissions Department, PO Box 480, Guilford, CT 06437.

Off the Beaten Path is a registered trademark of Morris Book Publishing, LLC.

Editor: Amy Lyons
Project Editor: Heather Santiago
Layout: Joanna Beyer
Text design: Linda Loiewski
Maps: Equator Graphics © Morris Book Publishing, LLC

ISSN 1539-0845
ISBN 978-0-7627-7310-7

Printed in the United States of America
10 9 8 7 6 5 4 3

Contents

About the Authors

Diana and Bill Gleasner, an award-winning writer/photographer team, have 35 published books to their credit, including the popular *Popoki* series for children, as well as hundreds of articles for national and international magazines and newspapers. As professional travel photojournalists who have roamed the globe in search of fascinating travel experiences, they admit a continuing addiction to Florida. The Gleasners are members of the Society of American Travel Writers and the Travel Journalists Guild.

Introduction

Warning! Straying from the beaten interstate can be addictive. But is it ever fun!

By poking and prowling around this incredible state, we discovered a high-rise for bats, the world's smallest police station, a McDonald's complete with salt licks and hitching posts, and a museum dedicated to the inventor of air-conditioning.

Florida seems to have cornered the "world's largest" market. We saw the largest concentration of saw grass; the largest bald cypress tree; and the largest collections of Frank Lloyd Wright buildings, Art Deco buildings, Salvador Dalí artworks, and Tiffany glass in the world. We even strolled the world's longest continuous sidewalk.

We traveled by inner tube, pontoon boat, car, motor home, houseboat, sailboat, seaplane, canoe, motorized gondola, swamp buggy, and airboat. Our meanderings took us through Little Havana, the Greek community of Tarpon Springs, and a Miccosukee Indian village.

We heard a dolphin take a deep breath in the Everglades, toured a thoroughbred farm, and chatted with a cow hunter rounding up one of the few remaining herds of scrub cattle in existence. We saw manatees, wood storks, a herd of buffalo, and alligators romping in the surf!

We slept in a lighthouse, cheered ourselves hoarse at a rodeo, hunted for fossil shark teeth, lunched in an indoor swimming pool (luckily for us, it was dry), nibbled on alligator tail (lucky for us, it was no longer connected to the animal), and pitched a tent on more than a few of the Ten Thousand Islands.

In short, we have enjoyed an abundance of serendipitous experiences. But there are many more discoveries waiting to be made in Florida. Write us (c/o Globe Pequot Press, PO Box 480, Guilford, CT 06437, or editorial@Globe Pequot.com) and tell us your special finds.

Travel safely and have a terrific time!

Florida Facts

Name: Discoverer Ponce de León named it "Florida," the Land of Flowers, for its abundant flora.

Official nickname: The Sunshine State

Location: Southeastern US. Florida's southern tip is 1,700 miles (2,742 kilometers) north of the equator.

History: Florida has belonged to five different nations: Spain, England, France, the Confederacy, and the US.

Pensacola

NORTHWEST
FLORIDA ★Tallahassee

Jacksonville

NORTHEAST
FLORIDA

Orlando

C E N T R A L
F L O R I D A

Tampa

Sarasota

SOUTHEAST
FLORIDA

SOUTHWEST
FLORIDA

Miami

THE KEYS

State capital: Tallahassee was selected as the capital in 1824—a compromise between Pensacola in west Florida and St. Augustine on the east coast.

Population: With more than 18 million people, Florida is the fourth-most populous state in the US after California, Texas, and New York. The population increased 17.6 percent from 2000 to 2010. The largest concentration of Finns (17,000) outside of Finland lives in the Lake Worth/Lantana area. When asked where they would most like to live other than their current residence, most Americans made Florida their first choice.

Time: Most of Florida is in the eastern time zone. The area west of the Apalachicola River is in the central time zone.

Weather: Abundant sunshine, pleasant coastal breezes during summer months, and 53 inches of annual rainfall.

Average annual temperatures: Summer: 80.5 degrees Fahrenheit in north Florida and 82.7 in south Florida. Winter: 53 degrees Fahrenheit in north Florida and 68.5 in south Florida.

Geography: Total area is 58,560 square miles. From Pensacola to the southernmost point of Key West is 832 miles (1,342 kilometers).

Lakes: Florida is sprinkled with more than 7,800 lakes, ranging in size from an acre to the 448,000-acre Lake Okeechobee, the second-largest freshwater lake in the US.

Rivers: Florida has 34 major rivers. Certainly one of the best-known rivers (thanks to Stephen Foster's song "Old Folks at Home") is the Suwannee, in the northern part of the state.

Springs: There are 320 known springs in the state and 27 are classified as "first magnitude." First magnitude springs produce at least 100 cubic feet of freshwater per second. One of the longest underwater cave systems in the continental US (over 28,000 feet), Peacock Springs State Recreation Area is a popular place for cave diving.

Beaches: A beach is no more than 60 miles (96.7 kilometers) away no matter where you are in Florida. Sand beaches account for 1,200 miles (1,935 kilometers) of the state's 1,800 miles (2,903 kilometers) of coastline. Florida's beaches are rated among the finest in the country by University of Maryland coastal geologist Stephen Leatherman, who researches and rates the nation's beaches on 40 criteria.

Shoreline: Florida has more tidal shoreline than any other state except Alaska.

Islands: Florida has 4,510 islands that are 10 acres or more in size, more than any state except Alaska.

Elevations: Florida's highest point is Britton Hill, at 345 feet, near DeFuniak Springs (Walton County) in the northwest section of the state.

Tourism: Tourism is the state's number-one industry, followed by agriculture. In 2010, 82.6 million tourists visited Florida.

National parks: Florida has three national parks. Biscayne National Park has more than 180,000 acres of water. Here too is evidence of 10,000 years of human history, from pirates and shipwrecks to pineapple farmers and presidents. Everglades National Park, with more than 1.4 million acres, is the largest subtropical wilderness in the US. Dry Tortugas National Park in Key West, located 70 miles west of Key West, is an isolated outpost set apart from the mainland by the expansive waters of the Gulf of Mexico.

National forests: Florida's four national forests—Apalachicola (including Choctawhatchee), Osceola, Florida National Scenic Trail, and Ocala— cover more than 1 million acres. Nearly half the state is covered with uninhabited forests.

National sanctuary: Florida Keys Marine Sanctuary, the largest US marine sanctuary, covering 2,600 nautical square miles, extends from Biscayne National Park south to Fort Jefferson National Monument and northward to Everglades National Park on the tip of the Florida peninsula.

State parks: Florida's park system, consisting of more than 100 recreational areas, is one of the finest in the nation. All state parks have varying entrance fees, and open at 8 a.m. and close at sunset year-round.

Seaports: The Port of Miami is the busiest cruise port in the world, serving over 3 million passengers per year, which is ⅔ of the world's cruise-ship passengers.

Professional sports: Professional sports franchises in the state include:

- **National Football League:** Miami Dolphins, Tampa Bay Buccaneers, and Jacksonville Jaguars.

- **Arena Football:** Orlando Predators, Jacksonville Sharks, and Tampa Bay Storm.

- **National Basketball Association:** Miami Heat and Orlando Magic.

- **Major League Baseball:** Florida Marlins and Tampa Bay Devil Rays.

- **National Hockey League:** Tampa Bay Lightning and Florida Panthers.

Daily Newspapers

More than 150,000 circulation: *St. Petersburg Times* (www.sptimes.com); *Orlando Sentinel* (www.orlandosentinel.com); *Miami Herald* (www.herald.com).

100,000 to 150,000 circulation: *South Florida Sun-Sentinel* (www.sun-sentinel.com); *Tampa Tribune* (www.tampatrib.com); *Florida Times-Union* (www.jacksonville.com); *Palm Beach Post* (www.palmbeachpost.com).

Transportation

Car: Florida has spent far more money on highways than on mass transit, so it should come as no surprise that while public transportation opportunities are limited, the roads are excellent. The best way to travel in Florida is by car, and major airports have extensive fleets of rental cars with economical rates. Recreational vehicles (RVs) are also available for rent. Often the most economical way to vacation in Florida is a package deal that includes car rental and/or lodging with the cost of the flight.

Train: Amtrak serves Florida from both the East and West Coasts of the US. There are over 30 Amtrak stations, including ones in the following cities: Pensacola, Tallahassee, Jacksonville, Ocala, Sanford, Orlando, Tampa, West Palm Beach, Fort Lauderdale, and Miami. A rail pass providing unlimited travel during a certain period of time must be purchased from an Amtrak agent before arrival. Amtrak buses, known as "Thruway" buses, run from Winter Haven, near Orlando, to Fort Myers via St. Petersburg and Sarasota to connect with Amtrak rail services. Amtrak's Auto Train, for visitors who want to travel by train and then have use of their own car when they arrive, runs daily from Virginia to Sanford. For information on all rail service to Florida, call Amtrak toll-free at (800) USA-RAIL (872-7245), or visit the company's website at www.amtrak.com. Tri-Rail, linking 15 stations between Miami and West Palm Beach, runs frequently during the week, less often on weekends. Call (800) TRI-RAIL (874-7245) or visit www.tri-rail.com for more information.

Bus: Greyhound buses usually offer the best value in public transportation, and passes purchased in advance provide unlimited travel for set periods of time. Call (800) 231-2222 for more information, or visit www.greyhound.com.

For More Information

State parks: State Park Information Center, 3900 Commonwealth Blvd., Tallahassee; (850) 245-2157; www.floridastateparks.org.

State forests: Florida Division of Forestry, 3125 Conner Blvd., Tallahassee; (850) 488-6611; www.fl-dof.com.

Historical sites: Division of Historical Resources, Florida Department of State, R. A. Gray Building, 500 S. Bronough St., Tallahassee; (850) 245-6300; www.flheritage.com.

Attractions: Florida Attractions Association, 1114 N. Gadsden St., Tallahassee; (850) 222-2885; www.floridaattractions.org.

Sports: Florida Sports Foundation, 2930 Kerry Forest Pkwy., Tallahassee; (850) 488-8347; www.flasports.com.

Accommodations: Florida Hotel & Motel Association; www.fl-motels-review.com.

Florida Bed and Breakfast Inns: (877) 303-FBBI (3224); www.florida-inns.com or www.fl-bnb-review.com.

General information: Florida Chamber of Commerce, 136 S. Bronough St., PO Box 11309, Tallahassee 32302-3309; (850) 521-1200; www.fl chamber.com.

Vacationers planning a trip to Florida may receive a free official *Florida Vacation Guide* by contacting Visit Florida, 2540 W. Executive Center Circle, Ste. 200, Tallahassee; calling (850) 205-3865; or visiting www.visitflorida.com.

Please Note

Free attractions are noted; otherwise, expect an admission fee.

NORTHEAST FLORIDA

Curiosity and a sense of adventure will take you a long way. Oh yes, and an appetite. Each new edition of *Florida Off the Beaten Path* gives us a chance to make new discoveries and revisit longtime favorites. Our latest trip into the Sunshine State treated us to a wealth of things to see and do (and eat!). If you crave char-grilled crocodile, now you know where to go. (Hint: Check out Clark's Fish Camp and Seafood Restaurant.)

We discovered such treasures as we investigated the northeast section of the state. Looking for romance? Ponce Inlet Light Station is Florida's tallest lighthouse, but it may also be the most romantic, especially if you take advantage of the "Climb to the Moon" event. Plan your trip to Kanapaha Botanical Gardens in the summer, when the place explodes with color. Micanopy is a whole other world of rare books and fine antiques. (Hint: Bring money.)

For leisurely exploration, it's hard to beat an old, ocean-hugging route like SR A1A. Amelia Island, at the northern border of Florida, was the state's first resort destination. The southernmost in a chain of large barrier islands known as the Golden Isles, Amelia's beauty includes both expansive beaches with rolling dunes and lush interior forests.

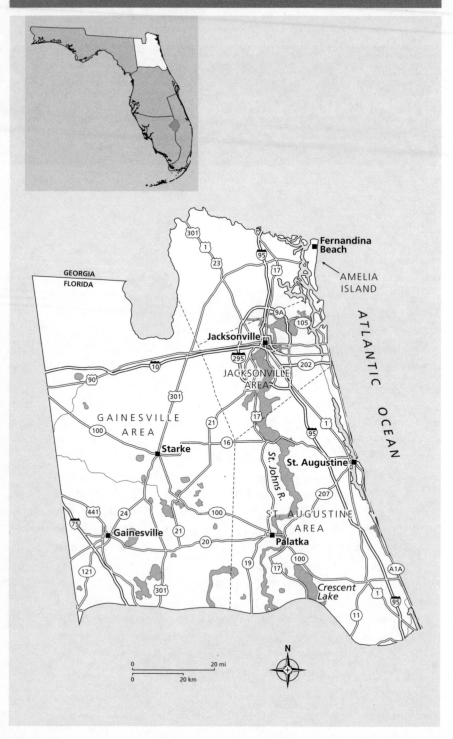

Continue south on SR A1A, via the Mayport ferry (a 10-minute ride across the St. Johns River), to Jacksonville and St. Augustine. After Bulow Plantation ruins (south of Palm Coast), turn inland via SR 100 to Palatka. Follow SR 20 to the Gainesville area, then take I-75 northward to O'Leno State Park and Ichetucknee Springs.

Amelia Island

Amelia Island, with its 13 miles of uncrowded sandy beaches, has already been discovered. In fact, it is the only US location to have been under eight different flags: French, Spanish, British, American Patriots (1812), Green Cross of Florida (1817), Mexican, Confederate, and American.

The resident Timucuan Indians' simple life was disrupted first by the French in the 16th century and then by the Spanish. The Union Jack was raised in 1763, but the Tories who converged on the island during the Revolutionary War left when Florida was ceded to Spain. A military adventurer, General Sir Gregor MacGregor, captured the island and claimed it as his own for a brief time but was ousted by a pirate who took over, ostensibly for Mexico. After the US government took formal possession, the claim was disputed by the Confederacy, which raised its flag here during the Civil War.

ameliaisland

"It is a place wonderfull fertill, and of strong scituation, the ground fat so that it is lekely that it would bring fourthe wheate and all other corn twise a yeare . . . yt is a country full of havens, rivers and islands of suche frutefullnes as cannot with tonge be expressed . . . the fairest, frute-fullest and pleasantest of all the worlde . . . ."

— Jan Ribaut, French colonizer, 1563

Federal occupation during the Civil War triggered a tourist boom. This, with an impressive flow of money created by the shipping business, made Fernandina Beach a prosperous community. Before long, handsome Victorian homes lined the residential streets. These architectural gems, dating from 1857 and ranging in style from old steamboat Gothic to Queen Anne, earned the 30-block Old Town district, also known as **Centre Street Fernandina,** a listing on the National Register of Historic Places. Be sure to stop at the chamber of commerce near the city docks for walking or driving tour directions to this gingerbread seaport.

It was from these docks that the country's first offshore shrimp trawlers sailed early in the 20th century. Be sure to be at the docks at sunset to watch the shrimping fleet return with the day's catch.

TOP EVENTS IN NORTHEAST FLORIDA

Hoggetowne Medieval Faire,
Gainesville, February, (352) 334-5064,
www.gvlculturalaffairs.org

Gatornationals (drag-racing spectacle),
Gainesville, March, Gainesville racetrack, (352) 377-0046; Gainesville Visitors Bureau, (866) 778-5002, www.visitgainesville.net

Isle of Eight Flags Shrimp Festival,
Fernandina Beach, May, (866) 4-AMELIA (426-3542), www.shrimpfestival.com

St. Augustine Birthday Festival
(since 1565),
St. Augustine, September, (904) 829-1711, www.visitoldcity.com

British Night Watch and Grande Illumination,
St. Augustine, December, (904) 825-1004, www.britishnightwatch.org

Stroll past the old *Palace Saloon,* or better yet, stop in to inspect its splendid carved mahogany bar, which a reliable source has called "the best bar east of Boise." Open noon to 2 a.m. daily. The Palace Saloon is at 117 Centre St., Fernandina Beach; (904) 491-3332.

Historic Centre Street bristles with fascinating shops and boutiques. *The Ships Lantern* (210 Centre St., Fernandina Beach; 904-261-5821) offers a fine selection of paintings, prints, woodcarvings, scrimshaw, jewelry made from shark teeth found in the area, and "lots of pirate stuff." Open 10 a.m. to 9 p.m. daily (may close earlier depending on how busy it is downtown).

Even if you can't stay in the *Bailey House,* be sure to take a good look at this 1895 Victorian former bed-and-breakfast inn in the heart of the historic district. Its turrets, gables, bays, fish-scale decoration, and stained-glass windows make it a showcase. No wonder it cost $10,000 to build—an outrageous amount in 1895! The Bailey House is at 28 S. 7th St., Amelia Island.

Fort Clinch State Park on Atlantic Ave. in Fernandina Beach welcomes visitors to the most northeasterly point in Florida. Its European-style brick masonry is unique in this country, and you'll get a splendid view of the Atlantic Ocean and Georgia's Cumberland Island from the fort's ramparts. On the first full weekend of every month, rangers and

piratesand smugglers

President James Monroe once called Fernandina Beach a "festering fleshpot" because of the pirates and smugglers who anchored there. Later it became Florida's first resort.

volunteers reenact the 1864 occupation in full period costume. The park's rec-reation facilities include saltwater fishing along a 1,500-foot-long lighted pier, swimming, camping, picnicking, mountain biking (6-mile trail), and hiking. The park opens at 8 a.m. and closes at sunset daily year-round. Fort Clinch State Park, 2601 Atlantic Ave., Fernandina Beach; (904) 277-7274; www.floridastate parks.org.

If you've always wanted to *stay in a lighthouse* right on the beach, this is your chance. Rent all four floors, which include three bedrooms (sleeps up to eight total), two and a half baths, a kitchen and dining area, and an obser-vation deck for expansive viewing of the great Atlantic Ocean. Wallpapered in nautical charts, this is the place for faraway dreams. Breakfast and the morn-ing paper are delivered to your door. The lighthouse is on the ocean side of SR A1A on the northern end of Amelia Island. Write to Amelia Island Lodging Systems, 98 S. Fletcher, Amelia Island; call (904) 277-4851 or (800) 772-3359; or visit www.ameliaislandvacations.com.

Amelia Island Plantation is a low-key, four-star resort offering a wide range of accommodations and amenities, from a beautiful beach and complete health club to a well-supervised children's program. Tennis enthusiasts have the run of 23 Har-Tru courts and golfers play on 54 challenging holes, which architect Pete Dye claims are the only true links on the East Coast. The fishing is fine whether it's deep-sea tarpon and kingfish charter, freshwater lagoon angling, or crabbing.

Nature lovers should follow the plantation's *Sunken Forest Trail.* The dense semitropical growth includes palms, magnolias, and live oaks festooned with Spanish moss. About a quarter of this resort community has been set aside as a nature preserve enjoyed by raccoons, opossums, armadillos, and alligators. There are 7 miles of bike and nature trails, and a staff of full-time naturalists offers tours daily.

Amelia Island Plantation is on the southern end of Amelia Island off SR A1A, 29 miles northeast of Jacksonville International Airport. Amelia Island Plantation, 6800 First Coast Hwy., Amelia Island; (904) 261-6161; www.aipfl.com.

Kayak Amelia offers visitors an opportunity to discover the tranquil backwaters of Amelia Island by kayak. Experienced guides teach visitors the how-tos of kayaking and will take them on guided tours of the island's many creeks, marshes, and rivers. Nature discovery tours are also available for the entire family. For more information, call Kayak Amelia at (904) 251-0016, write to 13030 Heckscher Dr., Jacksonville, or visit www.kayakamelia.com. Also contact (888) 30-KAYAK.

Jacksonville Area

Little Talbot Island State Park embraces a quiet curving beach hidden beyond the dunes and framed by graceful sea oats. This is a delightful spot to camp, swim, and picnic on an unspoiled beach. Open 8 a.m. to sunset daily year-round, Little Talbot Island is 17 miles northeast of Jacksonville, off SR A1A. For additional information, write 12157 Heckscher Dr., Jacksonville 32226, or call (904) 251-2320; www.floridastateparks.org.

The house at *Kingsley Plantation,* believed to be the oldest plantation house in Florida, has been restored in pre–Civil War style. Long rows of crumbling quarters are a mute reminder of the days of slavery. Open 9 a.m. to 5 p.m. daily; 11676 Palmetto Ave., Jacksonville; (904) 251-3537; www.nps.gov.

The *Marine Science Education Center* welcomes visitors to a marine museum, wet lab (with more than a dozen different aquaria), and a collection of marine specimens including everything from giant clam shells to huge whale vertebrae. The center, in the historic village of Mayport, is 1 block south of the ferry slip on SR A1A (1347 Palmer St.). The reason the center looks like a school is that it is one. Although this resource is primarily for students, visitors are welcome from 7 a.m. to 3:30 p.m. Mon through Fri except school holidays.

Time Warp

We camped at **Fort Clinch State Park,** which commands a splendid view of Georgia's Cumberland Island and the Atlantic Ocean. The park, the northernmost point in Florida, takes full advantage of its Atlantic beach, Cumberland Sound, and salt marsh. Besides, it's the only place for RVs on the island. Certainly it boasts one of the most impressive fishing piers (1,500 feet long with night lighting) we have ever seen. If the strings of fish coming off that pier are any indication, Amelia Island is an extremely fertile fishing ground.

The fort is a fascinating reminder of a less complicated time. We roamed the ramparts and inspected exhibits in the small museum. Quite by accident, we happened to be there the first full weekend of the month, when costumed rangers reenact the 1864 occupation of the fort. These folks really take this time-warp business seriously. They feigned total ignorance when we mentioned computers or men on the moon.

As we were leaving, a soldier stepped in front of us and ordered us to halt. Did we have permission to leave? Well, not exactly. We had to return to the office where a young man laboriously filled out the necessary form with a quill pen. Still not satisfied, the guard at the gate quizzed us as to the president's name. We stammered for a moment, finally came up with "Abraham Lincoln," and only then were granted permission to leave.

AUTHORS' FAVORITE ATTRACTIONS IN NORTHEAST FLORIDA

Castillo de San Marcos National Monument, St. Augustine; www.nps .gov/casa/

Centre Street Fernandina, Fernandina Beach; http:// ameliaislandliving.com/fernandina beach/amelia-island-travel-guide/ historic-district/

Colonial Spanish Quarter, St. Augustine; http://staugustine government.com/

Florida Museum of Natural History, Gainesville; www.flmnh.ufl.edu/

Fort Caroline National Memorial, Jacksonville; www.nps.gov/foca/index .htm

Fort Clinch State Park, Fernandina Beach; www.floridastateparks.org/ fortclinch/

Ichetucknee Springs State Park, north of Gainesville; http://floridastateparks .org/ichetuckneesprings/default.cfm

Marjorie Kinnan Rawlings Historic State Park, Hawthorne; www.floridastateparks.org/ marjoriekinnanrawlings/

Ravine Gardens State Park, 1 mile southeast of Palatka; www.floridastate parks.org/ravinegardens/

St. George Street, St. Augustine

Closed Fri during the summer. Call (904) 247-5973 or visit the center online at www.duvalschools.org/msec for more information.

Fort Caroline National Memorial commemorates the only French attempt to establish a colony in Florida (1564). The 138-acre park features exhibits, guided tours, and an interpretive model of the original fort. The story told is a tragic one, ending in the massacre of most of the French settlers by the Spanish from St. Augustine. The memorial is located about 5 miles from the mouth of the St. Johns River. Open 9 a.m. to 5 p.m. daily except Thanksgiving, Christmas, and New Year's Day. Fort Caroline National Memorial, 12713 Fort Caroline Rd., Jacksonville; (904) 641-7155; www.nps.gov. Free.

Jacksonville is Florida's largest and most populous city as well as its leading financial, industrial, transportation, and commercial center. Situated on a bend in the St. Johns River, this bustling and prosperous port is a skyscrapered showcase of sophisticated urban amenities. The St. Johns, the only major river in the US to flow from south to north, has been the focus of the city's development since Jacksonville was founded in 1822. An ambitious riverfront beautification program has spiffed up the south bank with its attractive *Riverwalk.* Be sure to stroll the boardwalk and enjoy a fine view of this bustling city.

Adjacent to the Riverwalk are several fine restaurants, an excellent museum, and one of the world's tallest fountains, which erupts after dark into a spirited rainbow of beautiful colors. The ***Museum of Science and History*** is a treasure-house of exploration for the whole family. Attractions include a 28-foot dinosaur skeleton, an exhibit of Florida Indian culture, and the ***Alexander Brest Planetarium***, with its daily multimedia productions. The museum is at 1025 Museum Circle in Jacksonville. Open 10 a.m. to 5 p.m. Mon through Thurs, 10 a.m. to 8 p.m. Fri, 10 a.m. to 6 p.m. Sat, and 1 to 6 p.m. Sun; (904) 396-6674; www.themosh.org.

parksareperks

Jacksonville boasts the largest urban park system in the US, providing facilities and services at more than 337 locations on more than 80,000 acres throughout the city. Many of these parks provide access to the St. Johns River and the Atlantic Ocean for those who want to boat, swim, fish, sail, Jet Ski, surf, and water-ski.

The ***Cummer Museum of Art and Gardens*** features a permanent collection particularly rich in baroque and American art, traveling exhibitions, an award-winning interactive education center known as Art Connections, and 2.5 acres of formal gardens on the west bank of the St. Johns River. Open 10 a.m. to 9 p.m. Tues, 10 a.m. to 4 p.m. Wed, Thurs, and Fri, 10 a.m. to 5 p.m. Sat, and noon to 5 p.m. Sun; closed Mon. The museum is located at 829 Riverside Ave., Jacksonville. Call (904) 696-8373 or visit www.cummer.org to learn more.

The brewmaster's art is on display at the ***Anheuser-Busch Brewery***. After your tour, enjoy a free taste of the product or soft drinks in the hospitality room. The brewery is at 111 Busch Dr., Jacksonville. Take I-95 north to the Busch Drive exit. Guided tours are available 10 a.m. to 4 p.m. Mon through Sat. For more information, call (904) 751-8118 or visit www.budweiser.com and prepare to be "carded" online. Free.

Ever dream of chocolate? ***Peterbrooke Chocolatier*** has the answer to your dreams. The store overflows with chocolate tennis rackets, golf balls, and teddy bears. The candy is made from a secret recipe (known only to three people), and you may view the hand-dipping on the premises.

The specialty here is fresh crème truffles, but you may also indulge in chocolate-smothered Oreos, chocolate-covered popcorn, fresh strawberries dipped in chocolate, or ice cream appropriately named Total Decadence (loaded with milk chocolate, semisweet chocolate, and mixed nuts).

The chocolatier ships products all over the world but maintains a keen interest in the local community. Peterbrooke was the inspiration for much of the impressive restoration around San Marco Boulevard, and you will want

Clark's Fish Camp Seafood Restaurant

As you probably know, you don't exactly "dine" in a fish camp—you eat. Usually bass, perch, or catfish, a small side of coleslaw, and a heap of hush puppies and wilted fries. But then the word "seafood" raises your expectations. Shrimp for sure, maybe crab, clams—oysters, if you're lucky.

Hold on to your appetite, folks. This is like no other greasy spoon (or plastic-fork) establishment you have ever been in. With more than 160 items, the menu is eclectic, to say the least.

Originally this was a bait and tackle shop with a super view of Julington Creek, a tributary of the St. Johns River. You may reach Clark's by land or by sea. If you come by land, be prepared for a weathered exterior and an unpaved parking lot. Don't be misled. The food is well worth the trip.

You may eat inside or creekside. In true fish-camp style, Clark's is comfortably rustic. The appetizers are described as huge, gargantuan, and filling, and they are not kidding. Though you could feed an entire zip code with the leftovers, you are cautioned not to feed the alligators who are, trust me, nearby. That should alert you to the fact that you are now on the wild side. Vegetarians beware.

Everything you ever wanted (such as bison, live lobster, or Dungeness crab) is offered, and, for sure, a number of things you'd never even think of ordering: charred python (as in snake), fried ostrich, yak, smoked eel, and kangaroo. And, no, they don't taste like chicken.

Be honest now. When was the last time you had a craving for char-grilled crocodile? How about gator eggs or fried antelope? Still hungry? A massive 3-pound prime rib with stuffed mushrooms. To turn that into a "surf and turf," throw in a Shrab Salad made with hot buttered crab and shrimp. And don't forget dessert. A fried dill pickle should do it.

The ambience is a whole other story, an impressive one at that. An entire menagerie of wild animals watches as you eat. The hundreds of beautifully preserved animals in museum-quality settings are a tribute to the taxidermist's talent. One of the largest private collections in the country, this includes lions, tigers, monkeys, bears, giraffes, deer, bobcats, and a whole passel of exotic animals you may not be able to name.

With swell service, cuisine done to perfection, and myriad choices, Clark's ranks right up there with the best of the Florida fish camps. When it comes to unusual fish camps, it takes the cake.

Located in Mandarin, less than 25 miles from Jacksonville, just off I-295 south of the city. Approach by land or by river (St. Johns River). Clark's Fish Camp Seafood Restaurant, 12903 Hood Landing Rd., Jacksonville; (904)268-3474; www.clarksfish camp.com.

to visit other shops and restaurants in the area. Open 9 a.m. to 9 p.m. Mon through Sat and 11:30 a.m. to 6 p.m. Sun. Peterbrooke is at 2024 San Marco Blvd., Jacksonville; (904) 398-2489 or (800) 771-0019; www.peterbrooke.com.

St. Augustine Area

St. Augustine, 40 miles south of Jacksonville, is an important repository of history, not only for the community and the state but for the entire nation. In a cheerful if sometimes unsettling mix, the city's carefully preserved past rubs shoulders with the most blatant commercialism, but it is impossible not to be impressed by the city's antiquity. A history that spans four centuries covers a lot of territory.

Ponce de León, landing in this general vicinity, claimed the region for Spain, but it was Pedro Menendez de Aviles, sent by the king of Spain to get rid of the French, who established the first settlement. Continuously occupied since 1565, St. Augustine was founded 42 years before the colony at Jamestown and 55 years before the ocean-weary Pilgrims set foot on Plymouth Rock! The St. Augustine visitor center, 10 Castillo Dr., is open 8:30 a.m. to 5:30 p.m. daily; (904) 825-1000.

Imposing ***Castillo de San Marcos National Monument*** is well worth a visit. The king of Spain spent $30 million on this fort, which took nearly a quarter century to build. Overlooking Matanzas Bay, this national monument

St. Augustine

In April 1513 Ponce de León landed in Florida. He may have been seeking the legendary fountain of youth, as the myth says. After all, he was over 50 and no doubt could have used an elixir guaranteed to roll back the years. More likely, he was hoping to increase his net worth. Other Spanish explorers had returned from adventurous forays into Central and South America laden with gold. Ponce de León had every reason to think this new land might be similarly endowed. The king of Spain promised treasures beyond imagining. All Ponce de León had to do was find them.

The intrepid explorer claimed the region for Spain, but it was Pedro Menendez de Aviles, sent by the king of Spain to get rid of the French, who first sighted land during the Feast of St. Augustine and named the settlement in honor of the saint.

Although sacked by pirates, burned by the British, attacked, counterattacked, and ravaged by a raging yellow fever epidemic, St. Augustine managed to serve as the capital of colonial East Florida for 259 years. Control shifted from the Spanish to the English, then back to the Spanish, who finally turned it over to the Americans in 1821.

Truly Weird

Ripley's Believe It or Not! Museum in St. Augustine, Ripley's original museum, has some displays that will make your skin crawl. This collection features bizarre and unusual oddities from around the world. So if it's a two-headed lamb you want to see, a bunch of shrunken heads, the "Oldest Mother," or the man with the largest nose, this is the place.

If these items don't entice you, perhaps the 2,000-year-old Egyptian mummified cat, a sculpture of the Last Supper made entirely of pecans, or a collection of paintings done on potato chips will. Not yet convinced? Wax figure heads of the Double-Eyed Man, the Human Unicorn, or a 17-inch dwarf named Alypius should do it.

A new addition is the Ripley's Red Sightseeing Trains, which give a 1.5-hour tour of St. Augustine and have 23 stops where you can get on and off the train. Tickets are good for 3 days. Open Sun to Thurs 9 a.m. to 7 p.m., Fri and Sat 9 a.m. to 8 p.m. 19 San Marco Ave.; (904) 824-1606; www.ripleys.com.

withstood many a siege but was never captured. Periodically, reenactors in Spanish uniforms provide plenty of smoke as well as action with their demonstrations of old-time firearms. Castillo de San Marcos National Monument, 1 S. Castillo Dr., St. Augustine. Open 8:45 a.m. to 5:15 p.m. daily except December 25; (904) 829-6506; www.nps.gov.

A faithful reconstruction of the 1750–1845 period centers on *St. George Street.* To absorb the old-world atmosphere, take a leisurely stroll by coquina-stone houses with overhanging balconies and walled garden patios that line the narrow streets. Be sure to visit the exquisite *St. Photios National Greek Orthodox Shrine* at 41 St. George St., St. Augustine (open 9 a.m. to 5 p.m. daily). Attractive shops and restaurants lure visitors. You'll want to follow your nose to the *Spanish Bakery* at 42 St. George St. Ask for Spanish meat turnovers, better known as empanadas, to eat in the picnic area. (The bakery is open 9 a.m. to 3 p.m. daily) The historic area is immediately south of the Old City gate.

Don't miss the *Colonial Spanish Quarter* in the restoration area. Here the daily lives of soldiers and their families are re-created by costumed guides and craftspeople who welcome your questions. Look for the red-and-white Spanish flag, and enter at 29 St. George St. Operated by the city, this quality attraction is open 9 a.m. to 5:30 p.m. daily. The visitor center is located at 29 St. George St., St. Augustine; (904) 825-6830; www.historicstaugustine.com.

St. Augustine experienced its first tourism boom at the turn of the 20th century, thanks to Henry Flagler. Impressed with the city's possibilities, he linked

St. Augustine and Jacksonville by railroad. While he was at it, Flagler turned the town into a fashionable resort by building two grand hotels, the **Ponce de Leon Hotel** and the **Alcazar Hotel.** Visitors should not leave the city without at least a look at these two lavish hotels, their gardens, and fountains. The Ponce de Leon serves as **Flagler College** (no charge to roam the campus), and the restored Alcazar at 75 King St. houses the **Lightner Museum,** with its three floors of fascinating collections. Open 9 a.m. to 5 p.m. daily; (904) 824-2874; www.lightnermuseum.org. Both are at Cordova and King Streets in St. Augustine.

What better spot to lunch than in the indoor swimming pool (fortunately, it was drained some time ago) of the fantastic Alcazar Hotel (now the Lightner Museum) at 75 King St. **Cafe Alcazar** is located in the rear of the museum (25 Granada St.) right in the center of the **Lightner Antique Mall.** You may investigate the antiques shops while waiting for a sandwich, enchilada, crepes, or salad. Appropriately, considering the grand setting, the dozen tables are set with real flowers, linen tablecloths, and china. Open 11 a.m. to 3 p.m. 7 days a week; (904) 825-9948. Inexpensive.

Those seeking a spot to spend the night that is as charming as it is convenient should make reservations at **The Kenwood Inn.** This bed-and-breakfast hostelry (built between 1865 and 1886) is located within the Historic District between the Oldest House and the famous Castillo de San Marcos National Monument. Most of St. Augustine's historic sights and fine restaurants are within walking distance.

The 13 rooms range in size from small and cozy to spacious; each has its own unique personality (choose Shaker, Colonial, or Victorian), and all have private baths. A small outdoor swimming pool is an appreciated extra, and innkeepers Pat and Ted Dobosz make everyone feel warmly welcome (no small children or pets). Contact the Kenwood Inn, 38 Marine St., St. Augustine, by calling (904) 824-2116 or visiting their website at www.thekenwoodinn.com.

O'Steen's restaurant is a St. Augustine institution. You don't go there for

ghosttown

Are there ghosts in St. Augustine? Are you kidding? Of course there are. Remember, this is the oldest continuously occupied European settlement in the continental US.

If you care to meet them, take a colorful **Ghost Tour** hosted by knowledgeable tour guides in period costume. As you wind through the narrow byways of the oldest city and feel the hairs on your neck stand on end, you'll understand why this is one of the city's most memorable tours. Call Ghost Tours of St. Augustine, (904) 829-1122, for information. Reservations are required. Carriage tours and walking tours are at 8 p.m. daily with additional, seasonably available times.

the ambience. Frankly, there isn't much, with the exception of a model ship on the mantle. This is simply a small, bare-bones, basic restaurant, but there is a reason you probably will have to get in line: fried shrimp done to perfection served with special sauce. Ahhh, now you know how fresh is supposed to taste. The veggie sides are homegrown delectable. All the seafood is good, but the shrimp is what the lines are all about. So be patient, and wait your turn. No wine, no beer, no credit cards, but you'll find your meal an excellent value. Open for lunch and dinner Tues through Sat from 11 a.m. to 8:30 p.m. On SR A1A across the Bridge of Lions on the right, about 2 blocks south toward the beach. 205 Anastasia Blvd., St. Augustine; (904) 829-6974.

The *St. Augustine Alligator Farm* has it all: Maximo, more than 15 feet long and weighing in at a hefty 1,250 pounds, weird albino gators from the bayous of Louisiana, and excellent wildlife shows, including hungry alligators leaping for their dinner. Also, this is the only zoo in the world where you can see all 23 species of crocodiles in one location. We know this sounds crazy, but our favorite exhibit has nothing to do with reptiles. It's the wild-bird rookery, where exotic residents court, nest, and raise their young within a few feet of the boardwalk. The birds are truly wild. No one feeds them. They come and go as they wish but hang out here because they feel relatively safe. Sure, an occasional hatchling gets eaten by the alligators, but these vigilant gators scare off the birds' worst enemies: raccoons, opossums, and snakes. If you enjoy photographing, or just watching, birds, this well-maintained zoological park will hold you spellbound. The birds have been setting up housekeeping here a long time: The Alligator Farm, listed on the National Register of Historic Places, was founded in 1893. Open 9 a.m. to 5 p.m. daily, 9 a.m. to 6 p.m. during the summer. 999 Anastasia Blvd. (SR A1A South), St. Augustine; (904) 824-3337; www.alligatorfarm.com.

Nice to know the *St. Augustine Lighthouse,* the city's oldest surviving brick structure, is still an official working aid to navigation. Completed in 1874, this 165-foot photogenic tower comes complete with a keeper's house. Converted to a museum, this house features exhibits on shipwrecks and regional maritime archaeology. For a grand view, climb the 219 steps to the observation deck. Sorry, but kids less than 44 inches tall aren't allowed on the stairs, and this historic structure has no elevator. Don't miss the gift shop's fine array of nautical treasures. From Anastasia Boulevard (SR A1A), turn onto Red Cox Road and go 0.2 miles. Open 9 a.m. to 6 p.m. daily except Thanksgiving, Christmas Eve, and Christmas Day. St. Augustine Lighthouse & Museum is at 81 Lighthouse Ave., St. Augustine; (904) 829-0745; www.staugustinelighthouse.com.

Our dictionary defines gunkholing as "sailing casually along a coast, anchoring from time to time in quiet coves and inlets." The waters around St. Augustine, especially the Matanzas River and Intracoastal Waterway, are ideally

Florida on a Budget

Perhaps it's time to treat your credit cards to a well-deserved rest.

Florida off the beaten path often translates to Florida on a budget. For the most economical rates, hit the beach during the low season. South Florida's low season generally runs from May through September, while in north Florida, low season lasts from November through March. Spring and fall rates vary but are considerably less than peak season.

Consider camping. Florida has more campgrounds and campsites than any other state. If you're looking for a real deal, head for the state parks.

You don't have to camp to take advantage of the wealth of educational and recreational opportunities in the state park system. You could make it a day trip. But if you stay the night, it will save money and allow you to experience some of the most beautiful areas of the state.

From its inception in 1936, the Florida state park system has developed into one of the largest and best systems in the country. It has twice been named the "Nation's Best State Park Service" by the National Recreation and Parks Association.

More than 160 state parks span 700,000 acres and 100 miles of glistening white beach across the state. From Perdido Key near Pensacola and Amelia Island in the northeast corner to Key West, the southernmost city in the continental US, these parks preserve both natural treasures and unique cultural resources.

Step back in time. Explore the tangled backwaters of central Florida that inspired Marjorie Kinnan Rawlings to write *The Yearling.* Hobnob with the soldiers guarding Fort Clinch. Wander through the Stephen Foster Culture Center while humming a few bars of "Old Folks at Home."

Or you may stretch out on a sun-drenched beach and snooze comfortably in the warm Florida sunshine. State park beaches—one more gorgeous than the next—run the gamut from palm-shaded Bahia Honda State Park in the Keys to glittering St. Andrews on the Florida panhandle.

When you've had enough sun, head for the downright chilly underground wedding room in Florida Caverns State Park near Marianna. Take a dip in the spring-fed pools in the Ocala National Forest. Or board a rented inner tube for a cool cruise down the Ichetucknee River.

Cost of entrance to state parks varies but generally runs between $2 and $5 per vehicle. Camping and cabin fees are extra.

suited for this type of boating. For those who don't need a destination or an itinerary and just want to poke around, we suggest renting a boat or a kayak. Watch for birds, dolphins, and manatees. Soak up the sun. Breathe deeply of salt-washed air.

Devil's Elbow Fishing Resort will rent you an easy-to-operate Carolina skiff or pontoon boat complete with instruction and safety equipment, and a bait shop is available, too. They now have 10 rental cottages as well as a swimming pool available for fishermen—or those who come with their fishermen but prefer other activities. Open 7 a.m. to 6 p.m. daily. 7507 SR A1A South; www.devilselbowfishingresort.com.

Let's say you want fresh seafood or some really great ribs. Or maybe you're in the mood for a "Florida Cracker" feast of frog legs, cooter, and alligator tail. You don't want to dress up, and a casual turn-of-the-century fish camp setting sounds good. Before getting all serious about food, you might want a little more information. What's a Florida Cracker? What's a cooter? Which turn of the century? Oh, yes, and define "fish camp setting." Florida Cracker refers to rural Florida folks and their old-fashioned, pioneer ways. A cooter is a soft-shelled turtle. In this case, "turn of the century" goes back to the beginning of the 20th century. The fish camp at ***Salt Water Cowboys*** includes handmade willow-twig furniture, old wooden floors, and rusted tin ceilings. The "decor" is highlighted by alligator and snake skins on the wall. Snake skins don't do much for us, and we don't mean to be narrow-minded, but the idea of a soft-shelled turtle doesn't stir us at all. Here's what does: Cowboys' award-winning creamy white clam chowder, smoked fish dip and crackers, Oysters Dondanville (prepared with garlic, butter, vermouth, and scallions), catch of the day grilled and basted with lemon butter scallion sauce. Oh boy. No wonder the place is always busy. Salt Water Cowboys, 299 Dondanville Rd., St. Augustine; (904) 471-2332; www.saltwatercowboys.com.

Matanzas is the Spanish word for "massacre." ***Fort Matanzas,*** a Spanish outpost built in 1742 to defend St. Augustine's south entrance, is well named. Spain's struggle with France to control the area erupted in a bloody encounter when, in 1565, Spanish soldiers came upon a shipwrecked French fleet. Without weapons or food, the French surrendered but refused to give up their Protestant faith as commanded. The Spanish, finding this unacceptable, slaughtered nearly 250 Frenchmen on the beach. In 1742 the construction of this watchtower fort was Spain's last effort to control Matanzas Inlet and stop British encroachments from the north. A ranger puts the events of those early struggles in historical perspective as you explore this 30-foot masonry tower and wonder what duty in this wilderness outpost was really like back in the 1700s. This gives the off-the-beaten-path concept a whole new dimension. Weather permitting, a free passenger ferry to the fort leaves the visitor center dock from 9:30 a.m. to 4:30 p.m. at half past the hour. The fort is open 9 a.m. to 5:30 p.m. daily except December 25. The fort, 14 miles south of St. Augustine, is reached by SR A1A on Anastasia Island. Fort

Matanzas National Monument, 8635 SR A1A South, St. Augustine; (904) 471-0116; www.nps.gov/foma.

Trouble sleeping? Try tuning in to the rhythmic slosh of ocean waves breaking on the beach. Thomas A. Mellon, of the well-known Pittsburgh banking family, did. On the advice of relatives, this wealthy insomniac arrived in Summer Haven in the early 1880s to escape the heat and get a good night's sleep. He was so enchanted with the area, he purchased a good chunk of real estate. His two properties, a rustic fisherman's cottage called The Hut (1882) and The Lodge (1895), became beloved family retreats. Thomas Mellon Schmidt, Mellon's great-great grandson, inherited the historic Lodge in 1987 and faithfully restored it to its former charm. Made of first-growth Florida pine and cedar, with original hand-rubbed wooden walls and ceilings and heart-of-pine floors, the five-bedroom, two-bath Cracker-style cottage is of classic "dogtrot" architectural style. Positioned between the Atlantic Ocean and the Summer Haven River, *The Lodge,* with its comfortable wraparound porch and breezeway separating the kitchen from the main living quarters, takes full advantage of the fresh ocean air. The location, with whales and dolphins cruising by and 105 bird species and countless butterflies identified without ever leaving the porch, is a nature lover's dream. The Hut and The Lodge are cherished remnants of the old pre-condo Florida. The string of notables who have visited here includes Marjorie Kinnan Rawlings, author of *The Yearling;* C. V. Whitney, founder of nearby Marineland; Owen D. Young, chairman of General Electric; Princess Angela Scherbatow, a Flagler County heiress; and Ilya Tolstoy, grandson of the Russian writer. And now you can add your name to that list. The Lodge, with a coquina-stone fireplace, period furnishings, and modern amenities, is available for weekly and monthly rentals. It comes complete with the hypnotic sound of ocean waves to lull you to sleep. *The Hut,* next door to The Lodge and also for rent, is a cozy place to get away from it all. Beginning as a rustic one-room fisherman's dwelling, it has grown by additions to include a bedroom, bathroom, kitchen, and long living room. A charming cupola provides a delightful spot to greet the sunrise emerging from the great Atlantic. Please contact www.vacationrentalpros.com or (904) 385-3888.

If you've been lucky, swimming with dolphins is somewhere on your lifetime list of most memorable experiences. If not, this is your golden opportunity. Remember *Marineland?* They're the folks who kicked off this whole discovery-of-the-oceans trend. In fact, they are the world's first oceanarium and America's oldest (1938) marine park. They've weathered hurricanes, economic downturns, and changing ideas about how people interact with marine mammals. Dedicated to preserving marine life by offering the public a unique combination of entertainment and education, they have successfully emerged

A Medieval Moment

Rolling into St. Augustine just about dusk, we spotted combatants in medieval garb hacking away at one another to the tune of flailing swords and clanking armor. All this on the library grounds, no less, and not a movie director in sight—our first clue that St. Augustine is not your everyday, run-of-the-mill city.

Since whacking one another with broadswords is not what folks in our hometown generally do in their spare time, we stopped to watch. These earnest warriors, we learned, belonged to a group dedicated to reenacting medieval battles as authentically as possible and were in dress rehearsal for a major contest in another state.

Strange as it seemed at first, this was oddly appropriate. After all, St. Augustine is old.

from a complete makeover. Their mammoth seawater lagoons are pristine, the dolphins as show-offy as ever. Marineland offers a whole menu of experiences from watching Nellie, the world's oldest (born in 1953) bottlenose dolphin, cavort to swimming with these gentle creatures in deep water. Whatever else you do in Florida, don't miss this experience. Open 8:30 a.m. to 4:30 p.m. daily. Marineland, 9600 Oceanshore Blvd., St. Augustine; (877) 933-3402 or (904) 471-1111; www.marineland.net.

Tranquility reigns at **Washington Oaks Gardens State Park.** It's a grand place for a leisurely stroll along the boulder-strewn beach, through the rose garden, and beneath majestic live oaks. Tucked between the Atlantic Ocean and the Matanzas River, this is an extremely productive area for both fishing and bird watching. Once part of Bella Vista Plantation and later owned by the chairman of the board of General Electric, this 410-acre estate was given to the state by his widow, Mrs. Owen D. Young. Hiking and biking trails and a lovely, shaded picnic area have been developed for visitors. The park is on SR A1A about 20 miles south of St. Augustine and 2 miles south of Marineland. Open 8 a.m. to sundown daily. Washington Oaks Gardens State Park, 6400 N. Oceanshore Blvd., Palm Coast; (386) 446-6780; www.floridastateparks.org.

South of St. Augustine are sights in Bunnell and Palatka not to be missed. The **Bulow Plantation Ruins Historic Site State Park** features an old sugar mill and the crumbling foundation of an ancient mansion destroyed during the Seminole Indian Wars. Guided tours are available on request. The ruins are southeast of Bunnell on Old Kings Road. Open 9 a.m. to 5 p.m. daily. For information, write CR 2001, Flagler Beach 32110; (386) 517-2084; www.florida stateparks.org.

If your thoughts turn to **Ravine Gardens State Park,** it's probably spring. During February and March the azaleas and camellias are at their peak. You may drive the road that loops around the edges of three steep ravines, jog the popular exercise course, or just stroll the paths thinking end-of-winter thoughts. One hundred thousand azaleas can't be wrong. Open 8 a.m. to sunset daily. Located about 1 mile southeast of Palatka at 1600 Twigg St. (off Moseley Avenue), Palatka; (386) 329-3721; www.florida stateparks.org.

Gainesville Area

Marjorie Kinnan Rawlings found inspiration in the backwater community of Cross Creek. This semitropical low country was the setting for her Pulitzer Prize–winning novel, *The Yearling*. The author's rambling farmhouse, complete with old-fashioned canned goods on the kitchen shelves and her antique typewriter on the screened porch, looks as though she just stepped out for a moment.

Rawlings quickly grew to love this place and its people, which she immortalized in her autobiographical book, *Cross Creek*. Her neighbors were "Crackers," rural folk native to the region who were used to "making do." They made what living there was from the land, put on no airs, and wore their Southern heritage with pride. The author also compiled a book of regional recipes titled *Cross Creek Cookery*. The ***Marjorie Kinnan Rawlings Historic State Park*** is in Cross Creek, off CR 325.

Although you can see inside the historic home every day, access inside is by guided tour only. Tours are available Thurs through Sun at 10 a.m. and 11 a.m., and 1, 2, 3, and 4 p.m. The house is closed Aug and Sept but the grounds and trails are open year-round from 9 a.m. to 5 p.m. Marjorie Kinnan Rawlings Historic State Park, 18700 S. CR 325, Cross Creek; (352) 466-3672; www.florida stateparks.org.

Florida's home where the buffalo roam is ***Paynes Prairie Preserve State Park,*** just south of Gainesville. Indian artifacts dating back to 7000 BC

Marjorie Kinnan Rawlings, author of *The Yearling:*

"When I first came to the Creek, and knew the old grove and farmhouse at once as home, there was some terror, such as one feels at the first recognition of a human love, for the joining of persons to place, as of persons to person, is a commitment of shared sorrow, even as to shared joy."

have been unearthed here. The visitor center (863-375-4717) contains interesting exhibits on the natural and cultural history of the preserve. Open 9 a.m. to 4 p.m. daily. (It was once a large Spanish cattle ranch.) A nearby observation tower provides a scenic overlook of this vast, marshy sea of grass.

The park offers boating (no gasoline-powered boats allowed) and fishing in Lake Wauberg, as well as camping, bird watching, and horseback riding (bring your own horse). The entrance is on US 441, 10 miles south of Gainesville. Open 8 a.m. to sunset daily year-round. For more information, contact Paynes Prairie Preserve State Park, 100 Savannah Blvd., Micanopy; (352) 466-3397; www.floridastateparks.org.

Micanopy, tucked between I-75 and US 441, just southeast of Gainesville, is a small, friendly town that will reset your inner clock and refresh your spirit.

Founded in 1821, **Micanopy** (pronounced Mick-can-OH-pee) is Florida's oldest inland settlement. Most of the buildings are on the National Historic Register. Spanish moss envelopes ancient oaks with a misty gray veil of antiquity. The pace seems light years away from that of the theme parks clustered in and around Orlando. Antiques shops are crowded with treasures from another era. This is the place to find first editions and other rare and unusual books. When white men arrived, they found remnants of the Southern Creek nation living here. They were called Seminoles, a Creek word meaning "runaway." This is a fine place to run away to when you've had it with the whole concept of speed dialing. Let's say you don't want to spend the whole day shopping. Maybe you're male, and there's a football game somewhere on TV. So you want the condensed version. Try **The Shop** on Cholokka Boulevard in historic downtown Micanopy. Yes, the name of this particular shop is The Shop.

castlewarden

Castle Warden, the building housing Ripley's Believe It or Not! Museum, was built in 1887 by William G. Warden, once a partner of John D. Rockefeller and Henry Flagler in the early development of the Standard Oil Company. Henry Morrison Flagler was convinced Florida would become the "Riviera of the Americas." He asked Warden to invest in the construction of a great railroad to connect St. Augustine with New York.

Warden went to Florida, studied the railroad project, and declared (the story goes) he would not put a cent into the railroad. However, he liked the climate and decided to build a large home here. He wanted to be in Florida, he said, to watch Flagler go broke.

The Warden family and its heirs lived here for many years until Marjorie Kinnan Rawlings, the well-known Florida author of The Yearling, bought the home in 1941. In 1950 Castle Warden became the original Ripley's Believe It or Not! Museum.

Gainesville's outstanding *Florida Museum of Natural History* offers fascination for all ages with its 14-foot-tall Columbian mammoth skeleton and a mastodon as well as a reconstructed Florida cave. (The cave comes complete with cave critters, but don't worry, they don't fly.) What a find! Don't miss the butterflies (lepidoptera) in the rain forest exhibit. The McGuire Center for Lepidoptera and Biodiversity is the world's largest lepidoptera research facility, with one of the world's largest collections of butterflies and moths (more than 9 million specimens and growing). The museum, with one of the largest natural history collections in the US, is on the University of Florida campus in Powell Hall at SW 34th Street and Hull Road. Admission is free but there is a charge for the rain forest exhibit. Open 10 a.m. to 5 p.m. Mon through Sat, and 1 to 5 p.m. Sun and holidays. Closed Thanksgiving and Christmas. Call (352) 846-2000, or check out the museum's website at www.flmnh.ufl.edu. The museum's two gift shops carry a fine selection of items relating to the natural and social sciences.

Just down the road from the museum is the lush *Lake Alice Wildlife Preserve,* home base for alligators that fit easily into the whopper category. Don't mess with them, but do enjoy this lovely spot. The preserve is on Museum Road, a mile west of SW 13th Street.

Some fossils that have shed light on Florida's ancient history were found in the northwest part of Gainesville at the *Devil's Millhopper Geological State Park.* This huge 5-acre sinkhole has yielded shark teeth and other evidence of the prehistoric sea that once covered the state. Some of the plants and animals in the 120-foot-deep collapsed caverns are more typical of the Appalachian Mountains than of Florida. Devil's Millhopper Geological State Park is located off SR 232 at 4732 Millhopper Rd., Gainesville; (352) 955-2008; www.florida stateparks.org. Open 9 a.m. to 5 p.m. Wed through Sun year-round.

Kanapaha Botanical Gardens features 24 major collections (62 acres), including the state's largest public display of bamboos and the largest herb garden in the Southeast. Kanapaha's signature plants include a premier stand of Chinese royal bamboo, giant Victoria water lilies, and Asian snake arums. The garden's name comes from the Timucua Indian words for "palmetto leaf" and "house." It refers to the thatched dwellings that were clustered on the western shore of 250-acre Lake Kanapaha. The inhabitants of this small Timucua village were residing here when European explorers made their first forays into inland Florida. To see the gardens at the height of their color, visit June through September. Don't bypass the gift shop. It offers an unusual array of tasteful items including original art and treasures from the natural world.

Every winter Kanapaha holds its Annual Winter Bamboo Sale. In early January a descriptive listing indicates which bamboos are being offered during January and February on a dug-to-order basis. Usually between 15 and 20 types are offered, often including the elegant black bamboo. Purchases are available for pickup within two weeks of ordering. Open Mon, Tues, Wed, and Fri 9 a.m. to 5 p.m., and Sat and Sun 9 a.m. to dusk. Closed Thurs. Kanapaha Botanical Gardens, 4700 SW 58th Dr., Gainesville; (352) 372-4981; www.kanapaha.org.

If Florida springs intrigue you, head for *Ginnie Springs Outdoors.* Here's an opportunity to tube, snorkel, or canoe down a remarkable river: the Santa Fe. (Canoe, tube, and snorkel equipment are available for rent.) The nine springs that feed the river are a favorite of scuba divers, who come from all over the world to explore the transparent 72-degree water. The resort offers a full-service dive center and air station, dive equipment rentals, and cavern- and cave-diving instruction. Spread over more than 200 acres of unspoiled forest, this lovely site offers everything from RV sites and cottages to riverfront wilderness camping. Located in north-central Florida near Gainesville and Lake City, Ginnie Springs Outdoors is just 20 minutes from I-75 at 5000 NE 60th Ave., High Springs; (386) 454-7188; www.ginniespringsoutdoors.com.

At *O'Leno State Park,* the scenic Sante Fe River performs a real disappearing act as it flows underground for more than 3 miles before coming to the surface. Other natural features of O'Leno are sinkholes, hardwood hammocks, a river swamp, and sandhill communities. You'll find a good view of the river from the suspension bridge built by the Civilian Conservation Corps in the late 1930s. This is a fine place to camp, canoe, fish, swim, or walk the nature trails. The park is off US 441, 35 miles northwest of Gainesville, and is open 8 a.m. to sunset daily year-round. O'Leno State Park, 410 SE Olena Park Rd., High Springs; (386) 454-1853; www.floridastateparks.org.

Tubing the Ichetucknee

The day was warm, the water cool (72 degrees). We parked all our cares on the river's banks, plopped into our inner tubes, and dedicated the day to drifting. We bobbed along beneath an emerald canopy on crystal-clear water. Sunlight flickering through Spanish moss created moving light patterns on the river floor. We could see each and every fish. A great blue heron fanned us with massive wings as it passed just overhead. Early tubers reported seeing beavers and otters.

We moved along at a good clip with only an occasional steering stroke. Every turn offered a new view of this dense wilderness area studded with cypress knees and limestone outcrops. There was no motor noise to spoil the tranquility.

We did our tubing one gorgeous Saturday in October; a day we'll remember always. This has to be one of Florida's most enjoyable (and economical) off-the-beaten-path adventures.

OTHER ATTRACTIONS WORTH SEEING IN NORTHEAST FLORIDA

Amelia Island Museum of History, Fernandina Beach

Kanapaha Botanical Gardens, Gainesville

Fountain of Youth Park, St. Augustine

St. Augustine Beach, St. Augustine

Jacksonville Zoo, Jacksonville

Ichetucknee Springs State Park features a pristine, crystal-clear river, but it is not exactly undiscovered. Floating down the scenic Ichetucknee in an inner tube has become so popular that the park limits the number of tubers to protect vegetation. Spending a day (or a few hours) on this river is a perfectly splendid thing to do. The current moves you effortlessly along so you can enjoy the surrounding beauty. No wonder this is such a popular pastime.

The river's source is a group of springs that boil out of limestone sinks and trickle out from under cypress tree roots to the tune of 233 million gallons a day. Ichetucknee is the state's third-largest spring, an impressive statistic in a state that claims more springs than any other.

At the park entrance you will receive a map of tubing options. No food, drink, tobacco, disposable items, or pets are allowed on the river. The peak season is May through September, when the park is apt to be most crowded. At other times you can occasionally have the river to yourself. The water is 72 degrees year-round. Local vendors rent tubes and canoes. The park, which is north of Gainesville off I-75 and 4 miles northwest of Fort White, off SR 27 and CR 238, is open 8 a.m. to sunset daily. The north entrance (off CR 238) is open Memorial Day through Labor Day. The south entrance (off SR 27) is open year-round. For maps and details, visit the north entrance of Ichetucknee Springs State Park on CR 238 (12087 SW US 27, Fort White), call (386) 497-4690, or visit www.floridastateparks.org.

State Parks in Northeast Florida

State park information: (850) 245-2157 or www .floridastateparks.org. For camping reservations in any state park, call (800) 326-3521.

Amelia Island State Park, (904) 251-2320

Anastasia State Park, (904) 461-2033

Big Shoals State Park, (386) 397-4331

Big Talbot Island State Park, (904) 251-2320

Bulow Creek State Park, (386) 676-4050

Bulow Plantation Ruins Historic State Park, (386) 517-2084

Cedar Key Museum State Park, (352) 543-5350

Cedar Key Scrub State Reserve, (352) 543-5567

Crystal River Archaeological State Park, (352) 795-3817

Devil's Millhopper Geological State Park, (352) 955-2008

Dudley Farm Historic State Park, (352) 472-1142

Fanning Springs State Park, (352) 463-3420

Faver-Dykes State Park, (904) 794-0997

Fernandina Plaza Historic State Park, (904) 277-7274

Forest Capital Museum State Park, (850) 584-3227

Fort Clinch State Park, (904) 277-7274

Fort George Island Cultural State Park, (904) 251-2320

Gainesville-Hawthorne State Trail, (352) 466-3397

Gamble Rogers Memorial State Recreation Area at Flagler Beach, (386) 517-2086

George Crady Bridge Fishing Pier State Park, (904) 251-2320

Guana River State Park, (904) 823-4500

Homosassa Springs Wildlife State Park, (352) 628-5343

Ichetucknee Springs State Park, (386) 497-2511, (386) 497-4690

Lafayette Blue Springs State Park, (386) 294-3667

Little Talbot Island State Park, (904) 251-2320

Manatee Springs State Park, (352) 493-6072

Marjorie Kinnan Rawlings Historic State Park, (352) 466-3672

Mike Roess Gold Head Branch State Park, (352) 473-4701

O'Leno State Park, (386) 454-1853

Olustee Battlefield Historic State Park, (386) 758-0400

Paynes Prairie Preserve State Park, (352) 466-3397

Peacock Springs State Park, (386) 776-2194

Pumpkin Hill Creek Preserve State Park, (904) 696-5980

Rainbow Springs State Park, (352) 465-8555

Ravine Gardens State Park, (386) 329-3721

River Rise Preserve State Park, (904) 454-1853

San Felasco Hammock Preserve State Park, (386) 462-7905

Stephen Foster Folk Culture Center State Park, (386) 397-2733

Suwannee River State Park, (386) 362-2746

Troy Spring State Park, (386) 935-4835

Waccasassa Bay Preserve State Park, (352) 543-5567

Washington Oaks Gardens State Park, (386) 446-6780

Withlacoochee Trail State Park, (352) 726-2251

Yellow Bluff Fort Historic State Park, (904) 251-2320

Yulee Sugar Mill Ruins Historic State Park, (352) 795-3817

Places to Stay in Northeast Florida

AMELIA ISLAND

Florida House Inn
22 S. 3rd St.
(904) 491-3322
www.floridahouseinn.com

The Ritz-Carlton, Amelia Island Resort
4750 Amelia Island Pkwy.
(904) 277-1100
www.ritzcarlton.com

Williams House
103 S. 9th St.
(904) 277-2328 or
(800) 414-9258
www.williamshouse.com

GAINESVILLE

The Magnolia Plantation
309 SE 7th St.
(352) 375-6653
www.magnoliabnb.com

JACKSONVILLE

Omni
245 Water St.
(904) 355-6664
www.omnihotels.com

PALATKA

Quality Inn & Suites Riverfront
201 N. 1st St.
(386) 328-3481
www.qualityinn.com

VISITOR INFORMATION FOR NORTHEAST FLORIDA

Amelia Island Tourist Development Council, 102 Centre St., Amelia Island; (904) 277-0717; www.ameliaisland.org

Flagler County Chamber of Commerce, 20 Airport Rd., Ste. C, Palm Coast; (386) 437-0106; www .flaglerchamber.org

Gainesville/Alachua County Visitors and Convention Bureau, 30 E. University Ave., Gainesville; (352) 374-5260; www.visitgainesville.com

Jacksonville and the Beaches Convention & Visitors Bureau, 208 N. Laura St., Ste. 102, Jacksonville; (800) 733-2668; www.visitjacksonville.com

Jacksonville and Jacksonville Beaches Chambers of Commerce, 3 Independent Dr., Jacksonville; (904) 366-6600; www.opportunityjacksonville .com

North Florida Regional Chamber of Commerce, 100 E. Call St., Starke; (904) 964-5278; www .northfloridachamber.com

Putnam County Chamber of Commerce, 1100 Reid St., PO Box 550, Palatka; (386) 328-1503; www .putnamcountychamber.org

St. Johns County Visitors and Convention Bureau, 29 Old Mission Ave., St. Augustine; (904) 829-1711 or (800) OLD-CITY (653-2489); www .sapvb.org

PONTE VEDRA BEACH

The Lodge and Club at Ponte Vedra Beach
607 Ponte Vedra Blvd.
Ponte Vedra Beach
(904) 273-9500 or
(800) 243-4304
www.pontevedra.com

Marriott at Sawgrass
1000 PGA Tour Blvd.
Ponte Vedra Beach
(904) 285-7777
www.marriott.com

Ponte Vedra Inn & Club
200 Ponte Vedra Blvd.
Ponte Vedra Beach
(904) 285-1111 or
(800) 234-7842
www.pontevedra.com

ST. AUGUSTINE

Monterey Inn
16 Avenida Menendez
(904) 824-4844
www.themontereyinn.com

Old City House Inn
115 Cordova St.
(904) 826-0113
www.oldcityhouse.com

Old Powder House
38 Cordova St.
(800) 447-4149
www.oldpowderhouse.com

Places to Eat in Northeast Florida

AMELIA ISLAND

Beech St. Grill
801 Beech St.
Fernandina Beach
(904) 277-3662
www.beechstreetgrill.com

The Grill
The Ritz-Carlton
Amelia Island Resort
4750 Amelia Island Pkwy.
(904) 277-1100
www.ritzcarlton.com

JACKSONVILLE

The Wine Cellar Restaurant
1314 Prudential Dr.
(904) 398-8989
www.winecellarjax.com

JACKSONVILLE BEACH

Aqua Grill
950 Sawgrass Village Dr.
Ponte Vedra
(904) 285-3017

ST. AUGUSTINE

Creekside Dinery
160 Nix Boatyard Rd.
(904) 829-6113
www.creeksidedinery.com

Le Pavillon
45 San Marco Ave.
(904) 824-6202
www.lepav.com

NORTHWEST FLORIDA

We found beaches so remote that at one time, they were left off the map. Zip-lines are sprouting up all over the country, but where can you zip through such magnificence as the tree canopy at Blackwater River State Park just north of Pensacola? Yolo (You Only Live Once) Boards are all the rage, as long as you know how to paddle your surfboard while standing up. Crab Island is a well-populated island that comes and goes with the tides and the seasons. Don't forget to howl with the wolves. We promise they'll howl back at you. More—much more. Read on.

From the Lake City area, the most direct route to Cedar Key is south on I-75 and west on SR 24. From Cedar Key, travel north on US 19/98 to Perry, then follow US 98 west as it passes one sugar-white beach after another, clinging to the Gulf of Mexico all the way to Pensacola. Side roads reveal all sorts of surprises, from dead lakes sprouting tree skeletons to verdant offshore islands.

If you take the northern route (I-10) from Pensacola to Tallahassee, you'll discover a Florida few folks are familiar with. Sometimes the scenery resembles Maine, Canada, or the foothills of Virginia. Byways off this main road lead to fall

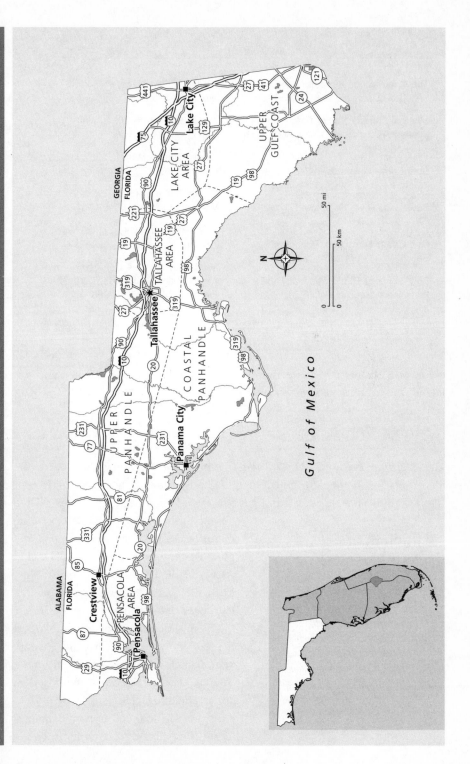

TOP EVENTS IN NORTHWEST FLORIDA

The Chautauqua Assembly, DeFuniak Springs, January, (850) 892-7613

Musical Echoes Native American Festival, Fort Walton Beach, April, (850) 243-4405

Springtime Tallahassee Festival, Tallahassee, April, (850) 224-5012

Suwannee River Jam, Live Oak, April, (386) 364-1683

Gulf Coast Triathalon, Panama City Beach, May, (850) 235-0720

Billy Bowlegs Pirate Festival, Destin/Fort Walton Beach, June, (800) 322-3319

Fiesta of Five Flags, Pensacola, June, (850) 433-6512

Pensacola Seafood Festival, Pensacola, September, (850) 434-1234

Boggy Bayou Mullet Festival, Niceville, October, (850) 729-4545

Destin Fishing Rodeo, Destin/Fort Walton, October, (850) 837-6734

Old Tyme Farm Days, Live Oak, November, (386) 364-1683

Winter Festival—A Celebration of Lights, Music, and Arts, Tallahassee, December, (800) 628-2866

color, one of only two perfectly round lakes in the world, stalactites and stalagmites, and the state's only waterfalls.

Lake City Area

The *Stephen Foster Folk Culture Center State Park* pays tribute to the man who made the Suwannee River famous, wrote "Old Folks at Home" (Florida's official state song), and gave us such long-standing favorites as "Oh Susannah" and "Camptown Races." One of America's best-loved composers, Stephen Foster was born in Pennsylvania in 1826 and died at the age of 37 in New York City with 35 cents in his pocket. He never did get to see the Suwannee, but you should. It's the second-largest river in the state, and you may camp, boat, fish, and explore nature trails here.

The *Foster Museum* is housed in an antebellum-style mansion that conjures up all sorts of romantic images of the Old South. The Carillon Tower

floridacool

Miami Beach pharmacist Benjamin Green invented the first suntan cream in 1944. Gatorade, created at the University of Florida for their football team, was named after the university's mascot, the Gators. Air-conditioning, refrigeration, and ice cubes in your drink are all thanks to Dr. John Gorrie. You can check out the John Gorrie State Museum in Apalachicola.

chimes forth hourly concerts of Foster favorites. Inside you may take a trip through yesteryear as you inspect Foster memorabilia, antique musical instruments, original manuscripts, and animated dioramas.

The **Florida Folk Festival,** an annual gathering of folk musicians and craftspeople held in May, is a well-attended event. The Jeanie Ball (named for "Jeanie with the Light Brown Hair") is the highlight of October; December features popular Christmas concerts. For a complete schedule of events, write Stephen Foster Folk Culture Center State Park, US 41 North, White Springs 32096; (386) 397-1920 or (877) 635-3655; www.floridastateparks.org. The Stephen Foster Center is open from 9 a.m. to 5 p.m. daily. White Springs is 3 miles east of I-75 and 10 miles northwest of Lake City at the junction of US 41 and SR 136.

Toe-tapping musicians can be found in abundance at **Spirit of Suwannee Music Park and Campground** near Live Oak, where impromptu jam sessions are the order of the day. You may even be lucky enough to catch a concert or music festival; a regular schedule features top-name groups. How serious are these folks about their music? The outdoor amphitheater seats 5,000. Be sure to take the Music Park's paddleboat ride on the Suwannee. The river, which begins in the Okefenokee Swamp on the Florida/Georgia border, owes its fame to Stephen Foster's song "Old Folks at Home." Other activities include canoeing, kayaking, miniature golf, swimming, and horseback riding. Besides camping, accommodations at the park include cottages, an elegant "tree house," and an extensive RV park. Spirit of Suwannee Music Park and Campground is located within 4 miles of the I-75 (exit 85) and I-10 (exit 40) interchanges on SR 129 North at 3076 95th Dr. in Live Oak; (800) 224-5656; www.musicliveshere.com.

waydownupon thesuwannee river

In the late 1700s the Suwannee River was called the Little San Juan, possibly because a Spanish mission, San Juan de Guacara, was located on its banks. Some historians suspect local dialect changed the name to San Juanee and hence Suwannee. Others believe the river's name was derived from the Creek Indian word *suwani,* which means "echo."

For another look at this well-known river, head west for **Suwannee River State Park.** The overlook above the confluence of the Suwannee and the Withlacoochee provides a commanding view of both rivers as well as a fine place for a picnic. Notice the remains of Confederate earthworks built to protect the railroad bridge across the Suwannee. Oaks bearded with moss and cypress trees canopy the tranquil river, creating a scenic setting for those who enjoy camping, boating, fishing, and hiking. Open 8 a.m. to sunset daily. The park is 13 miles west of Live Oak off US 90 at 3631 201st Path, Live Oak; (386) 362-2746; www.floridastateparks.org.

Upper Gulf Coast

The **Forest Capital Museum State Park,** just south of Perry ("Tree Capital of the South"), pays tribute to forestry, the state's third-largest industry. This cypress geodesic dome features an old turpentine still as well as exhibits on such things as modern-day turpentine production and the sex life of the pine tree. After learning about Florida's 314 known species of trees and the 5,000 products manufactured from the longleaf pine tree, take time to wander through the turn-of-the-20th-century **Cracker Homestead** behind the visitor center. This log cabin home has a "dogtrot" (a breezeway), mosquito netting on the beds, and a kitchen that is separated from the house in case of fire. Near the well, tubs for washing clothes stand ready for action. (Keep in mind, these are the "good old days.") A grape arbor, outhouse, pantry house, chicken pen, barn, corncrib, cane grinder, and smokehouse round out the self-sufficient scene of yesteryear.

andthebeach goeson

Plunk yourself down anywhere in Florida and you're never more than 60 miles from the beach—1,350 miles (2,160 km) of its coastline are sand beaches. Florida has more miles of tidal shoreline than any other state in the continental US, and half the state is less than 100 feet above sea level.

The Visitor Center Museum and Cracker Homestead are off US 19 and 27A just south of Perry. The center is open 9 a.m. to noon and 1 to 5 p.m. Thurs through Mon except Thanksgiving, Christmas, and New Year's Day. Forest Capital Museum State Park, 204 Forest Park Dr., Perry; (850) 584-3227; www .floridastateparks.org.

In October the **Florida Forest Festival** celebrates by crowning a Forestry Queen and holding chainsaw championships and arts and crafts shows. For festival information call the festival office at (850) 584-8733.

If you're looking for Old Florida with a touch of class, **Steinhatchee Landing Resort** is a good choice. The resort, on the meandering Steinhatchee River, is just 3 miles from the Gulf of Mexico. This secluded riverfront retreat, tucked beneath lush native live oaks, pines, and palms, is an ideal base for exploring the area. Seven scenic state parks, most featuring springs, are within a short drive. Fresh- and saltwater fishing are favorite Steinhatchee activities throughout the year, and if you're lucky enough to be there during scallop season (July 1 through September 10), you can "bag" your own supper. An afternoon of scalloping is usually followed by a delectable feast. No wonder this is such a popular summer pastime.

You may swim in the resort's riverfront pool, play tennis, bike, or ride horseback. Or perhaps you'd prefer to canoe 8 miles down the Steinhatchee River, ending up at the resort. Overnight accommodations, Victorian and Cracker cottages, are as comfortable as they are attractive. Contact the Steinhatchee Landing Resort, 203 Ryland Circle, PO Box 789, Steinhatchee 32359; (352) 498-3513; www.steinhatcheelanding.com.

A pleasant drive will take you to **Keaton Beach,** 17 miles north of Stein-hatchee. Follow SR 361 north and turn left at the stop sign. When you reach Keaton Beach, you'll find an uncrowded beach, picnic pavilions, a 700-foot fishing pier, and the best lunch in town at the **Keaton Beach Hot Dog Stand.** Want to hear tales of the latest hurricane? This is the place—the beach's unofficial "information center," looking very much like a hot-dog stand sprouting

jailtime

Longing for the good old days? Perhaps a visit to the *Old Jail* in Jasper will cure that longing. Inspect the hangman's noose—13 knots swinging freely in the hanging tower constructed over the front entrance—and the dungeon, where the most dangerous criminals were kept. Photos of what is believed to be the last legal hanging in Florida are on display. The Old Jail is at 501 NE 1st Ave. in Jasper. The museum is open 10 a.m. to 2 p.m. Mon through Fri. Call (386) 792-3850 to schedule a tour on the weekend.

Ghost Ship

If you haven't done any underwater sightseeing lately, perhaps the time has come. For almost 100 years, from 1834 to the 1920s, more than 50 steamboats plied the Suwannee River. Today the remains of a dozen steamboats can be found along the riverbed, including the especially well-preserved **City of Hawkinsville,** the largest and last steamboat to be stationed on the Suwannee. Looking like a storybook ghost ship, the wreckage can be viewed by swimmers and divers.

The site, accessible only by boat, is located in shallow water on the river's west bank, south of the railroad trestle at Old Town. The *City of Hawkinsville* is marked by a series of buoys on its starboard side and by mooring buoys approximately 50 feet downstream from its stern. Visitors are asked to tie up to the mooring buoys to prevent anchor damage to the boat. This underwater archaeological site is a well-preserved but fragile piece of Florida history. Please take care to leave it as you found it. For more information, contact the Office of Cultural, Historical and Information Programs, 500 S. Bronough St., Tallahassee; (850) 245-6300; www.flheritage.com.

the head of a ferocious shark over the door. You may indulge in a luscious hot dog or go all the way and order the Fisherman's Platter (flounder, shrimp, clams, scallops, crab cake, and oysters) followed by a slice of French silk pie. If you've spent the day fishing, bring in your cleaned catch and they'll cook it for you. Open 11 a.m. to 8:30 p.m. Mon through Thurs, 11 a.m. to 9:30 p.m. Fri, and 7 a.m. to 9:30 p.m. Sat and Sun. For more information, contact the Keaton Beach Hot Dog Stand, 21239 Keaton Beach Dr., Perry; (850) 578-2675.

Halfway between Tallahassee and Tampa but a world apart from both, **Cedar Key** is far enough off the beaten interstate to have preserved the flavor of Old Florida. (Take SR 24 off I-19 and I-98.) This tiny fishing village is on the largest of more than 100 islands clustered in the Gulf of Mexico. Three miles from the mainland, Cedar Key is officially on Way Key, which is connected to the mainland by a causeway. Local restaurants, the beneficiaries of fishing, crabbing, scalloping, and oystering, are known for their sumptuous repasts.

Settled in the early 1840s, Cedar Key began to blossom in 1861 with the completion of Florida's first major railroad, which ran from Fernandina in the northeast corner of the state to Cedar Key. This led to a boom in the lumber business and brought trainloads of tourists. It seems incredible today, but Cedar Key was once the second-largest city in Florida.

After the Civil War, Cedar Key developed a reputation as a center for ship-building and manufacturing of wooden pencils. When the cedar forests had all been leveled, residents turned to the sea for their living. For a brief time, the manufacture of brushes and brooms from palmetto fiber created a flurry of economic activity, but the discovery of plastics decisively ended that enterprise. As if it needed a final "blow," this once-bustling port was devastated by the hurricane of 1896, from which it never fully recovered.

All these ups and downs are carefully documented at two pleasant little museums, **Cedar Key Museum State Park** and the **Cedar Key Historical Society Museum.** Cedar Key Museum State Park is open 10 a.m. to 5 p.m. Thurs through Mon; 12231 SW 166 Ct., Cedar Key; (352) 543-5350; www.florida

When Was the Last Time You Went Scalloping?

Hint: If you can snorkel, you can do it. The season begins July 1 and continues through the end of August. A study conducted by the Marine Fisheries Commission reported the highest density of bivalves in the Steinhatchee River, the best area in Florida for scalloping. The River Haven Marina sells snorkel gear and provides boat rental service. 1110 Riverside Dr., PO Box 898, Steinhatchee; (352) 498-0709.

stateparks.org. The Cedar Key Historical Society Museum, on the corner of 2nd and D (SR 24) Streets (609 2nd St.), is open 11 a.m. to 5 p.m. Sat, 1 to 4 p.m. Sun through Fri. For more information, call (352) 543-5549 or visit www.cedar keymuseum.org.

Cedar Key's *National Wildlife Refuge,* covering three islands, gives rattlesnakes the same preferential treatment as birds. Sea views are embellished by the pink flash of a rare roseate spoonbill, freewheeling frigates, and pelicans crashing into the Gulf in search of supper. The refuge is strictly an environmental study area and not open for visitor use. But birders who rent a boat and cruise near the islands will be well rewarded.

Festival followers flock to the Cedar Key Sidewalk Arts Festival in April and the Seafood Festival in mid-October. For information, contact the Cedar Key Area Chamber of Commerce at PO Box 610, Cedar Key 32625, call (352) 543-5600, or visit www.cedarkey.org.

Coastal Panhandle

St. Marks National Wildlife Refuge, 25 miles south of Tallahassee, comprises nearly 70,000 acres of forests, water areas, and the coast on the Gulf of Mexico. Stop in the visitor center for a look at the interpretive displays, to pick up leaflets and maps, and to browse in the gift shop. Then take the 7-mile wildlife drive to the *St. Marks Lighthouse,* one of the oldest in the Southeast.

If you are a birder or alligator-watcher, you will be in your glory. (You'll feel even more glorious if you remembered the bug repellent.) Hike miles of primitive walking trails, including a 42-mile section of the *Florida National Scenic Trail,* and enjoy a picnic lunch overlooking the water near the lighthouse. The visitor center, 3 miles south of US 98 on Lighthouse Road (1255 Lighthouse Rd., St. Marks), is open 8 a.m. to 4 p.m. Mon through Fri and 10 a.m. to 5 p.m. Sat and Sun. You are welcome in the refuge anytime during daylight hours to picnic, launch a boat, crab, or fish. Call (850) 925-6121 or visit www.fws.gov.

San Marcos de Apalache Historic State Park is also the site of a fort first built in 1679 by the Spaniards. The fort was held at various times by the British, Spanish, and Confederate forces. Its capture by General Andrew Jackson in 1818 was an important factor in the US acquisition of Florida the next year. The museum contains artifacts spanning the area's history from the Spanish occupation to the Civil War. A lovely trail winds through Confederate earthworks, climbs to the top of a powder magazine, follows fort walls along the banks of the Wakulla River, and ends at the original site of early Spanish fortifications where the Wakulla and St. Marks Rivers merge. The museum is

24 miles south of Tallahassee on SR 363 (148 Old Fort Rd.) in St. Marks; (850) 925-6216. Open 9 a.m. to 5 p.m. Thurs through Mon. For more information, contact the Tallahassee–St. Marks Geo Park at 1022 Desoto Park Dr., Tallahassee; (850) 922-6007.

Folks from Tallahassee head to the coast for fresh seafood, and one of their favorite destinations is *Spring Creek Restaurant.* This family operation hides out under live oaks festooned with Spanish moss where, according to the menu, "fresh spring water merges with the Gulf, creating the finest seafood in the world." Spring Creek serves up generous portions of mullet, crab fingers, oysters, lobster, deviled crab, and grouper, to name just a few. If you are partial to truly fresh seafood, the owners raise their own soft-shell crabs. The salad bar comes to the table so you can build your own. Specialties are cheese grits and homemade desserts such as chocolate peanut-butter pie and coconut cream pie. Take US 363 (S. Monroe Street) south from Tallahassee and go west on US 98 and south on CR 365 to the tiny community of Spring Creek. Open noon to 9 p.m. Sat and Sun, 5 to 9 p.m. Tues through Fri; closed Mon. Prices are mostly in the moderate range. Spring Creek Restaurant, 33 Ben Willis Rd., Crawfordville; (850) 926-3751.

Once you've started, there's no stopping. Fresh seafood is a fun addiction. The roomy wraparound deck at *Angelo's Seafood Restaurant* is just the place to relax in a rocking chair and have a cocktail while the sun sets over the river. Try the charbroiled grouper and, for sure, their Greek salad. Each table is served a corked wine bottle full of dressing. Angelo's "over the water" restaurant is right by the bridge in Panacea. The owners take a lot of pride in their handsome restaurant, which is open 4:30 to 11 p.m. Fri and Sat, noon to 10 p.m. Sun, and 4:30 to 10 p.m. every other day but Tues. Prices are mostly moderate. 5 Mashes Sands, Panacea; (850) 984-5168.

You really shouldn't drive through Carrabelle without tipping your hat to the *world's smallest police station.* You can't miss it. It's a public phone booth right on the main drag with an American flag painted on it. Often the patrol car is parked beside it waiting for the next call. If it is, why not wave?

A British fort once stood at the *Fort Gadsden* historic site. Held for a time by Indians and runaway slaves, it was destroyed by American forces in 1816.

wholiveswhere

There's nothing quite like stumbling upon celebrities in their own turf. In the Ocala area, watch for John Travolta and Bo Derek. Orlando is home to golf great Tiger Woods and the boy bands Backstreet Boys and *NSYNC. Russian-born tennis star Anna Kournikova frequents Miami's hot spots with Enrique Iglesias, and golf legend Jack Nicklaus calls Palm Beach home.

In 1818 Andrew Jackson ordered the fort to be rebuilt, but today only a bare outline is visible. A miniature replica of Fort Gadsden, some British muskets, and Indian artifacts are on display in an open-sided interpretive center. You may picnic, fish, and explore the nature trails in Apalachicola National Forest. A short walk will take you to the remains of the renegade cemetery where grave robbers left nothing but shallow depressions. Fort Gadsden is 24 miles north of US 98 just off SR 65 (21 miles of good road, the last 3 miles are rough) or 6 miles south of Sumatra off SR 65. Open 8 a.m. to sunset daily. Free.

If you love the beach—the sand, the sea, and the sky—uncluttered by honky-tonk attractions, head for *St. George Island State Park* at the end of Apalachicola Bay. The miles of undeveloped beaches, sand dunes, and marshland are not totally wild. You'll find nature trails, boardwalks, observation platforms, picnic and camping areas, and bathhouses. Take the turnoff from US 98 that leads across the bridge to St. George Island. Open 8 a.m. to sunset daily; 1900 E. Gulf Beach Dr., St. George Island; (850) 927-2111; www.florida stateparks.org.

Apalachicola's *Trinity Episcopal Church,* one of the oldest (1830s) in the state, was cut in sections in New York and floated by schooner down the Atlantic Coast and around the Florida Keys. The original church bell was melted down to make a Confederate cannon. Trinity, sometimes called the nation's first prefabricated church, is at 79 6th St., a block off US 98, across from the Gorrie Museum in Apalachicola. Write PO Box 667, Apalachicola 32329, call (850) 653-9550, or visit www.mytrinitychurch.org to learn more.

st.marks lighthouse

The original St. Marks Lighthouse was built in 1829 by Winslow Lewis of Boston for $11,765, but the structure was judged unacceptable because the tower walls were found to be hollow rather than solid. Calvin Knowlton reconstructed the 80-foot tower using limestone blocks taken from the stone quarry at Fort San Marcos de Apalache. The reflector lens, from Paris, was installed in 1829. On a clear evening the light, now triggered by an electric eye, can be seen from 15 miles away.

Whether you know it or not, you owe a lot to John Gorrie. He's the physician whose inventions make it possible for you to enjoy air-conditioning, refrigeration, and ice cubes in your drink. Back in the days when ice had to be shipped all the way from the Great Lakes, it was a precious commodity in Florida. Dr. John Gorrie wanted a way to cool the rooms of patients suffering from malaria. The only problem was that the pipes in his experimental machine kept clogging with ice. When he realized the importance of this accidental discovery, he immediately built a small ice-making machine. You may inspect a replica of the machine (patented in 1851, the original machine is in the Smithsonian Institution) that paved the way for modern refrigeration and air-conditioning in the *John Gorrie State Museum.* This one-room museum also has displays on cotton, lumbering, fishing, and other aspects of early Apalachicola history. The museum is at Avenue D and 6th Street, 1 block off US 319/98 in Apalachicola. Open 9 a.m. to 5 p.m. Thurs through Mon. For more information, write John Gorrie State Museum, 46 6th St., Apalachicola 32320, or call (850) 653-9347.

The *Bryant House Bed and Breakfast* is conveniently located a short walk from the waterfront and downtown Apalachicola. Built in 1915 and awash with authentic antiques, this European-style bed-and-breakfast offers old-world hospitality in a Victorian setting. Not every lodging has its own personable parrot (named Einstein) to greet you. You will sleep well knowing you will not leave hungry. Brigitte Schroeder's full German breakfast includes juice, assorted cheeses, hams and sausages, just-baked bread and rolls, honey, homemade jams, a boiled egg, and fresh-brewed European coffee. If you can't summon up the appetite to do justice to this feast, Brigitte will wrap it up for you to take to the beach. She'll even provide directions to the best beaches. The Bryant House Bed and Breakfast is located at 101 6th St., Apalachicola; (888) 554-4376; www.bryanthouse.com.

Don't leave Apalachicola without sampling its famous homegrown oysters. *Boss Oyster,* a shanty by the water, serves incredibly delicious oysters every

Abandon Hope

If you're into snakes—really dangerous, poisonous snakes—have we got a place for you. *Tate's Hell Swamp* (shown on some maps as Tate's Hell State Forest) is not a tourist attraction where a friendly herpetologist demonstrates how to milk snakes. It's a real, live swamp located just north of Apalachicola. Well named, it is infested with deadly water moccasins. Abandon hope, all ye who enter.

Get lost in this 70,000-acre swamp and you're apt to be lost a long time. Fossils found in the tangled interior indicate it may have been a bog for more than 100 centuries. According to the lumber company that owns the land, some of the trees deep in the swamp are more than 600 years old.

No one's quite sure whether Old Man Tate, who gave his name to this watery wilderness, is still in there or not. Legend has it he was mad as hell because a panther had been killing his cattle. Following the panther's tracks, Tate disappeared into the morass. Some claim he was bitten by a snake and died somewhere deep in the quagmire. A folk song says he lived just long enough to tell of the hell he'd been through. In any case, he was not a pretty sight. Don't say you weren't warned.

which way in addition to a variety of other fresh seafood. Don't dress up. This down-home-style eatery, attached to a tin "shuck house," has cornered the market on funkiness. You've got your oysters, a small arsenal of hot sauces, and a roll of paper towels. What more do you want out of life? Boss Oyster is open for lunch and dinner 11:30 a.m. to 9 p.m. Sun through Fri, 11:30 a.m. to 10 p.m. Sat, and is located at 123 Water St., Apalachicola; (850) 653-9364.

Loggerhead Run is 8 miles of paved path parallel to Cape San Blas Road. Named for the endangered loggerhead sea turtles that nest along the beaches, Loggerhead Run ties into the state park at the tip of the cape. Remember the fable about the tortoise and the hare? Well, get going. Bicycle rentals: Salty's Beach Shack, (850) 229-6611, or Scallop Cove, (850) 227-1573.

theforgottencoast

Gulf County and its 43 miles of pristine shorelines earned their sobriquet, "Florida's Forgotten Coast," the hard way. In the 1990s state tourism officials literally left it off the map. However, over the years, this has worked in this unspoiled area's favor. Some folks truly enjoy getting off the beaten path, and apparently you're one of them.

You dream up a romantic scenario: a leisurely horseback ride on the beach. Florida provides the setting: the hidden beaches of Cape San Blas, a long and lovely stretch of soft sand. The good folks at *Broke-A-Toe* will provide horses and guides who know what they're doing. After all, they have been at this for more than a decade. They want you to enjoy the ride, so they take it slow and keep it safe.

Your responsibility is to soak up the scenery. Not a bad job. Sunset. Moonrise. The surf highlighted by moonglow. Broke-A-Toe will take care of all the details—whatever you want—from champagne and tasty appetizers to a bonfire on the beach. A time to pop the question. A special anniversary. Or perhaps you want to take the whole family along. The kids will talk about this ride the rest of their lives. Check out the rates and times by calling (850) 899-7433 or visiting www.brokeatoe.com.

St. Vincent National Wildlife Refuge on St. Vincent Island is a bridgeless gem given over to some interesting animals and birds. White-tailed deer, wild hogs, raccoons, and opossums share the triangular-shaped refuge with sambar deer, which were imported from India by early owners. Red-tailed hawks, peregrine falcons, bald eagles, and a host of songbirds and waterfowl come and go. The deserted beaches are a favorite nesting ground for sea turtles. Most alligators hang around the freshwater ponds and marshes, while a few individualists choose to sun on the beach and enjoy the surf—something to remember when taking a swim! This splendid place, with mile after mile of unspoiled beach, can be reached only by water. Contact the refuge manager for information on freshwater fishing, island exploration, and the cost of managed hunts for deer and wild hogs. There is no charge for using the island, but you'll have to make your own arrangements to get there. Contact Refuge Manager, St. Vincent National Wildlife Refuge, PO Box 447, Apalachicola 32329; (850) 653-8808; saintvincent@fws.gov.

The city of St. Joseph was a dream. With a beautiful gulfside setting and a natural deep-water port, it attracted trade from around the world. In July 1836 it was incorporated as a city and described as a "place of importance." Its founders had nothing to do but sit back and let the world's treasures come. But there was more than treasure in the ship's hold that fateful July day in 1841. St. Joseph, so rich in promise, was annihilated by yellow fever brought in by a ship from the West Indies. What was left of the dream city was buried beneath the sand by a vicious hurricane in 1844. Almost overnight, it had become a place of broken dreams.

A new city, incorporated in 1913 and called Port St. Joe, replaced the old. With no aspirations to rival the great ports of Charleston and New Orleans, the community counted its blessings. Being off the beaten path was just fine, thank you. The folks of Port St. Joe were no longer seeking riches other than the clear emerald water of the Gulf and the glistening sands of their beaches. They had their dream. Now all they had to do was to protect its bounty and enjoy the day-to-day pleasures it afforded.

If you would like to see where the first of Florida's five constitutions was written, stop in at *Constitution Convention Museum State Park* in Port St. Joe. Here you'll view an impressive replica of the Convention Hall's west wing, see 18th-century artifacts, and learn the story of the town of St. Joseph, which vanished forever after the 1844 hurricane. The museum is a quarter-mile east of US 98, just south of Port St. Joe, at 200 Allen Memorial Way. Open 9 a.m. to noon and 1 to 5 p.m. Thurs through Mon; (850) 229-8029; www.floridastateparks.org.

Strange as it may seem, the *Dead Lakes* are alive with fish—largemouth bass, bream, and flathead catfish. Named for the thousands of cypress, oak, and pine trees that drowned in the natural overflow of the Chipola River, Dead Lakes enjoys a reputation as one of the best freshwater fishing spots in Florida. In this majestic 80-square-mile preserve, a longleaf pine forest shelters a tranquil picnic and camping area. Ospreys perch in the treetops, and wood ducks come and go. Large stands of bare trees and ancient cypress stumps create a place of haunting beauty. Open 8 a.m. to sunset year-round. Dead Lakes is located 1 mile north of Wewahitchka on SR 71, at 510 Gary Rowell Rd., Wewahitchka 32465; www.visitgulf.com. Call Gulf County Welcome Center, (850) 229-7800.

To make a pound of honey, the bees in the colony must fly the equivalent of twice around the world. Hey, that's a lot of miles. Think how tired those bees must be. Now think how good it is for you! Honey is loaded with vitamins, minerals, and antioxidants. (One unique antioxidant called pinocembrin is found *only* in honey.) The L. L. Lanier family has been harvesting world-renowned tupelo honey from the Apalachicola River basin for 100 years. In fact, this river valley is the only place in the world where tupelo honey is commercially produced. Why here? Because this is where the tupelo gum trees grow, and these bees love the nectar of the tupelo blossoms. The bees are placed on elevated platforms along the river banks, and harvest season is during April and May, when the tupelo trees blossom. According to the L. L. Lanier family, "We do our own processing and packaging to ensure our customers get the real 'unadulterated tupelo honey.' Ours is as pure and natural as extracted honey can be." Stop in at the local Piggly Wiggly store in Apalachicola and pick up a jar. Or you can call to order at Smiley's, (850) 639-5672; www.florida tupelohoney.com.

> ## surprise!
>
> Mexico Beach is in Florida, not Mexico, and when you get there you will find times they are a-changing—unless you're already on central time.

A state recreation area that takes advantage of the Panhandle's gloriously white beaches is **St. Andrews State Park** near Panama City. The water is unusually clear, the dunes are picturesque, and the pine woods shade fine campsites. Be sure to take a look at the restored old-time "Cracker" turpentine still. Open daily 8 a.m. to sunset. St. Andrews is 3 miles east of Panama City Beach on SR 392, 4607 State Park Ln., Panama City; (850) 233-5140; www.floridastateparks.org.

While in Panama City be sure to visit the **Man in the Sea Museum,** which chronicles man's attempt to explore the depths of the ocean. We've come a long way since using animal-skin bladders to help us breathe underwater. Check out early scuba gear, submersibles, commercial diving equipment, and the latest deep-dive gear to see just how far we've come. Kids will want to visit the saltwater touch pool, try on an undersea helmet, and see what it's like to travel in a submarine. Exhibits include treasures from the *Atocha,* a 17th-century Spanish galleon that went down in a hurricane off Key West. Open 10 a.m. to 4 p.m. every day except Mon and Thanksgiving, Christmas, and New Year's Day. The museum is located 0.5 mile west of the intersection of Panama Beach Parkway and SR 79 at 17314 Panama City Beach Pkwy., Panama City Beach. Call (850) 235-4101 for more information or visit www .maninthesea.org.

Florida wineries are off and running. Consider **SeaBreeze Winery** in Panama City Beach, opened in 2003 and already producing award-winning muscadine wines. The first vines, planted in 1996, have now grown to cover 100 acres, reportedly the largest single vineyard in Florida. The grapes grow in Kyotee vineyards, 35 miles north of Panama City Beach in the deep sand lands of an ancient beach. The vineyards produce a variety of wines, from dry to sweet. Blueberry and blackberry wines have proved to be popular, as have premium port and sherry. SeaBreeze Winery is open daily from 10 a.m. to 5 p.m. for complimentary wine tastings. Be sure to try SeaBreeze Magnolia semidry, the winery's celebrated white wine, made with the magnolia variety of muscadine grapes. Tour the winery and visit the gift shop full of clever gift items and wine-related accessories. The winery is located at 13201 Hutchison Blvd. (Middle Beach Road), Panama City Beach. Call (850) 230-3330 or visit www.seabreezewinery.com.

One of the most popular boat trips along the Panhandle Gulf Coast is to **Shell Island.** This undeveloped treasure of long, white beaches and wind-swept dunes is perfect for barefoot beachcombers and those who enjoy uninterrupted views of the Gulf between swims. Seven and a half miles long and more than a mile wide, this pristine island boasts a freshwater lake and teems with wildlife. From St. Andrews State Park, boats leave every half hour from 9 a.m. to 5 p.m. Call (850) 233-0504. You can reserve a boat or WaveRunner or

AUTHORS' FAVORITE ATTRACTIONS IN NORTHWEST FLORIDA

Alfred B. Maclay Gardens State Park, Tallahassee; www.floridastateparks.org/maclaygardens

Cedar Key

Falling Waters State Park, Chipley; www.floridastateparks.org/fallingwaters/default.cfm

Florida Caverns State Park, Marianna; www.floridastateparks.org/floridacaverns

Gulf Islands National Seashore, Gulf Breeze; www.nps.gov/guis

National Museum of Naval Aviation, Pensacola; www.navalaviationmuseum.org

Seville Square, Pensacola

Stephen Foster Folk Culture Center State Park, White Springs; www.floridastateparks.org/stephenfoster

Tallahassee Museum of History and Natural Science, Tallahassee; http://tallahasseemuseum.org/

Edward Ball Wakulla Springs State Park, Wakulla Springs; www.floridastateparks.org/wakullasprings

YOLO (You Only Live Once)

You see them all along the Gulf Coast: large surfboards manned by a paddler standing upright and wielding a long paddle. "I can do that," you say, and the next thing you know, you're under way. Lessons? You simply paddle into calm water, start on your knees, then gradually progress to a standing position. If you can paddle a canoe, you can certainly paddle a YOLO board. Beginners won't have any problems negotiating their craft from here to there. As you become more proficient, you will appreciate the nuances of the sport. There are 18 different YOLO boards made for every age, skill, and size. Some are designed for parent and child, others to carry gear, and those with a need for speed will opt for the racing model.

This is yet another way to enjoy the glorious waters of the Gulf. A terrific bonus is that you improve your balance and coordination and strengthen your core muscles while enjoying the scenery. You are in charge as you glide along the surface of the crystal-clear water, your mind in kickback mode, your life on "pause."

Cofounders Jeff Archer and Tom Losee developed the boards in Santa Rosa Beach and named their company YOLO for You Only Live Once.

For Yolo board lessons, rentals, and group paddles, contact YOLO Board Adventures. 820 N. CR 393, 1 mile north of US 98, Santa Rosa Beach; visit www.yolo board.com, or call (850) 622-5760.

schedule a tour from Treasure Island Marina on Thomas Drive (3605 Thomas Dr., Panama City) at Grand Lagoon in Panama City. To inquire about sightseeing and dinner cruises, call (850) 234-7245; www.shellislandtours.com.

The **Beaches of South Walton** span 26 miles along the clear blue-green waters of the Gulf of Mexico in northwest Florida. Between Destin to the west and Panama City Beach on the east, these 18 small beach neighborhoods specialize in dazzling white sand hugging the Gulf's gentle waters.

These beaches have always been favorites for summer vacations, but they are quickly becoming a year-round destination. Along with mild temperatures, fall, spring, and winter bring quiet, peaceful beaches and low-season prices. Winter, with an average temperature of 68 degrees Fahrenheit, means sweater weather for Florida residents but feels like Indian summer to most people. The average high fall and spring temperatures are 79 and 80 degrees Fahrenheit, respectively. October and November are the least humid months of the year.

These communities take a great deal of pride in being one of the most pristine destinations in Florida. Of 53,000 acres, an astonishing 23,000 are undeveloped state-owned property. With nary an amusement park, chain motel, T-shirt shop, or honky-tonk bar in sight, these relaxed beach communities still offer plenty of fascinating things to see and do. For more information, contact

Beaches of South Walton, 25777 US 331 South, Santa Rosa Beach; (800) 822-6877; www.beachesofsouthwalton.com.

For a sample of the natural splendor of the area, head straight for **Grayton Beach State Park.** This beach was retired in 1994 as the "Nation's Best Beach." (Dr. Stephen Leatherman, or "Dr. Beach," professor of environmental studies at Florida International University in Miami, names certain US beaches "best beach." After a beach is given this honor, it becomes ineligible for the designation for 10 years.) Chosen from 650 US beaches for its quality of sand, accessibility, natural beauty, water temperature, pristine nature trails, and safe, uncrowded environment, Grayton Beach State Park is the beach of your fantasies. Here sugar-white sand dunes crested by dense stands of sea oats and wind-sculpted trees lure artists to capture stunning seascapes. What's more, each year the University of Maryland Geological Survey, an independent study, ranks the beaches of South Walton among the best in the nation.

Grayton Beach State Park offers an extensive, self-guided trail system that provides an up-close look at the diverse ecosystems that make up northwest Florida's coastal areas. Dramatic examples of dune migration and dune building are seen along the trail. Open 8 a.m. to sundown daily. (Park closes at 5 p.m. during the winter months.) Grayton Beach State Park is located on CR 30-A, 1 mile east of Grayton Beach, about 25 miles east of Fort Walton Beach by way of US 98 and CR 30-A. Grayton Beach State Park, 357 Main Park Rd., Santa Rosa Beach; (850) 267-8300; www.floridastateparks.org.

Cassine Garden Nature Trail and boardwalk meanders through 3 scenic miles of marshlands, forests, and pure white-sand beaches and includes a 1-mile fitness trail. Visitors are welcome to use the trail at any time, but it is

OTHER ATTRACTIONS WORTH SEEING IN NORTHWEST FLORIDA

Civil War Soldiers Museum,
Pensacola, www.cwmuseum.org

Manatee Springs State Park,
Chiefland, www.floridastatepark.org

Gulfarium, Fort Walton Beach, www
.gulfarium.com

Museum of Commerce, Pensacola,
www.historicpensacola.org

Gulf Breeze Zoo, Gulf Breeze, www
.gulfbreezezoo.org

"Miracle Strip," Panama City,
www.miraclestripamusementpark
.panamacitysun.com

A Restaurant by Any Other Name . . .

Elegant restaurant names, wherefore art thou?

Start the day with a "Bad Ass" cup o' joe at **Bad Ass Coffee** (1708 Scenic Gulf Dr., Miramar Beach, Destin). Move on to **Another Broken Egg Cafe** (979 Highway 98 E, Ste. F, Destin) to break the fast. Lunch at **Stinky's Fish Camp** (5960 CR 30-A, Santa Rosa Beach). Dinner is a toss-up between **Goatfeathers** (C-30A, Santa Rosa Beach) and **Gravel Road** (4935 E. CR 30A, Santa Rosa Beach). Finish off your culinary adventures with a flaming dessert at **Fire** located at 7 Town Center Loop, Santa Rosa Beach.

not lighted at night. For more information, call (850) 231-5721 or visit www .destin-ation.com.

Established in the late 19th century, *Grayton Beach* is a community of sand streets, lots of trees, and homes made of weathered cypress. Ask a friendly local to point out the "Washaway" house built in the early 1900s by a veteran of the Civil War.

Topsail Hill Preserve State Park, just off US 98, is a 3-mile stretch of beach held in trust by the state as a nature conservatory. High dunes, a longleaf pine forest, and two freshwater lakes create a safe haven for wildflowers, plants, and native wildlife. This 3-mile undeveloped beachfront has been identified as the most pristine and environmentally protected piece of coastal property in Florida. When you've had it with the clang, clatter, and fax warbles of modern living, Topsail is an ideal antidote. The park is located at 7525 W. Scenic Hwy. 30-A, Santa Rosa Beach; (850) 267-8330; www.floridastateparks.org.

For a serene glimpse of the area's past, you'll want to tour the landscaped grounds and mansion of *Eden Gardens State Park,* overlooking Choctawhatchee Bay. Once the hub of a large sawmill complex, the lumber baron's antebellum residence now stands alone, framed by gnarled oaks dripping with Spanish moss. Camellias and azaleas add color to the enchanting scene, especially during the peak bloom season around mid-March.

The stately white-columned mansion with a fireplace in every room and the second-largest known collection of Louis XVI furniture in the US preserves a fragment of the 1800s, the Old South that has mostly gone with the wind. You may picnic, fish, and take a guided tour of this splendid old home. A picnic area with adjacent parking is available at the old mill site on Tucker Bayou. Five miles north of Grayton Beach, Eden Gardens State Park is on CR 395, 1 mile north of US 98 in Point Washington. For a small fee, tours of the house are offered Thurs through Mon on the hour from 9 a.m. to 4 p.m. The park is open 8 a.m. to sunset daily. Eden Gardens State Park, CR 395, Santa Rosa Beach; (850) 267-8320; www.floridastateparks.org.

The beaches of South Walton offer an impressive array of dining choices. The primary focus is on fresh seafood from the Gulf. And why not? It comes straight from the harbor docks of the largest charter boat fleet in the state. But just about everything else, from Cajun and Caribbean cuisine to down-home Southern cooking, is also on tap.

goingtothedogs

Only in Grayton Beach would local artists devote a long wall to paintings of neighbor dog portraits, past and present. Only in Grayton Beach would they take pride in the motto "Great dogs, weird people." Only in Grayton Beach . . .

You don't want to leave Florida without proof that you were chummy with an alligator or two. They bill it as *Gator Beach,* but the gators aren't really on the beach. They are in an enclosure (aren't you feeling better already?) within the *Fudpucker's* restaurant. And though the restaurant isn't free, the gators are. You'll find them at 20001 US 98 East in Destin. Just enter as if you were stopping for a bite to eat and tell the hostess you are there for the alligators. The folks in Florida don't mess around when they're dealing with gators. Here are 100 or so gators just waiting to see you, to be fed by you, and for you to have your picture taken while holding a live gator. There's lots to learn about these fascinating reptiles and fun for the whole family. Open daily at 11 am. When you're done gawking at alligators, you'll find Fudpucker's is a handy place for lunch, at 20001 US 98 East in Destin; (850) 634-4200; www.gatorbeach.com.

Pray tell . . . good-bye, God, I'm going to Florida. You were going to take a vacation from church, but then you arrived in the Destin area. The ocean sparkled, the sun shone, and you listened to weather reports from the Midwest. You were so thankful to be walking the beach instead of shoveling the driveway that you had to express your gratitude. What better place than a chapel that welcomes all faiths? Besides, church is almost always a fertile field for meeting new friends. If you want to meet a flock of snow birds, not unlike yourself (you know the species—eats early and enthusiastically, flits about, wants to see and do everything unless it interferes with his afternoon snooze in the sun), visit the *Chapel at Crosspoint.* This friendly, nondenominational congregation embraces all who show up and is an all-volunteer effort emphasizing music and a sense of humor. You've got to love a place of worship that asks the congregation to "please turn off your cell phones—God will not be calling you during the service." The chapel serves up a casual (the pastor often wears jeans) but meaningful worship experience. The chapel is at 1477 S. CR 393, Santa Rosa Beach; (850) 267-3146.

If you aren't an artist already, **Seaside** will make you long to be one. Perhaps the most widely painted and photographed community in northwest Florida, this pretty pastel town fronts a wide, sugar-white beach. Wood-frame cottages with front porches, tin roofs, gazebos, and picket fences evoke a feeling of nostalgia. Brick streets designed for leisurely strolling lead to lovely pavilions opening onto the beach. Town Center, with a village green, colorful shops, and restaurants, is but a short stroll away. Internationally acclaimed for its distinctive architecture and vision of what beach living should be, Seaside is a stunning success as well as a visual treat. Seaside Reservations Department, PO Box 4730, Seaside 32459; (866) 891-4600; www.seasidefl.com.

Perspicasity, a Mediterranean-type open-air bazaar, has an intriguing selection of clothes, accessories and shoes. On the beach side of CR 30-A in Seaside, its hours vary by the season, so call first at (850) 231-5829. **Modica Market,** surely one of north Florida's most unusual grocery stores, is the place to go when you're fresh out of Scottish smoked salmon or just have a taste for a New Orleans–style muffaletta or just-made tiramisu. Be sure to sample their freshly squeezed lemonade. Modica Market, open 7 a.m. to 7 p.m. daily,

What Is Crab Island?

Sometimes it's an underwater island. Sometimes it's a significant sandbar. Crab Island is a stretch of shallows that rises to the surface during the low-tide winter months. Once a haven for nesting birds and a fine place to hunt hermit crabs, today it is an ideal spot for water lovers to congregate. The transparent water ranges from 2 to 10 feet deep depending on time, tides, and where you anchor. **Crab Island** is a water playground where you can fish, tube, wade, bask in the sun, and play water football, volleyball, and Frisbee. This is also a favorite spot for anglers and party boats to drop anchor for a day. During the summer, floating vendors do a brisk business selling everything from hamburgers, ice cream, and boiled peanuts to steamed shrimp. Holiday weekends are a bit crazy. Look out for the locals.

Where is Crab Island? Crossing the Destin Bridge from April to November, on the north side of the bridge, look down and you will see from 10 to several hundred boats at anchor. Most of the time it looks like clear shallow water, but rest assured, that is Crab Island, and they are having a splendid time. You might want to join them.

Here's how: Rent a boat at **Sunshine Pontoon Rentals**—rent for a full or half day. Scout for dolphins, soak in the sun, or set out for Crab Island. Sunshine Pontoon Rentals is located at 500 Harbor Blvd., Destin; (850) 837-2299; www.sunshinepontoons.com.

Or try **Harbor Water Sports** at 390 Harbor Blvd., Destin; (850) 650-0390; www.harborwatersports.com; where you can parasail, take a dolphin tour, rent a pontoon or Jet Ski.

is located at 109 Seaside Central Sq., Santa Rosa Beach; (850) 231-1214; www .modicamarket.com.

Fred Gannon Rocky Bayou State Park provides an opportunity to see what the real Florida looks like. Located within Eglin Air Force Base, this park sits on the arm of Choctawhatchee Bay known as Rocky Bayou. A freshwater lake by the unlikely name of Puddin Head is home to largemouth bass, alligators, and a colony of beavers; nature trails wind through a pine forest shading reindeer moss and scrub oaks. The area is good for camping, swimming, boating, and fishing. Open 8 a.m. to sunset daily; located 3 miles east of Niceville off SR 20. For information, write to Fred Gannon Rocky Bayou State Park, 4281 SR 20, Niceville 32578; call (850) 833-9144; or visit www.floridastateparks.org.

panhandlesand

Don your darkest shades and prepare to be bedazzled. The brilliant white beaches of northwest Florida glitter and gleam their way through 343 sunny days each year.

How is this sand different? For starters, it's not beige, nor is it made of pulverized seashells. It's 99 percent pure quartz crystal formed in the Appalachian Mountains and refined by a millennium of grinding, polishing, and bleaching during its long river journey to the Gulf of Mexico. It's soft, squeaks underfoot, and is as clean and white as fresh snow.

Florida Panhandle history takes on new meaning at the **Heritage Museum** in Valparaiso. Besides an extensive library of old documents and maps (including *The Complete and Official Records of the Union and Confederate Armies*), the museum houses a collection of artifacts that provide insight into the social and economic challenges faced by Native Americans and early pioneers. You'll want to inspect the steam-powered cotton gin as well as tools used in farming, lumbering, and producing turpentine. Classes are offered in weaving, quilt-making, needlepoint, tatting, and basket-weaving, and handcrafted items are for sale. The Heritage Museum is at 115 Westview Ave. in downtown Valparaiso. Open 10 a.m. to 4 p.m. Tues through Sat; (850) 678-2615; www.heritage-museum.org.

The **Air Force Armament Museum** is outside the west gate of Eglin Air Force Base, the largest air force base in the world. The awesome SR 71 Blackbird spy plane and other military aircraft outside compete with interior displays and ongoing movies. The museum is open 9:30 a.m. to 4:30 p.m. Mon through Sat except on federal holidays. Eglin Air Force Base is 7 miles northeast of Fort Walton Beach on SR 85; 100 Museum Dr. For information, call (850) 651-1808 or visit www.afarmamentmuseum.com.

The historic fishing village of Destin was founded in the 1830s when Captain Leonard A. Destin sailed into Choctawhatchee Bay and decided it was a fine place to raise his family. The ***History and Fishing Museum*** is full of artifacts and photos that tell of the early days of this community. The staff may be able to help with genealogical research on early Destin families. The museum is on Stahlman Avenue, across from the Destin Library, and is open 10 a.m. to 4 p.m. Tues to Sat. History and Fishing Museum, 108 Stahlman Ave.; (850) 837-6611; www.destinhistoryand fishingmuseum.org.

In 1933 the isolated fishing village of Destin underwent a dramatic change: A wooden bridge was built connecting it to the outside world. Before long, folks began to notice Destin was not only the "luckiest fishing village" but also had some of the finest beaches anywhere. From red snapper to yellowfin tuna, an abundance of incredibly fresh and delectable seafood lands in area restaurants. Emerald Coast favorites include ***Marina Cafe,*** open 5 to 10 p.m. daily (404 Harbor Blvd., Destin; 850-837-7960; www.marinacafe.com), where the menu

union stronghold

After Florida left the Union in 1861, nearly all federal property in the state was seized by Secessionists, but a notable exception occurred at Pensacola. Rebel troops were never able to take Fort Pickens, but they did take control of all other installations in the area. In a November 1861 battle, Fort Barrancas had its flagstaff shot away and its walls slightly scarred, but casualties were light due to the strong walls. That combat turned out to be the last for the fort. In May 1862 the Confederates pulled out of Pensacola, and Union forces reoccupied all the harbor installations.

will have you struggling to make a choice. Rates are moderate to expensive. For lunch, savor a seafood combo at Fudpucker's (20001 Emerald Coast Pkwy., Destin; 850-654-4200; www.fudtv.com; inexpensive), or the superb char-grilled amberjack sandwich, served with a side-order view of parasailers and other assorted beach action, at the ***Back Porch*** (1740 US 98 East, Destin; 850-837-2022; www.theback-porch.com). Open 11 a.m. to 9 p.m. daily and until 11 p.m. during the summer. Rates are inexpensive to moderate.

Indians were dining on fresh seafood long before the Europeans "discovered" Florida. Some of them were mound builders, and they left a fine example of their work on the main drag in ***Fort Walton Beach.*** Imagine 500,000 basket-loads of dirt hauled one at a time to create this impressive landmark. To learn more about the seven pre-Columbian cultures who inhabited this area for more than 10,000 years, drop in at the ***Indian Temple Mound Museum*** on the east flank of the mound. Here you'll see the re-creation of an ancient temple, a four-legged bowl that has been called the most unique ceramic artifact in the Southeast, and various artifacts from recent archaeological excavations.

The museum and mound (which is a National Historic Landmark), at 139 Miracle Strip Pkwy. SE (US 98), are owned and operated by the City of Fort Walton Beach. The mound may be viewed during daylight hours. The museum is open noon to 4:30 p.m. Mon through Fri and 10 a.m. to 4:30 p.m. Sat. For more information call (850) 833-9595 or visit www.museumstuff.com.

Once upon a time, a buccaneer known as Billy Bowlegs decided being a run-of-the-mill pirate wasn't classy enough, so he assembled a group of followers—Indians, deserters, bandits, and the like—and proclaimed himself king of Florida. He did all the things pirates were supposed to do: scared folks out of their wits, took their money and buried it, and, in general, made a nuisance of himself. Since 1955, Fort Walton Beach has been annually reviving his swashbuckling spirit in the rollicking *Billy Bowlegs Pirate Festival.* The first week in June erupts in mock pirate attacks, parades, concerts, boat races, crafts exhibits, and, of course, treasure hunts. For information on the area, write Greater Fort Walton Beach Chamber of Commerce, PO Box 640, Fort Walton Beach, 32549; (850) 244-8191; www.fwbchamber.org.

Pensacola Area

Beach lovers can rest easy. *Gulf Islands National Seashore* protects shimmering white sand and swaying sea oats along a 150-mile stretch of islands and keys between Destin, Florida, and Gulfport, Mississippi. The Florida section of the national seashore includes *Naval Live Oaks Area* (where you may hike through groves once prized for shipbuilding), part of Perdido Key, the forts on the *Pensacola Naval Air Station,* and part of *Santa Rosa Island.*

Joe Patti and Anna Patane, born fewer than 10 miles apart in Sicily, had to cross the ocean to find each other. They met in Pensacola, Florida, in 1928 and started their own business in 1931. Captain Joe caught fresh bay shrimp, and Anna sold it from the back porch of their family home.

Theirs is the classic American story—combine hard work and the land of opportunity, and the result is success. Not only has it become the second-most popular tourist attraction in Pensacola (after the Naval Air Museum) and third in the nation in retail seafood markets, but *Joe Patti's Seafood* has become world renowned for its fresh and frozen seafood. The world seems to have beaten a path to this place, so is Joe Patti's Seafood really off the beaten path? First of all, it's crowded, so the secret is out. But there is a way to negotiate the system so you don't just stand there looking like you've lost your way. Work your way to the middle of the store, where someone is standing next to a customer-number machine handing out paper slips to new arrivals as they stream in. A number? To buy seafood? Yes, and it works.

Project GreenShores

Project GreenShores is systematically establishing a salt-marsh, seagrass and oyster reef habitat across from the Pensacola visitor center along the Bayfront Parkway. This 12-acre habitat was created by the Florida Department of Environmental Protection and local partners to boost estuarine habitat. The project won the Gulf Guardian Award, given by the Environmental Protection Agency. Project GreenShores was designated as part of the Great Florida Birding Trail. More than 400 local and migratory birds seem to enjoy the setting atop 10,000 tons of the limestone rock that is part of a man-made oyster reef. Get an up-close look at marine life and learn how salt-marsh grasses help create a healthier marine environment.

Birders know this area has been good for species such as osprey, brown pelican, and royal tern, but as the salt-marsh grasses take root, birders are spotting additional species. Yellow-crowned night herons, semipalmated plovers, and black-necked stilts can be seen on the flats and shoreline.

Park at Wayside Park near the bridge and walk the waterfront to the west along the bay shore. The restoration project continues past the Missing Children's Memorial on Hawkshaw Lagoon (across from Veterans Park) to Batram Park.

From I-10 North of Pensacola, take I-110 South to exit 1B (Chase Street) and head east. Continue east on Chase Street until it ends at US 98 (Bayfront Parkway) and turn left. The site and parking are approximately 0.3 miles on right, just before the Pensacola Bay Bridge. Open daily, dawn to dusk; (850) 436-5655. Take a self-guided tour or join a representative of the Florida Department of Environmental Education for a hands-on tour of Project GreenShores, a habitat restoration project. Visit www.dep.state.fl.us for additional information.

As frenzied as it may seem, the customers keep moving. Service is well choreographed and highly efficient. Browse the offerings. Tell the employee who takes your number what you want, and watch as your fish is filleted or otherwise prepared at gleaming stainless steel tables. After your purchase is weighed and bagged, head to the checkout counters in the back to have it professionally packed in ice for the drive home. Those visiting by plane get an airline-approved cooler. Unless you catch it yourself, you'll never have fresher seafood. But wait, don't leave. You'll want to check out *Amangiari Gourmet Shop* next door for imported olive oils, fresh bread, gelato, cannoli, and all kinds of interesting fare including Chinese pot stickers. At Patti's Sushi bar behind the deli, you can either dine in or take out. And then there's *Anna's Wine Shop,* with an awesome selection of wines from around the world. Be sure to inquire in advance about a behind-the-scenes tour or wine tasting for groups. Joe Patti's Seafood, 524 S. B St., Pensacola; (850) 432-3315 or (800) 500-9929; www.joepattis.com.

If you miss the **Fish House Restaurant,** you have missed Pensacola at its best. Location—right on the bay—is the first thing you should consider. Then scrutinize the menu, and when you get to World-Famous Grits à Ya Ya, STOP right there. If you don't have a big appetite, go out and run a marathon or something, because you've found what you came for. Here are the ingredients: spiced Gulf jumbo shrimp atop a sauté of spinach, portobello mushrooms, applewood-smoked bacon, garlic, shallots, and cream over a heaping bed of smoked Gouda cheese grits. The grits alone are worth the price of admission. You can work all day cooking this dish, but in the end you might as well face it—it just tastes better when you eat it in the Fish House. A selection of Southern sides rounds out the meal—"Ma's fresh collard greens," fried okra, black-eyed peas, etc. They're all outstanding. Save a little room for a slice of key lime pie (authentically yellow, not green) or the triple chocolate cheesecake. You will not leave hungry. The Fish House Restaurant, 600 S. Barracks St., Pensacola; (850) 470-0003; www .goodgrits.com.

world'slargest artificialreef

The **USS** Oriskany, a retired aircraft carrier sunk in 2006, is definitely off the beaten path. The massive, 911-foot wreck is 24 miles southeast of Pensacola Pass, but you need to be a certified diver to explore it. The variety of marine life is astonishing. It's definitely worth the trip.

The heart of Pensacola is in **Seville Square,** a historic district between East Government and South Alcaniz Streets where shops, restaurants, museums, and art galleries inhabit a hodgepodge of restored 18th- and 19th-century cottages and mansions. Pick up a free map and brochures at the visitor information center, 1401 E. Gregory St. (at the foot of the bridge), Pensacola; open 8 a.m. to 5 p.m. Mon to Fri, 9 a.m. to 4 p.m. Sat, and 11 a.m. to 4 p.m. Sun; (850) 434-1234 or (800) 874-1234; www.visitpensacola.com.

Stop in at the **Pensacola Historical Museum** for local history, including everything from displays on ancient Indian culture and Mardi Gras costumes to a fully equipped 1915 kitchen. Open 10 a.m. to 4 p.m. Tues through Sat. The museum is located at 115 E. Zaragosa St., Pensacola; (850) 433-1559; www .historicpensacola.org.

For a delightful glimpse into Pensacola's past, browse the **Museums of Industry and Commerce** (200 E. Zaragosa St., Pensacola; 850-595-5985), chat with costumed interpreters in five house museums, and shop a wide variety of attractive boutiques in **Historic Pensacola Village** (205 E. Zaragosa St., Pensacola; 850-595-5985). Don't miss the truly weird collection (including both shrunken heads and a petrified cat) in the *T. T. Wentworth Jr. Florida State Museum.* Kids love Discovery!, the lively hands-on children's museum upstairs. The museum is at 330 S. Jefferson St., Pensacola; open 10 a.m. to 4 p.m. Tues to Sat; (850) 595-5990; www.historicpensacola.org.

Not to be missed is *Seville Quarter* with *Rosie O'Grady's Good Time Emporium* and seven other saloons and restaurants. Even if you're not hungry, thirsty, or in need of entertainment, you really should stop in for a look. Besides an impressive collection of local antiques, the gaslights are from Liverpool, the parliament benches are from London, the disco booth was once an English pulpit, the ships' wheels in Coppersmith's Gallery are from schooners that made tea and spice runs to China, and Rosie's main door at one time graced a mansion in Mobile, Alabama.

Seville Quarter overflows with choices. Should you down a Flaming Hurricane drink at Rosie's, catch the show on a big-screen TV in *Lili Marlene's World War I Aviators Pub*, or tap your feet to *Apple Annie's* wonderful bluegrass music? While you're deciding, you might want to experience the flavors and ambience of New Orleans's French Quarter in the *Palace Cafe* by sampling some coffee and a plate of hot beignets. The Seville Quarter is at 130 E. Government St. in Pensacola, and the prices range from inexpensive to expensive; (850) 434-6211; www.sevillequarter.com.

Take a ride, or better yet a walk, through *North Hill Preservation District.* This 50-block area, bounded by LaRua, Palafox, Blount, and Reus Streets, is a treasure trove of fancy turn-of-the-20th-century houses. You'll be able to appreciate the details—the wide verandas, turrets, and elaborate gingerbread trim—better on foot. For more information call (850) 439-3384 or visit www.historicnorthhill.com.

The expansive *National Naval Aviation Museum* is a real prize—a beautifully designed, fascinating tribute to aviation history on the grounds of the world's largest naval air station. You'll follow the growth and development of our country's naval aviation from the first aircraft the navy purchased in 1911 (replica) to the Skylab command module. Especially fascinating is the movie of the inspiring Great Flight, the first successful crossing of the Atlantic Ocean by air in 1919. The only museum in the world devoted exclusively to naval aviation, this one has something for everyone. You can try out the controls of a jet trainer, wander among full-size aircraft, or browse the bookstore and gift shop. An impressive wing features a dramatic 7-story atrium with 4 full-size Blue Angel Sky Hawks soaring in permanent diamond formation. Use the main entrance of the Naval Air Station. In Pensacola take Palafox Street south to Garden Street, which becomes Navy Boulevard (SR 295). Follow the signs to the Naval Air Station, 1750 Radford Blvd., Ste. C/Naval Air Station,

Pensacola; (850) 452-3604; www.navalaviationmuseum.org. Open 9 a.m. to 5 p.m. daily. Closed Thanksgiving, Christmas, and New Year's Day. A real bargain—it's free.

The **Pensacola Naval Air Station** features a number of other attractions visitors sometimes miss because they simply don't realize they are so close by. The **Spanish Fort San Carlos de Barrancas** (part of the Gulf Islands National Seashore) is practically across the road from the museum. First stop in the visitor center to get some background information, then explore the fort and enjoy its commanding view. Be careful in the dark, steep, and sometimes slippery tunnel to the water battery.

Guaranteed to get your adrenaline pumping! Take a look at **Sherman Field,** home of the famous precision flying team known as the Blue Angels. Watch as they practice over the Naval Air Station most Tuesdays and Wednesdays from March to November. On Wednesday the Blue Angels team visits the museum to answer questions and sign autographs following their practice flight. Practices are at 8:30 a.m. sharp in back of the Naval Museum. Arrive 30 minutes before the practice, park at the Naval Museum, and bring sunscreen and bottled water. Limited bleacher seating is available or bring a lawn chair. Reserved seating is available for groups.

Or watch the Blues from the top of the Pensacola Lighthouse. Forget about a bird's-eye view—you will be eye to eye with the Blue Angels. Now this is a unique vantage point from which to view the show.

A night tour of one of America's most haunted lighthouses will prickle your skin. Keep in mind that this is a working lighthouse. Climb to the top for an awesome view of moonlit Pensacola Bay. Listen to chilling tales of ghosts who have been coming and going for many a blue moon. Call (850) 393-1561 or visit www.lighthousereservations.org. The **Old Pensacola Lighthouse** has been operating since 1825. The Pensacola Naval Air Station main entrance is on Navy Boulevard, SR 295; the facility is open 9 a.m. to 5 p.m. daily. Free.

While you're in the area, take advantage of the fine facilities at **Big Lagoon State Park,** where you may picnic, camp, boat, fish, and swim. An elaborate boardwalk network and observation tower at East Beach provide birders with an excellent view overlooking the marsh. This is definitely the place to watch the great blue heron stalk his dinner! Also, you may soak up panoramic vistas of Big Lagoon, the park, and Gulf Islands National Seashore across the Intracoastal Waterway. The park is about 10 miles southwest of Pensacola off SR 292A. Big Lagoon State Park, 12301 Gulf Beach Hwy., Pensacola; (850) 492-1595; www.floridastateparks.org.

Upper Panhandle

It's your turn to tour the treetops—not just any treetops but the world's largest contiguous longleaf pine/wiregrass ecosystem. You step off the tower for the first time and your adrenaline kicks in. From there, exhilaration is part of the package. Glide over historic areas and rare geological sites. Soar through four unique ecosystems. Zip across two creeks—Wolfe Creek and Coldwater Creek. Your guides will tell you tales of this beautiful natural area and make sure that everyone in your group is safe as you fly through the treetops above ***Blackwater River State Forest.*** Look down. You are viewing one of America's most unusual sights. Coldwater Creek is stunning, with its snow white sandbars, vast ravines, and crystal-clear water rippling under a canopy of cedar, maple, and cypress trees. Be alert. Especially at dawn or dusk you may see wildlife—deer, turkey, and bobcat. Sign up for "Forest Flight," a series of nine zip-lines and one sky bridge. Three hours will fly by like a minute. Or you may elect "Soaring Stream," a series of 5 zip-lines. For the ultimate zip adventure, brave 14 zip-lines, 2 sky bridges, and 2 towers. You will fly 900 feet over Coldwater Creek, dipping down and almost touching the water. Are you are between 70 and 250 pounds and longing for a bird's-eye view of the world below? If you are, call Adventures Unlimited for information, (850) 623-6197, or visit www.adventures unlimited.com.

Canoeists and campers will appreciate ***Blackwater River State Park*** on the shores of one of the cleanest rivers in the country. Dark water contrasts with dazzling white sandbars at bends in the river. Especially good for novice paddlers and inner-tubers, the river winds its way from Alabama to Blackwater Bay at the leisurely rate of 3 to 4 miles per hour. The park is 15 miles northeast of Milton, 3 miles off US 90. Open 8 a.m. until sunset daily. Blackwater River State Park, 7720 Deaton Bridge Rd., Holt; (850) 983-5363; www.florida stateparks.org.

Since Milton has been officially designated Canoe Capital of Florida, you should really take advantage of the splendid surrounding waterways. ***Adventures Unlimited Outdoor Center*** on Coldwater Creek is the way to go. This family-oriented wilderness resort offers everything from a ropes challenge course to camping, hiking, biking, and inner-tubing. But most come here to canoe. Area rivers, shallow and free of dangerous rapids, are unbelievably scenic. The friendly staff will help you plan your canoe trip and choose your rental equipment and will even pack you a picnic basket. Lodging choices include cabins, Granny Peaden's Cracker-style cottage, or the attractively restored Wolfe Creek Schoolhouse Inn nestled in the secluded woods. Adventures

Unlimited Outdoor Center, 8974 Tomahawk Landing Rd., Milton 32570; (850) 623-6197 or (800) 239-6864; www.adventuresunlimited.com.

Put on your hiking shoes and heed the call of the *Jackson Red Ground Trail.* Located in Blackwater River State Forest, this old 21-mile Indian trading trail was used by General Andrew Jackson on his historic 1818 journey to the Florida Territory. Follow the orange paint marks on trees from Karick Lake to the Red Rock Bridge over a combination of footpaths and forest roadways.

The Jackson Red Ground Trail, which is part of the National Recreation Trail System and designated as a section of the Florida Trail System, has two camping shelters, one at Peaden Bridge and one south of SR 4. Open 7 a.m. to 4 p.m. weekdays. For information, contact Blackwater Forestry Center, 11650 Munson Hwy., Milton; (850) 957-6140.

asinkingfeeling

Falling Waters Sink, a cylindrical, smooth-walled chimney 100 feet deep with a diameter of 15 feet, is in Falling Waters State Park near Marianna. Here a small stream creates a waterfall and then flows into an underground cavern at the bottom of the sink, where hand-hewn timbers of an early gristmill can still be seen. This is a classic example of one of Florida's notable geological features, the limestone sinkhole.

Lake DeFuniak, halfway between Pensacola and Tallahassee, is well worth a visit. For one thing, this claims to be one of only two perfectly round lakes in the world; for another, the area has a rich and fascinating heritage. During the 1880s a railroad executive envisioned a splendid winter resort here. Later, the Chautauqua Committee decided this would make a fine winter site for its program of concerts and lectures given each summer at Lake Chautauqua, New York. Take some time to admire the late-19th-century Chautauqua Assembly Building and the grand old homes that surround the lake. The US Department of the Interior and the National Parks Service have placed the Town of DeFuniak Springs on the National Register of Historic Districts, citing some 285 structures of significant historic value. The Great Depression ended this glorious era, but an annual festival helps preserve memories of the past. The lake is in DeFuniak Springs near US 90 and SR 83. For information on the festival, call the Walton County Chamber of Commerce at (850) 267-0683 or visit www.waltonareachamber.com.

Welcome to the warmth and hospitality of another era. Located in the heart of the historic village of DeFuniak Springs, *Hotel DeFuniak* was built in 1920. Meticulously restored in 1998, it is furnished with 19th-century European and American antiques. Each room is unique; guests may choose from a variety of elegant styles including French country, Dutch romantic, and safari. The feeling is of another time—a slower, more gracious time. Guests may stroll to more than

200 historic sites and Victorian homes. No need to drive—lovely Lake DeFuniak is just a few steps from the hotel. When hunger calls, you won't even need to leave the hotel. ***Bogey's Bar and Restaurant*** awaits, ideal for a business lunch or romantic dinner for two. This is the Florida of yesteryear. The Hotel DeFuniak is on the corner of 8th Street and US 90. From I-10 take exit 85 (US 331), and go north 2 miles. Turn right (east) onto US 90 for 3 blocks. Located 1 block west of the Walton County courthouse and government offices. 400 E. Nelson Ave. (US 90), DeFuniak Springs; (850) 892-4383 (hotel), (850) 951-2233 (restaurant), (877) 333-8642; www.hotel defuniak.com.

strolling lake defuniak

A relaxing after-dinner ramble to view the Victorian homes surrounding Lake DeFuniak makes for an idyllic outing. Elaborate architectural details, including turrets, double verandas, classic fluted columns, gingerbread trim, and window dormers, create an architectural feast for the eyes.

Don't miss seeing one of the town's most historically significant structures, the ***Walton-DeFuniak Library.*** Opened on December 20, 1887, this is believed to be the state's oldest public library continuously operating in its original building. Its one room measured 24 by 17 feet and cost just under $580 when built. This charming library holds 30,000 volumes, including some rare books as old as the library itself.

You really wouldn't expect to find a fine European armor collection in such a modest little library, but that is one of the bonuses of getting off the beaten path. When Wallace Bruce was ambassador to Scotland and living in Edinburgh in the 1880s, his son Kenneth began collecting armor. The family came to DeFuniak Springs around 1890 when Mr. Bruce became president of the Chautauqua winter program. Some of the pieces of this unusual collection date back as far as the Crusades (AD 1100 to 1300). Besides European pieces, there are Kentucky rifles from the Daniel Boone era.

The entire collection was willed to Palmer College, but when the college closed in the 1930s, it was given to the city in partial payment of its debts. The city had no suitable place for it, so it eventually wound up in the library for visitors to enjoy. You won't have any trouble finding the library. Just drive around Lake DeFuniak on Circle Drive and look for a tiny building. Closed Sunday. For information, contact the library at (850) 892-3624.

You'll want to stop for a sip or two of wine at the ***Chautauqua Winery*** in DeFuniak Springs. Opened in 1989, the winery has earned more than 150 medals and awards in national and international competitions. The wines run the gamut from dry, barrel-fermented wines to traditional Southern favorites

Howling with Wolves

We are huddled in small groups on the ground at the **Seacrest Wolf Preserve** (3449 Bonnett Pond Rd., Chipley; (850) 773-2897; www.seacrestwolfpreserve.org). It is a raw day, overcast, with intermittent rain. That brilliant sun that Florida is famous for is noticeably absent. Crouching on the dirt, we are trying to ignore the bone-chilling cold. We are here to see the wolves.

Yes, wolves in Florida. And our plan is to do more than look. We will walk among them, touch them, and, yes, howl with the best of them. They call this an experience, and they are not kidding. If we huddle together in small groups, the wolves will be less threatened, more comfortable. I don't know much about wolves, but if the experts say they don't want their wolves uncomfortable, I will do as I'm told.

The first thing I notice about the wolves is that they are sporting fur coats, whereas we are severely underdressed. After all, we were expecting Florida sunshine and had optimistically packed the high-powered sunscreen. We learn there are all kinds of rules for getting close and personal with these fascinating animals. After all, they are wild, whether raised by humans or not. So they might become confused. Or worse.

We are cautioned to have nothing dangling, such as a purse, pony tails, even mittens. The wolves will think these things are toys and want to play with them and with you. Wolf play can be quite uncomfortable, but then so can sitting in the dirt. The wolves have had a bad rap that started in ancient times. Did you know that in 14th-century England the king accepted wolf heads instead of money for payment of taxes?

Remember listening to *Little Red Riding Hood*? That children's fairy tale should put the fear of God into anyone who has ever contemplated death by being eaten. When Little Red Riding Hood notices her grandmother's large teeth, the wolf, all decked out in the grandmother's PJs and nightcap, replies, "The better to eat you with, my dear."

The stories of wicked wolves crossed the Atlantic with the first settlers. The wolves were always depicted as a treacherous, murdering clan, and yet, we are told, in reality they are quite the opposite. In fact, they are monogamous, take good care of

like sweet muscadine and blueberry wine. Other popular offerings include juice and gourmet items, such as grapeseed cooking oil. Visitors are invited to tour the winery and learn about the process of grape growing and winemaking seasons, from pruning and harvesting to crushing and bottling. The winery is open daily, and the tastings and tours are always free. Chautauqua Vineyards and Winery, 364 Hugh Adams Rd., DeFuniak Springs; (850) 892-5887; www.chautauquawinery.com.

How nice is Niceville? Very nice, indeed. In fact, it's a center of creative energy showcasing a wide variety of cultural offerings. This is the home of their babies, and are loyal to their family units. They organize themselves into packs, understand their place in the pack, and do the job assigned to them.

We are learning a great deal about this highly endangered species. Gray wolf does not refer to its color, which ranges from grizzled gray and cinnamon to coal black and pure white, but rather to its species, and that species is close to being exterminated from the face of the earth. It would be hard not to come away from this wolf sanctuary without holding them in high regard. Their keepers are passionate, to say the least. The gray wolf used to roam the entire country, and now this noble breed has been reduced to less than 50 specimens here in Florida and a scattering of wolf packs in some western states. The answer is education. While we may be thoroughly convinced as to the merits of saving the wolves, cattle ranchers in Idaho might feel less enthusiastic after discovering yet another cow gutted by wolves in the night.

All this time we have been shivering on the ground, and now they are encouraging the wolves to interact with us. They turn out to be shy at first and then, when they have lost their fear, they become downright playful.

I'm sorry to be less than ecstatic when a wolf wants to lick my face, but Red Riding Hood was a staple in my early childhood reading repertoire. Now they are leaping about, warming to their mission to show off for the visitors. This could have something to do with the fact that one of the keepers is handing out the wolves' favorite appetizer, nuggets of raw meat. Before they start eyeing us as part of the main course, I slink out. I'm convinced. They are handsome animals, and I am pleased to come away with all my fingers intact.

My favorite part of the wolf experience was communicating with this threatened species. We learned to cup our frozen hands around our mouth and howl to our heart's content. Then we were to be very quiet and listen. What came back was mystical. Off in the woods somewhere . . . an answer. A pack of wolves, in captivity, reporting in with us. They have heard our call. Their howls reverberate through the night. An eerie, lonely cry passed down, wolf to wolf, from the earliest of times. A message that says *find a place for me. I'm here to stay.* If that makes your skin crawl, so be it.

Mattie Kelly Arts Center, northwest Florida's premier arts complex located on the *Northwest Florida State College* campus. You may enjoy the best of Broadway touring shows, listen to international guest artists, and attend concerts by the Northwest Florida Symphony Orchestra. Two fine art galleries, McIlroy and Holzhauer, draw from the surrounding communities to feature rotating exhibits. The Holzhauer Gallery displays the college's multimillion-dollar permanent art collection, which includes Emil Holzhauer's paintings and drawings, the Sublette Collection of New Guinea Sculpture, the I. R. Davis Flint Glass Collection, and over 100 Salvador Dalí original woodblock prints. Mattie Kelly Arts Center, 100

College Blvd., Niceville; (850) 729-6000; www.mattiekellyartscenter.org. Gallery is open Mon through Thurs 9 a.m. to 4 p.m., Sun 1 to 4 p.m. Closed Fri, Sat, and holidays. All exhibitions and programs are free and open to the public

Waterfalls in Florida? Strange as it may seem, they do exist in *Falling Waters State Park.* Though they don't exactly create a neck-craning Niagara, these waters do, just the same, fall. You see, some of the most notable geological features in Florida are the sinkholes. A small stream meanders into a 100-foot sinkhole, and voilà, a "waterfall"! A few caveats: You will be looking down, not up, and during the dry season there may not be any water to fall.

Not to worry. This forested area, the site of the first attempt (1919) to find oil in Florida, is lovely to stroll through. Limestone sinkholes that honeycomb the hilly terrain may be viewed from a series of boardwalks. Take the self-guided nature trails, picnic, camp, and swim. Located 3 miles south of Chipley, off SR 77A, the area is open 8 a.m. to sunset daily year-round. Falling Waters State Park, 1130 State Park Rd., Chipley; (850) 638-6130; www.florida stateparks.org.

Florida's caverns are another feature to come under the heading of strange quirks of geology. Over the millennium, mineral-rich drops of water have created the enchanting formations in *Florida Caverns State Park.* Among other sights, you'll see the *Waterfall Room,* the *Cathedral Room,* and the *Wedding Room*—all decked out in natural splendor. The caverns are as impressive, if not as large, as some of the country's most famous underground attractions. An enlightening audiovisual show in the visitor center explains how the caverns were formed, and exhibits on natural and cultural history shed some light on the early Indians who found shelter here.

The park also has a disappearing river, a natural bridge, and a natural beach rimming Blue Hole Springs. You may camp, swim, fish, canoe, and picnic. The park, off SR 166, is 3 miles north of Marianna. Open 8 a.m. to sundown daily. Cave tours are offered 9 a.m. to 4 p.m. daily except Tues and Wed. Florida Caverns State Park, 3345 Caverns Rd., Marianna; (850) 482-9598; www.floridastateparks.org.

If New England and Canada seem a trifle far to go for fall color, try *Torreya State Park.* Here rugged bluffs and ravines forested by flowers and hardwoods common to the North Georgia Appalachians provide the state's prettiest autumn display. The park, a botanist's paradise, protects the Torreya tree, which is native only to the 20-mile surrounding area. Be sure to tour the restored *Gregory Mansion* (1849), once the home of an affluent cotton planter, and hike the trails to the Apalachicola River. The park, on CR 1641 (which is off SR 12) between Bristol and Greensboro, is open 8 a.m. to sunset daily year-round. Guided tours of the house are given during the week at 10 a.m. and on weekends and holidays at 10 a.m., 2 p.m., and 4 p.m. Torreya State Park, 2576 NW Torreya Park Rd., Bristol; (850) 643-2674; www.florida stateparks.org.

The fishing is fine at **Three Rivers State Park.** Named for the Chatta-hoochee and Flint Rivers, which merge to form the Apalachicola, this scenic area includes 4 miles of shoreline on Lake Seminole at the Florida/Georgia border. Home to a slew of alligators and huge alligator snapping turtles as well as fish, Three Rivers is the place to wet a line, boat, picnic, or camp. Located 2 miles north of Sneads off SR 271, it's open 8 a.m. to sunset daily year-round. Three Rivers State Park, 7908 Three Rivers Park Rd., Sneads; (850) 482-9006; www.floridastateparks.org.

Tallahassee Area

At the **Alfred B. Maclay Gardens State Park** near Tallahassee, the peak blooming season begins in December and continues through April, when dog-wood, redbud, and more than 100 varieties of camellias and azaleas create a fairyland of flowers. The gardens are an oasis of beauty all year, but spring is spectacular! This 307-acre park was once the home of Alfred B. Maclay, a New York financier who made his winter home here starting in 1923.

He developed the grounds as a hobby, using exotic plants to comple-ment the native varieties and adding reflecting pools and avenues of stately palms. Stroll the brick walkways to the tiny walled garden where a graceful fountain provides the only sound except for the distant coo of the doves. If it's serenity you're after, you've come to the right place. Picnic grounds overlook Lake Hall, which is fine for swimming and boating (only electric motors allowed).

The park is open 8 a.m. to sunset daily year-round. The gardens and the **Maclay House Museum** are open 9 a.m. to 5 p.m. daily. The Maclay Gardens are north of Tallahassee, half a mile from exit 30 on I-10. Alfred B. Maclay Gardens State Park, 3540 Thomasville Rd., Tallahassee; (850) 487-4556; www .floridastateparks.org/maclaygardens.

The tradition of wintering in Florida was apparently started by Hernando de Soto in 1539. He and his men celebrated Christmas mass in the vicinity of **Lake Jackson Mounds Archaeological State Park** in what is believed to have been the first Christmas in the New World. That doesn't seem like such a long time ago when you consider that, on the basis of recent excavations, archaeologists now speculate the area was inhabited as early as 1,300 years before the birth of Christ.

The dominant features of Lake Jackson Mounds Archaeological State Park are impressive pyramid-shaped mounds that are the remains of the largest known Native American ceremonial center in north Florida. A way of life flourished here from AD 1300 to 1600 that revolved around a village, six temple mounds, and a burial mound. The people who lived here were farmers who traded their surplus crops with nearby villages. After you climb to the top of the highest mound, you will more fully appreciate the fact that these mounds were created by people carrying sand and clay, one basketful at a time! This is a lovely spot for a picnic and a walk through the woods. The Butler Mill Trail through a hardwood ravine and upland pine woods leads to an early 1880s gristmill site. The mounds are located 6 miles north of Tallahassee off US 27 at 3600 Indian Mounds Rd.; (850) 922-6007; www.floridastateparks.org.

For more information about ancient Florida—its ice age, huge mastodons, resourceful native tribes, and Spanish explorers—stop in at the ***Museum of Florida History*** in downtown Tallahassee. This is the place to learn about Florida's role on the high seas, to inspect a pre–Civil War dugout boat, and to view precious gold doubloons. Florida's wild booms and busts, complete with a colorful cast of characters from pirates to lumber tycoons, are all part of the story. Fascinating for all ages, the museum is housed in the R. A. Grey Building (500 S. Bronough; 850-245-6400; www.museumoffloridahistory.com) across from the Florida State Supreme Court in Tallahassee. Open every day (except Christmas and Thanksgiving) 9 a.m. to 4:30 p.m. Mon through Fri, 10 a.m. to 4:30 p.m. Sat, and noon to 4:30 p.m. Sun. Free.

The ***Tallahassee Antique Car Museum*** is chock-full of surprises. We expected cars, lots of cars, and we got them—immaculate, glistening, and champing at the bit. From the Stanley Steamer, Plymouth Prowler, and 1931 Duesenburg Model J to a Studebaker stunt car masquerading as a Tucker, they were in prime condition. As were the rest of the collections, from Indian artifacts, knives, and cash registers (!) to vintage outboard motors. While kids were drawn to a fantastic collection of pedal cars, Abraham Lincoln's horse-drawn hearse sent a somber historic shudder through the adults. The biggest surprise? A fantastic lineup of antique pianos—each a masterpiece of creative craftsmanship. My favorite? A re-creation of the original Alma-Tadema Art Case Steinway, hand-carved using 22 species of wood, with griffin legs and names of Greek muses inlaid on its lid. Museum owner De Voe Moore doesn't even play the piano, but he knows quality when he sees it. This one was described by Christie's in London as "the most artistic piano ever produced." 6800 Mahan Dr., Tallahassee; (850) 942-0137; www.tacm.com.

Bradley's Country Store is the place to go for a whiff of the past and the true taste of country smoked sausage. While you're there, pick up a couple of bags of Bradley's Country Milled Grits. Why are these products in such demand? Four generations of Bradleys have had a long time to get it right. The sausage is seasoned and smoked according to a recipe perfected a century ago by Grandma Mary Bradley, who started selling sausage from her kitchen in 1910. The Bradleys built a cane press and syrup furnace in 1915. The grits have been ground in the mill house behind the store with the same care for nearly a century. The store stocks such old-time favorites as hogshead cheese, liver pudding, and cracklings. Opened in 1927 and listed on the National Register of Historic Places, Bradley's Country Store is on Centerville Road, 12 leisurely miles from Tallahassee beneath a canopy of moss-draped oaks. The store is open Mon through Fri from 8 a.m. to 6 p.m. and Sat from 8 a.m. until 5 p.m. Bradley's Country Store, 10655 Centerville Rd., Tallahassee; (850) 893-1647; www.bradleyscountrystore.com.

Long before Americans set their spring vacation sights on Florida, Tallahassee was a popular place. Way back in the late 1600s, more than 1,400 Apalachee Indians and several hundred Spanish lived side by side in and around ***Mission San Luis.*** The mission, presently being reconstructed on its original site, was once the western capital of Spanish Florida. Unfortunately, this center for military, religious, and administrative activity was burned to the ground in 1704. In fact, of more than 100 mission settlements scattered around Spanish Florida, none has survived. Luckily, we have this impressive reconstruction to show us how folks lived in the 17th century.

The Pole-Vaulting Fish

At **Wakulla Springs** we took both boat trips offered, the jungle cruise and the glass-bottom-boat tour, and saw all manner of birds and fish. The endangered limpkin thrives here, primarily because its food, the apple snail, is abundant in the area. Often called the "crying bird," the limpkin's distinctive call has been described as sounding like "a woman lost forever in the swamps." This is one bird that has perfected extracting escargots down to a science, judging from the empty shells piled along the banks of the Wakulla.

We saw an alligator carrying several small progeny on its head, mullet jumping all over the place, and, yes, a pole-vaulting fish. Now Henry, the fish, doesn't pole-vault just for the fun of it. Our guide worked awfully hard to pull off this particular feat.

"Henry," he called out loudly, "I want you to meet us at the pole." Well, that didn't do it. After calling again and again in a special singsong that apparently is supposed to provoke action, our guide was reduced to pleading. He tried in a more threatening tone: "Henry! Henry Junior! Henrietta!"—all to no avail. Then suddenly a fish appeared, grinned, and vaulted over the pole. Everyone cheered.

Strolling this lovely 60-acre, largely undisturbed archaeological park is to wander into the past. Costumed interpreters bring the whole complex to life. You may meet a young monk as you enter the Franciscan church, watch Spanish colonists tend their gardens, and question the Spanish officer in charge at the fort. Or you can chat with a native Apalachee in the council house. This massive building can hold 3,000 people and is the largest known historic-era building in the southeastern US.

You may also learn that the height of the bunks circling the building's interior is no accident. They were designed just high enough so fleas, with limited jumping abilities, couldn't infest the sleeping Indians. Clearly the interpreters are just itching to have fun while imparting some very useful information. Mission San Luis, 2100 W. Tennessee St., Tallahassee; (850) 245-6406. Open Tues through Sun from 10 a.m. to 4 p.m. Closed Mon, New Year's Day, Easter, 4th of July, Thanksgiving Day, and Christmas Eve and Day.

The *LeMoyne Center for Visual Arts* is an oasis of peaceful beauty tucked into the middle of Tallahassee. The area's leading artists are represented in this compact gallery. In the Helen Lind Sculpture Garden, a few metal sculptures adorn a lovingly cared for three-quarter-acre garden behind the gallery. Open 10 a.m. to 5 p.m. Tues through Sat, For information, write to LeMoyne Art Foundation, 125 N. Gadsden St., Tallahassee 32301; (850) 222-8800; www .lemoyne.org.

The *Florida State University Flying High Circus* serves up excitement the first two weekends in April. Students perform under the Big Top at Florida State University at West Pensacola Street and Chieftain Way. Performances are at 7 p.m. Fri and Sat with a matinee at 2 p.m. on Sat afternoon. For details, call (850) 644-4874. Campus tours and maps are available at the visitor information center; (850) 644-3246; www.circus.fsu.edu.

The *Tallahassee Museum of History and Natural Science* is a favorite haunt for adults as well as children who are curious about the way things were. At this authentic 1890 pioneer farm and community, you'll see demonstrations of blacksmithing, syrup making, sheep shearing, spinning, and weaving during fall farm days. There are nature trails, exhibits of wild animals native to the area, a one-room schoolhouse, a gristmill, and the Bellevue Plantation, once the home of Prince and Princess Murat. The museum is at 3945 Museum Dr., Tallahassee, on Lake Bradford bordering Apalachicola National Forest. Open 9 a.m. to 5 p.m. Mon through Sat and 12:30 to 5 p.m. Sun; (850) 575-8684; www.tallahasseemuseum.org. Recorded information: (850) 576-1636.

If you'd like to peer into the world's deepest spring, head south of Tallahassee to *Edward Ball Wakulla Springs State Park,* where limestone-filtered water gushes forth at more than 600,000 gallons per minute. Wakulla has been a sanctuary for wildlife and people ever since Indians fished its 185-foot depths and Spanish explorers refreshed themselves in its clean, clear waters. Tourists after the Civil War thought the springs well worth the trip, as did underwater filmmakers, who came as early as the mid-1940s.

The resort still has an old-fashioned flavor due to its emphasis on conservation rather than razzle-dazzle tourism. This 2,888-acre wildlife sanctuary provides a glorious glimpse into precondominium Florida. Jungle cruises and glass-bottom-boat tours reveal an enchanting blend of scenery and wildlife. You'll see lots of alligators and elegant birds, including snowy egrets, herons, and ibises.

One common meaning given for the Indian word *wakulla* is "mysteries of strange waters." The spring has its share of mysteries, including complete mastodon skeletons, which have been found in the bottom of the spring. It seems appropriate that this was the location for the filming of *Creature from the Black Lagoon*.

After exploring the nature trails or taking a swim, enjoy historic **Wakulla Springs Lodge.** This Spanish-style inn, built in the 1930s of Tennessee marble, has unusual wood ceiling beams decorated with Florida scenes and flowers. The lodge dining room serves up Southern cooking at reasonable prices. Wakulla Springs is 15 miles south of Tallahassee on SR 267. The lodge is open 24 hours; the park closes at dusk daily. Edward Ball Wakulla Springs State Park and Lodge, 550 Wakulla Park Dr., Wakulla Springs; (850) 926-0700; www.floridastateparks.org.

Civil War buffs will not want to miss the **Natural Bridge Battlefield Historic State Park.** Young cadets from West Florida Seminary (now Florida State University) and old men (Gadsden County Grays) joined Confederate forces to inflict heavy casualties on Union soldiers here on March 6, 1865. Thanks to their efforts, Tallahassee was the only Southern capital east of the Mississippi that did not fall into Union hands. Each year, in early March, the battle is reenacted.

This is a fine place to do a little fishing in the St. Marks River or have a picnic, but don't go looking for an impressive arch like Virginia's Natural Bridge. This was originally a place where the river flowed underground for a distance, but the county has modified the "bridge" for drainage purposes. The battlefield site is 10 miles southeast of Tallahassee. Take US 363 to Woodville, then go east on Natural Bridge Road. For more information, write the Tallahassee–St. Marks Geo Park, 7502 Natural Bridge Rd., Tallahassee 32301; (850) 922-6007; www.floridastateparks.org.

State Parks in Northwest Florida

State park information: (850) 245-2157 or www .floridastateparks.org. For camping reservations in any state park, call (800) 326-3521.

Alfred B. Maclay Gardens State Park, (850) 487-4556

Bald Point State Park, (850) 349-9146

Big Lagoon State Park, (850) 492-1595

Blackwater River State Park, (850) 983-5363

Camp Helen State Park, (850) 233-5059

Cedar Key Museum State Park, (352) 543-5350

Cedar Key Scrub State Reserve, (352) 543-5567

Constitution Convention Museum State Park, (850) 229-8029

Deer Lake State Park, (850) 267-8300

Dr. Julian G. Bruce (St. George Island) State Park, (850) 927-2111

Econfina River State Park, (850) 922-6007

Eden Gardens State Park, (850) 267-8320

Edward Ball Wakulla Springs State Park & Lodge, (850) 926-0700

Falling Waters State Park, (850) 638-6130

Florida Caverns State Park, (850) 482-9598

Forest Capital Museum State Park, (850) 584-3227

Fred Gannon (Rocky Bayou) State Park, (850) 833-9144

Grayton Beach State Park, (850) 267-8300

Henderson Beach State Park, (850) 837-7550

John Gorrie Museum State Park, (850) 653-9347

Lake Jackson Mounds Archaeological State Park, (850) 922-6007

Lake Talquin State Park, (850) 922-6007

Letchworth Mounds, (850) 922-6007

Manatee Springs State Park, (352) 493-6072

Natural Bridge Battlefield Historic State Park, (850) 922-6007

Ochlockonee River State Park, (850) 962-2771

Perdido Key State Park, (850) 492-1595

Ponce de Leon Springs State Park, (850) 836-4281

Rocky Bayou State Park, (850) 833-9144

St. Andrews State Park, (850) 233-5140

St. George Island State Park, (850) 927-2111

St. Joseph Peninsula State Park, (850) 227-1327

San Marcos de Apalache Historic State Park, (850) 925-6216

Stephen Foster Folk Culture Center State Park, (386) 397-2733

T. H. Stone Memorial (St. Joseph Peninsula) State Park, (850) 227-1327

Tallahassee–St. Marks Historic Railroad Trail State Park, (850) 245-2052

Tarklin Bayou Preserve State Park, (850) 492-1595

Three Rivers State Park, (850) 482-9006

Topsail Hill Preserve State Park, (850) 267-8330

Torreya State Park, (850) 643-2674

Waccasassa Bay Preserve State Park, (352) 543-5567

Wes Skiles Peacock Springs State Park, (386) 776-2194

Places to Stay in Northwest Florida

APALACHICOLA

Gibson Inn
51 Avenue C
(850) 653-2191
www.gibsoninn.com

CEDAR KEY

Island Hotel and Restaurant
2nd and B Streets
373 2nd St.
(352) 543-5111
www.islandhotel-cedarkey.com

DEFUNIAK SPRINGS

Best Western Crossroads Inn
2343 Freeport Rd.
(850) 892-5111
www.bestwestern.com

FORT WALTON BEACH

Four Points by Sheraton
1325 Miracle Strip Pkwy.
(850) 243-8116
www.starwoodhotels.com/fourpoints

Ramada Plaza Beach Resort
1500 Miracle Strip Pkwy.
Southeast
(850) 243-9161
www.ramadafwb.com

LAKE CITY

Holiday Inn
213 SW Commerce Dr.
(386) 754-1411
www.hilakecityfl.com

MARIANNA

Quality Inn
2175 SR 71 South
(850) 526-5600
www.qualityinn.com

PANAMA CITY

Comfort Inn
1013 E. 23rd St.
(850) 769-6969
www.panamacitycomfortinn.com

PANAMA CITY BEACH

Edgewater Beach Resort
11212 Front Beach Rd.
(800) 874-8686
www.edgewaterbeachresort.com

Holiday Inn SunSpree Resort
11127 Front Beach Rd.
(850) 234-1111 or
(800) 633-0266
www.hipcbeach.com

Marriott's Bay Point
4200 Marriott Dr.
(800) 874-4025
www.marriottbaypoint.com

PENSACOLA

Best Western Blue Angel Inn
2390 W. Detroit Blvd.
(850) 477-7474
www.bestwestern.com

Hampton Inn
2 Via DeLuna
(850) 932-6800

Holiday Inn Express
130 Loblolly Ln.
(850) 944-8442

New World Inn
600 S. Palafox St.
(850) 432-4111
www.newworldlanding.com/newworldinn.htm

TALLAHASSEE

Cabot Lodge
1653 Raymond Diehl Rd.
(850) 386-7500 or
(800) 255-6343
www.cabotlodge.com

Governors Inn
209 S. Adams St.
(850) 681-6855 or
(800) 342-7717
www.thegovinn.com

Super 8
2801 N. Monroe St.
(850) 386-8286
www.super8.com

Places to Eat in Northwest Florida

APALACHICOLA

Apalachicola Seafood Grill & Steakhouse
100 Market St.
(850) 653-9510

VISITOR INFORMATION FOR NORTHWEST FLORIDA

Alachua County Visitors & Convention Bureau, 30 E. University Ave., Gainesville; (866) 778-5002; www.visitgainesville.com

Apalachicola Bay Chamber of Commerce, 122 Commerce St., Apalachicola; (850) 653-9419; www.apalachicolabay.org

Columbia County Tourist Development Council, PO Box 1847, Lake City 32056-1847; (386) 758-1312; www.columbiacountyfla.com

Destin Area Chamber of Commerce, 4484 Legendary Dr., Ste. A, Destin; (850) 837-6241; www.destinchamber.com

Emerald Coast Convention & Visitor Bureau, 1540 Miracle Strip Pkwy., Fort Walton Beach; (800) 322-3319; www.emeraldcoastfl.com

Greater Fort Walton Beach Chamber of Commerce, 34 Miracle Strip Pkwy., Fort Walton Beach; (850) 244-8191; www.fwbchamber.org

Gulf County Chamber of Commerce, 150 Captain Fred's Place, Port St. Joe; (850) 227-1223; www.gulfchamber.org

Hamilton County Chamber of Commerce, 1153 US 41 Northwest, Ste. 9, Jasper; (386) 792-1300; www.hamiltoncountychamber.com

Hamilton County Tourist Development Council, 1153 US 41 Northwest, Ste. 2, Jasper; (386) 792-6828; www.hamiltoncountyflorida.com

Levy County Business Development Council, PO Box 1324, 620 N. Hathaway Ave., Bronson 32621; (352) 486-3396; www.visitnaturecoast.com

Panama City Beach Convention & Visitors Bureau, 170001 Panama City Beach Pkwy., Panama City Beach; (850) 233-5070 or (800) 722-3224; www.visitpanamacitybeach.com

Pensacola Convention & Visitor Center, 1401 E. Gregory St., Pensacola; (850) 434-1234 or (800) 874-1234 (US only); www.visitpensacola.com

Perry-Taylor Chamber of Commerce, 428 N. Jefferson St., Perry; (850) 584-5366; www.taylorcountychamber.com

Santa Rosa Tourist Development Council, 8543 Navarre Pkwy., Navarre; (850) 939-2691 or (800) 480-SAND (7263) (US only)

South Walton Tourist Development Council, 25777 US 331 South, Santa Rosa Beach; (800) 822-6877 (worldwide); www.beachesofsouthwalton.com

Suwannee County Chamber of Commerce, 816 S. Ohio, Live Oak; (386) 362-3071; www.suwanneechamber.com

Tallahassee Area Convention & Visitors Bureau, 106 E. Jefferson St., Tallahassee; (850) 606-2305 or (800) 628-2866; www. visittallahassee.com

Wakulla County Chamber of Commerce, 23 High Dr., Crawfordville; (850) 926-1848; www.wakullacountychamber.org

CEDAR KEY

Blue Desert Cafe
12518 SR 24
(352) 543-9111

Island Hotel and Restaurant
373 2nd St. (2nd and B Streets)
(352) 543-5111 or
(800) 432-4640
www.islandhotel-cedarkey
.com

FORT WALTON BEACH

Staff's Seafood Restaurant
24 Miracle Strip Pkwy. Southeast
(850) 243-3482
www.staffrestaurant.com

MARIANNA

Tony's
4133 W. Lafayette
(850) 482-2232

PANAMA CITY

Uncle Ernie's Bayfront Grill and Brewhouse
1151 Bayview Ave.
(850) 763-8427
www.uncleerniesbayfront
grill.com

PANAMA CITY BEACH

Boar's Head Restaurant
7290 Front Beach Rd.
(850) 234-6628
www.boarsheadrestaurant
.com

Capt. Anderson's Restaurant & Waterfront Market
5551 Lagoon Dr.
(850) 234-2225
www.captanderson.com

PENSACOLA

The Angus (Greek)
1101 Scenic Hwy. (US 90)
(850) 432-0539
www.anguspensacola.com

The Fish House
600 Barracks St.
(850) 470-0003
www.fishhouse.goodgrits
.com

TALLAHASSEE

Andrew's 228
228 S. Adams St.
(850) 222-3444
www.andrewsdowntown
.com

Chez Pierre
1215 Thomasville Rd.
(850) 222-0936
www.chezpierre.com

CENTRAL FLORIDA

Mount Dora—charming, friendly, and close to the glitzy attractions of Orlando—but a world away. And if it's tranquility you're after, Bok Tower will give you a double dose. Highland Hammocks State Park is one of our favorites in Florida's long list of outstanding state parks.

Starting in Daytona, you can travel a roughly circular route to see central Florida, but be sure to allow plenty of time for exploration off the beaten path. Whenever you can use SR A1A (which parallels the great Atlantic) rather than US 1, try to do so, but on occasion the ocean intercedes and pushes you inland.

The Orlando area is so congested, it's probably best to take major routes to your destination. The benefits of getting there outweigh the pleasures of wandering. As soon as you drop south of Orlando, you'll begin to enjoy less hectic travel by taking Alternate US 27 instead of US 27 through the orange-grove country surrounding peaceful Bok Tower.

The Tampa–St. Petersburg area is another driving challenge, but look at it this way: There isn't any snow or ice to contend with. Traveling north from Tampa on US 19 is a pleasant way to reach attractions on or near the Gulf. Take

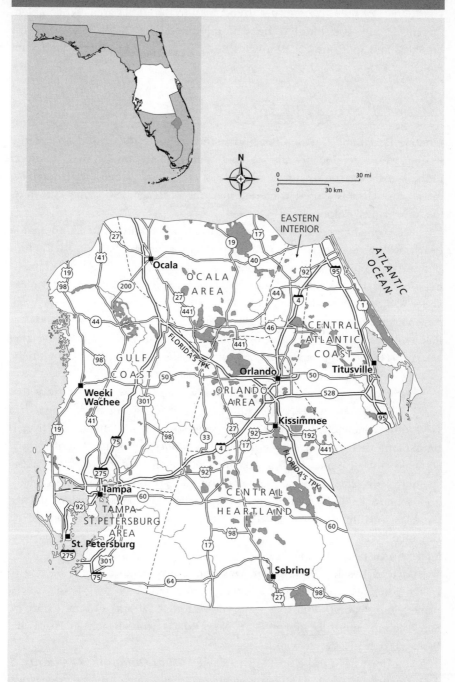

CENTRAL FLORIDA

N

0 ——— 30 mi
0 ——— 30 km

EASTERN
INTERIOR

ATLANTIC
OCEAN

27

41   19

19   98   200

98   44

GULF
COAST

Weeki
Wachee

19   41

75   98

Ocala

OCALA
AREA

27   441

FLORIDA'S TPK

50   301

33

4

92

27   40

19   17

92   95

44

441

46   1

CENTRAL
ATLANTIC
COAST

Orlando

ORLANDO
AREA

27

17   92

50   528   Titusville

Kissimmee

192   441

FLORIDA'S TPK   95

275

Tampa   60

92

TAMPA-
ST.PETERSBURG
AREA

St. Petersburg

275

301

75   64

92

CENTRAL

HEARTLAND

98   60

17

27   98   Sebring

your choice of little roads to get from US 19 to the Ocala area. To complete the circle, drive east through the sand pine woods of Ocala National Forest on SR 40 and south on US 19 toward Blue Springs and Hontoon Island State Parks.

Central Atlantic Coast

Ormond Beach and Daytona Beach owe their starts to the irrepressible Henry Flagler, who extended his railroad south and built the ornate Hotel Ormond in the late 1880s. The moneyed set was not far behind. When the Vanderbilts, Astors, and Goulds started wintering in Ormond Beach, it became known as the Millionaires' Colony.

Rich men shipped their automobiles to Florida because the 500-foot-wide beach, with its hard-packed sand, was perfect for running flat out. By the turn of the 20th century, Henry Ford, Louis Chevrolet, and R. E. Olds were comparing times on the beach's measured mile. Things moved quickly. In 1903 Alexander Winton set a world record of 68 miles per hour on the sands of Daytona. A Stanley Steamer was clocked at 127.66 miles per hour in 1906. The next year Ralph Owens made the first car trip from New York to Daytona in an amazing 17 days. Thirteen auto speed records were set here between 1902 and 1935, earning the area the reputation as the "birthplace of speed."

Faster cars and larger crowds gradually outgrew the oval raceway that had been dug into the Daytona dunes. A 2½–mile asphalt track, opened in 1959, offered new challenges to the growing sport. World attention is riveted on the famous *Daytona International Speedway* during the Fourth of July 400-mile stock car race and its Daytona 500 in February. No tours of the speedway are offered during races and special tests, but at other times a half-hour tram tour will fill you in on all the details. For tickets to special events, write Daytona International Speedway, 1801 W. International Speedway Blvd., Daytona 32114; call (386) 254-2700 or (800) 748-7467; or visit www.daytona internationalspeedway.com.

Daytona Beach's *Museum of Arts and Sciences* has a fine collection of Cuban paintings, a skeleton of a giant ground sloth, interesting fossils, and a planetarium. Open 9 a.m. to 5 p.m. Tues through Sat and 11 a.m. to 5 p.m. Sun. The museum is located at 352 S. Nova Rd. (Daytona Beach) in Tuscawilla Park; (386) 255-0285; www.moa.org.

You don't have to be an RVer to stay at *Great Outdoors RV/Nature & Golf Resort,* but most are. If you love the natural beauty of the outdoor world and enjoy golf, fishing, and the camaraderie of other like-minded folks, this is definitely the place for you.

Medium Well

If you are hungering for spiritual growth or would like to communicate with a deceased loved one, perhaps you should seek out the **Cassadaga Spiritualist Camp.** Designated a historic district on the National Register of Historic Places, the Southern Cassadaga Spiritualist Camp Meeting Association is the oldest active religious community in the southeastern US. The association originated in 1894.

While residents may own the homes they live in within the campgrounds, the church retains ownership of the land and offers lifetime leases to the homeowners. Incidentally, there are no camping facilities in Cassadaga. "Camp Meeting" is an old term referring to the annual gathering of a religious group.

Cassadaga, complete with an education center devoted to the science, philosophy, and religion of Spiritualism, is a sanctuary where Spiritualists live and work together. Spiritualists believe that life continues after "the change called death" and that those who have passed through this transition can communicate with the living through mediumship.

About 25 of the camp's residents are mediums who offer counseling from their homes. According to the Spiritualists of America, a medium—a spiritual counselor with proven capabilities of communicating with the Spirit through various forms of phenomena—acts as a channel for information between the Spirit and Earth Planes.

The camp welcomes the curious and skeptical as well as believers to its Sunday services, Wednesday night services, and candlelight healing services on the second Friday of each month.

Contact the Camp Bookstore for a listing of all certified mediums in the camp and call the medium of your choice for a private appointment. Or you may wish to attend a workshop, seminar, or educational program listed on the camp's fascinating schedule. Office hours are Mon through Thurs 10 a.m. to 4 p.m. Cassadaga Spiritualist Camp is located at 1325 Stevens St. in Cassadaga, midway between Daytona and Orlando, and is easily accessed from I-4, exit 114; (386) 228-2880; www.cassa daga.org.

No wonder this is considered one of the finest RV destinations in the South. Miles of scenic nature trails through forests and around lakes and wetlands reveal the beauty of these 3,000 acres. Woodlands shelter Sabal palms, holly, pines, wax myrtles, palmettos, and huge live oaks dripping with Spanish moss.

Besides fishing and golf, the Great Outdoors has two swimming pools, lighted tennis and shuffleboard courts, a health club with a well-equipped exercise room, sauna and steam rooms, a recreation hall with a dance floor, a restaurant, a lounge, bathhouses with laundry facilities, a beauty salon, a hobby shop, croquet lawn, a library, a post office, a bank (with golf-cart

AUTHORS' FAVORITE ATTRACTIONS IN CENTRAL FLORIDA

Bok Tower Gardens, north of Lake Wales; http://boktowergardens.org/

Homosassa Springs Wildlife State Park, Homosassa; www.floridastate parks.org

Merritt Island National Wildlife Refuge, near Titusville; www.fws.gov/merrittisland

Ocala National Forest, east of Ocala; http://fs.usda.gov/ocala

Salvador Dalí Museum, St. Petersburg; http://thedali.org

Silver Springs, east of Ocala; www.silversprings.com

Weeki Wachee Springs, Weeki Wachee; www.weekiwachee.com

drive-through), a church, and a country store complete with deli, golf-cart rentals, and RV repair center. The Great Outdoors RV/Nature & Golf Resort, 125 Plantation Dr., Titusville, is on SR 50 just west of I-95, 6.5 miles from the Kennedy Space Center; (321) 269-5004 or (800) 621-2267; www.tgoresort.com.

The **Kennedy Space Center Visitor Complex,** just south of Titusville, will test the limits of your imagination. Here the past, present, and future of our country's inspiring probe into the mysteries of outer space are packed into one memorable visitor attraction. Admission and parking are free, as are the Gallery of Spaceflight, NASA Art Exhibit, the outdoor Rocket Garden, and live shows on a variety of current space-related topics presented in Spaceport Theater. The Spaceman, who loves to pose for photographs, appears for several hours daily.

You'll want to purchase tickets for a bus tour of **Kennedy Space Center's Launch Complex 39,** where NASA prepares and launches the Space Shuttle. Also available are tours of the historic **Cape Canaveral Air Force Station,** where the US space program began in the early 1960s.

Don't miss the three impressive IMAX movies shown on a 5.5-story screen in the **IMAX Theatre.** Call or check the website for current showings. The **Astronaut Memorial (Space Mirror Memorial),** honoring US astronauts who gave their lives in the name of space exploration, was dedicated on May 9, 1991. This memorial, which has the astronauts' names brilliantly lit by reflected sunlight, sits beside a quiet lagoon on six acres of land.

The Kennedy Space Center Visitor Complex is open 9 a.m. to 5:30 p.m. every day except Christmas and certain launch days. Plan to arrive early. The complex is less busy on weekends than weekdays. Lunch is available at either the Orbit Cafeteria or the Launch Pad restaurant. Board a full-scale replica of the Space Shuttle Explorer, tour the rocket garden, and take a bus tour of the complex. Located on Florida's Space Coast, 1 hour east of Orlando, the visitor complex is off SR 405, NASA Parkway, 7 miles east of US 1. Use exit 78 off I-95. Take SR 407 north if you're eastbound on the Beeline (SR 528). For visitor or launch information, call (866) 737-5235, write DNPS, Kennedy Space Center, 32899, or visit www.kennedyspacecenter.com. To purchase tickets, go online or call (321) 449-4444.

The Kennedy Space Center is flanked by the *Canaveral National Seashore* and the sprawling Merritt Island National Wildlife Refuge. All that's left of 600 years of fresh oyster dinners consumed by early Florida Indians is the 40-foot historic *Turtle Mound* at the northern tip of the national seashore. Because this shell mound was the highest point of land for miles around, it served as an important landmark and appeared on 16th-century maps. Climb the boardwalk to the top for an impressive view of river and ocean. Turtle Mound is 10 miles south of New Smyrna Beach on SR A1A. Canaveral National Seashore is 7 miles east of Titusville. Call (386) 428-3384 or visit www.nps.gov/cana for information on the Apollo Beach/Turtle Mound area.

Swimmers, surfers, and beachcombers head for Playalinda Beach at the south end of Canaveral, where sea oats and shifting dunes create a lovely seascape. The national seashore is one of the last sections of undeveloped beach on the east coast of Florida. The beach, open daily during daylight hours (except when the road is closed due to NASA launch-related activities), is free. Call (321) 267-1110 for Playalinda Beach information.

The *Merritt Island National Wildlife Refuge* protects more endangered species of birds, mammals, and reptiles than any other area of the continental US. The Audubon Society has registered one of the highest counts of bird species in the country here. Gulls, terns, egrets, herons, ibises, and storks are a common sight. You may even be lucky enough to spot a pretty pink roseate spoonbill or a bald eagle. Open daily from sunrise to sunset. www.fws.gov/merrittisland or www.nbbd.com. Free.

If you are intrigued by tropical foliage, you will want to see the *Botanical Gardens* on the grounds of the Florida Institute of Technology in Melbourne, with more than 300 species of palms, ferns, and other plants. The institute is at 150 W. University Blvd., Melbourne, off of Country Club Road, a mile south of New Haven Avenue; (321) 674-8125; www.fit.edu. Open dawn to dusk daily.

The sign at the entrance to *Ponce de Leon Lighthouse* reads: "Nothing indicates the Liberality, Prosperity or Intelligence of a Nation more clearly than the Facilities which it affords for the Safe Approach of the Mariner to its Shores." How can you resist the tallest lighthouse in Florida? Well, the answer is that you can't, especially when you learn that it is one of the best-preserved, most complete light stations in the nation. Thanks to decades of restoration by the Ponce de Leon Inlet Lighthouse Preservation Association, the light station was designated a National Historic Landmark in 1998. Completed in 1887, this stately structure was built when the area was known by the unfortunate, but perhaps well-earned, name of Mosquito Inlet.

Visitors climb 203 steps to the top of this 175-foot lighthouse for a spectacular view of Ponce Inlet, New Smyrna, and the surrounding area. A marine museum displays much of the original lighthouse equipment, and the restored keeper's cottage and several other outlying buildings are open to the public. The Ayres Davies Lens Exhibit building houses one of the finest collections of

TOP EVENTS IN CENTRAL FLORIDA

Epiphany Celebration, Tarpon Springs, January, (727) 937-3540

Gasparilla Pirate Fest, Tampa, January, (813) 353-8070

Cracker Country, Tampa, February, (813) 627-4225

Daytona 500 NASCAR Stock Car Race, Daytona Beach, February, (800) 748-7467 (Daytona International Speedway ticket office)

Fiesta Day, Ybor City, February, (813) 241-8838

Florida State Fair, Tampa, February, (813) 621-7821

Annual Chasco Fiesta, New Port Richey, March, (727) 842-7651

Florida Strawberry Festival, Plant City, March, (813) 754-1996

Kissimmee Bluegrass Festival, Kissimmee, March, (800) 831-1844

Daytona Beach Car Show and Swap Meet, Daytona Beach, March and November, (386) 255-7355

Sun 'N Fun EAA Fly-in, Lakeland, April, (863) 644-2431

Fun 'N Sun Festival, Clearwater, April/May, (727) 562-4800

Zellwood Sweet Corn Festival, Zellwood, May, (407) 886-0014

Annual Harvest Festival, Clermont, June, (800) 768-WINE (9463)

Flagler County's Fabulous Fourth Festivities, July, (386) 439-0995 or (800) 298-0995

Coke Zero 400 Stock Car Race, Daytona Beach, July 4, (800) 748-7467 (Daytona International Speedway ticket office)

Taste of Clearwater, Clearwater, September, (727) 461-0011

Biketoberfest, Daytona Beach, October, (866) 296-8970

Clearwater Jazz Holiday, Clearwater, October, (727) 461-5200

Great Florida Triathlon, Clermont, October, (352) 394-1320

Guavaween, Ybor City, Tampa, October, (813) 248-3712

Christmas in the Park, Winter Park, December, (407) 645-5311

restored Fresnel lenses in the world, including the rotating first-order Fresnel lens from the Cape Canaveral lighthouse and the restored original Ponce Inlet lighthouse first-order Fresnel lens. Today's modern beacon flashes every 10 seconds and can be seen for 16 nautical miles.

The "Climb to the Moon" tour is offered once a lunar month when the moon is at its fullest. Romantics toast the sunset and moonrise while enjoying astronomical views with a sparkling beverage while a knowledgeable docent sheds light on the lighthouse's unique history and tells tales of yesteryear. Limited to 25 per event. The lighthouse is 12 miles south of Daytona Beach in the town of Ponce Inlet, on the north bank of Ponce Inlet where the Halifax and Indian Rivers empty into the Atlantic Ocean. Ponce de Leon Inlet Lighthouse Preservation Association, 4931 S. Peninsula Dr., Ponce Inlet; (386) 761-1821; www.poncelighthousestore.org. Open 10 a.m. to 6 p.m. daily. Last admission is 1 hour before closing.

Orlando Area

The **Maitland Art Center** is a special place. Originally designed to be a retreat for avant-garde artists, it is now an attractive complex housing a fascinating permanent collection and monthly rotating exhibits by contemporary artists. The buildings, adorned with murals and ornamental carvings in a Aztec-Mayan motif, are well worth seeing, as is the tranquil garden and courtyard area. When you visit the Garden Chapel, with its trellised walkway, you'll understand why this is such a popular place for weddings. Maitland Art Center, 231 W. Packwood Ave., Maitland. Open 11 a.m. to 4 p.m. Tues through Sun; closed on major holidays. Call (407) 539-2181; www.maitland artcenter.com.

If you love birds, you'll be very happy at the **Florida Audubon Center for Birds of Prey,** which includes a large collection of live birds, such as eagles, hawks, and owls, in an aviary. The center is one of the leading raptor-rehabilitation facilities in the state; it's open 10 a.m. to 4 p.m. Tues through Sun; closed federal holidays. You are encouraged to report injured or orphaned birds of prey to the center at (407) 644-0190. The center is at 1101 Audubon Way, Maitland; www.audubon.org.

The most comprehensive collection of Tiffany glass and jewelry in the world resides at the **Morse Museum of American Art** in Winter Park. This gallery features late-19th- and 20th-century art and decorative arts including leaded stained-glass windows, lamps, blown glass, pottery, paintings, and furniture. Open 9:30 a.m. to 4 p.m. Tues through Sat, plus 4 to 8 p.m. Fri Nov through Apr, and 1 to 4 p.m. Sun. The Morse Museum of American Art, 445 N.

Park Ave., Winter Park; (407) 645-5311; www.morsemuseum.org. Admission to the gallery is free on Friday evenings.

Don't be fooled by T-shirts that boast "I climbed Mount Dora." The town, built on a bluff overlooking Lake Dora, is a scant 184 feet above sea level. Just 30 miles northeast of Orlando, it seems several worlds away from the hustle and bustle of that tourist mecca. *Mount Dora* is fine place to wander on foot, browsing the many antiques and crafts shops and strolling the grounds of Lakeside Inn. The inn is a rambling winter resort with a high-class guest list that over the years has included President Calvin Coolidge, President Dwight Eisenhower, Thomas Edison, and Henry Ford. Listed on the National Register of Historic Places, the inn was built in 1883. The Donnelly House, built in 1893, is a 3-story, beautifully maintained, heavily gingerbreaded example of Victorian steamboat architecture located at 5th Avenue and Donnelly Street. .

One fun way to really appreciate the lovely lake-dotted Orlando area is to take a *Scenic Boat Tour.* The boat leaves hourly between 10 a.m. and 4 p.m. from the eastern foot of Morse Boulevard on Lake Osceola in Winter Park. The 1-hour narrated ride takes you through various Winter Park lakes and canals, by estates, the Isle of Sicily, Kraft Azalea Gardens, and Rollins College. Scenic Boat Tour, 312 E. Morse Blvd., Lake Osceola, Winter Park; (407) 644-4056; www.scenicboattours.com. Closed Christmas. Cash or check only.

Central Florida's major city, Orlando, was settled by soldiers who decided to stick around after the Seminole wars in the 1830s. It was little more than a cattle-country trading post until the railroad's arrival brought an influx of people and business in 1880. Then the town eased into a string of unremarkable years as a shipping center for citrus fruits and vegetables.

Over the years Orlando capitalized on its best features—54 lakes within the city limits and a year-round average temperature of 72 degrees Fahrenheit. The community protected its venerable groves of live oaks by creating 47 parks. A loyal contingent of Northerners who appreciated both the beauty and the climate enjoyed the town's relaxed pace each winter.

Those were the days before the nation's launch into space from nearby Cape Canaveral and before the coming of Walt Disney World. The city is still pretty, with all its lakes and parks intact, but the relaxed pace is a memory. Orlando is one of the fastest-growing metropolitan areas in the US, and the face of central Florida has been forever changed.

Loch Haven Park in Orlando offers two quality attractions. Parking is easy and you may spend all day enjoying the *Orlando Museum of Art* and Orlando Science Center. The museum has a growing permanent collection of American art, pre-Columbian artifacts, African art, and changing exhibitions from internationally renowned museums and private collections. Gallery hours are 10 a.m. to 4 p.m. Tues through Fri and noon to 4 p.m. Sat and Sun; call for information and times regarding special exhibits; 2416 N. Mills Ave., Orlando; (407) 896-4231; www.omart.org.

Those who find their earth weight discouraging may take consolation in learning their moon weight, one of many neat things you can do at the **Orlando Science Center.** This is one of those places where you learn a great deal while having a good time, and it is especially good for families. Ask about the daily planetarium shows at Dr. Phillips Cinedome. Open 10 a.m. to 5 p.m. Sun through Tues and Thurs through Sat; closed Wed. Orlando Science Center and Dr. Phillips Cinedome, Loch Haven Park, 777 E. Princeton St., Orlando; (407) 514-2000; www.osc.org.

The **Orange County Regional History Center** began in 1942 when a group of women set up a pioneer kitchen in the 1892 redbrick courthouse for a countywide centennial. It has evolved into a handsome museum that will take you on a trip down memory lane. Here you'll travel back to the time when Florida was a wilderness, learn about the Big Freeze of 1894–95 that destroyed the citrus industry, and ride the roller-coaster real estate boom-and-bust days of the 1920s. On display are a 1,000-year-old Timucuan Indian canoe, a newspaper composing room in the hot-type tradition, a Victorian parlor, and the hide of a 15-foot alligator. Open 10 a.m. to 5 p.m. daily. Orange County Regional History Center, 65 E. Central Blvd., Orlando; (407) 836-8500 or (800) 965-2030; www.thehistorycenter.org.

When the hustle and bustle of Orlando is too much for you, a walk through **Leu Gardens** provides a welcome tonic. Acres of trees, flowering shrubs, roses, camellias, and azaleas border Lake Rowena. Varieties bloom

OTHER ATTRACTIONS WORTH SEEING IN CENTRAL FLORIDA

Busch Gardens, Tampa, www.buschgardens.com

Cypress Island, Kissimmee

Fantasy of Flight, Winter Haven, www.fantasyofflight.com

International Drive, Orlando

Sea World, Orlando, www.seaworld.com

Universal Studios, Orlando, www.universalorlando.com

Walt Disney World Resort, Lake Buena Vista, www.disneyworld.disney.go.com

all year. The peaceful setting includes a tropical stream and butterfly garden. A museum house, which shows how a well-to-do Florida family lived at the turn of the 20th century, is open 10 a.m. to 4 p.m. daily; tours are on the half hour; museum house closed the month of July. The gardens are open 9 a.m. to 5 p.m. daily except for Christmas and are free to everyone on the first Mon of each month from 9 a.m. to 5 p.m. Leu House and Gardens, 1920 N. Forest Ave., Orlando; (407) 246-2620; www.leugardens.org.

The *Arabian Nights* dinner show features a legendary black stallion and a cast of other incredibly talented horses—horses who provide comedy as well as high drama. Sixty-five horses made up of 14 breeds—from Arabian and Appaloosa to Canadian Warmblood—all perform in the world's largest indoor equestrian arena along with 30 human-type performers in elaborate costumes. There's snow, fog, a flaming jump-through hoop, square dancing on horseback, bareback riding, and chariot races. Throw in a generous dose of glamour, royalty, old-fashioned romance, and an adrenaline-spiked Wild West adventure and you have an award-winning family show. All this and they feed you dinner, too. Strategically located on US 192 in Kissimmee, a half mile east of I-4, it's not really off the beaten path location-wise. But we're talking Arabian Nights here, and that's something you're not likely to experience anywhere else anytime soon. 3081 Arabian Nights Blvd., Kissimmee; (497) 239-9223; www .arabian-nights.com.

Camping sounds like fun, but you want a real vacation complete with daily maid service, cable TV, and air-conditioning. Surprise! You can have it all at *Walt Disney World's Fort Wilderness Campground.* Fully equipped cabins and a lodge allow you to enjoy all the comforts and conveniences of a fine hotel while enjoying the rustic beauty of the great outdoors.

Hearty fare and wholesome fun are close by. The *Hoop-Dee-Doo-Revue* at Pioneer Hall is the second-longest-running show at Walt Disney World. A cast of six "stagecoach passengers" keeps everyone in stitches for almost 2 hours. In between laughs, fill up on fried chicken, barbecued ribs, corn on the cob, and strawberry shortcake. Afterward, it's home-sweet-home to your trailer/ tent/cabin/lodge room under the trees. For information about Fort Wilderness, write Walt Disney World Central Reservations, PO Box 10100, Lake Buena Vista 32830, or call (407) 934-7639; www.disneyworld.com.

Gatorland should also be in your plans. Don't worry about the huge alligator jaws you walk through to enter. This isn't just another hokey attraction, but a fine zoo with thousands of alligators and crocodiles (Gatorland claims to be the world's largest alligator farm attraction) and some rather exotic animals including snakes and birds. An interesting artificial-insemination program for alligators is in full swing here.

Allow plenty of time to stroll the boardwalk through the eerie beauty of a cypress swamp. This sanctuary, lush with wild orchids and ferns, offers a welcome reprieve from the hectic pace some sightseers set for themselves. Open 9 a.m. to 6 p.m. daily, rain or shine. Gatorland is on US 441 next to Tupperware. Mailing address: 14501 S. Orange Blossom Trail, Orlando 32837; (407) 855-5496; www.gatorland.com.

Ahhh, the romance of medieval times when brave knights defended their kingdoms, and castles were scenes of great feasts and much revelry. This is now a possible dream thanks to *Medieval Times Dinner and Tournament.* Slip back to Europe in the 11th century and admire valiant knights on richly attired horses. A "serving wench" brings a delicious meal to be eaten with your hands.

Spectacular pageantry, splendid horses galloping at full tilt, and knights who duel to the death (well, almost) combine to make quite an evening. Just when you thought chivalry was dead, a knight shows up and throws you a flower. A knight to remember! Medieval Times is on US 192 (4510 W. Irlo Bronson Memorial Hwy.) in Kissimmee. Hours are Mon through Fri 9 a.m. to 5 p.m. Call ahead for reservations, (407) 396-1518; www.medievaltimes.com.

Kissimmee had a long proud heritage as the capital of cattle country before being billed as the Gateway to Walt Disney World. Spanish explorers brought livestock to the New World, and when Florida became a US territory in 1821, the open range and scrub cattle descended from Spanish cows lured home-steaders to the Florida frontier. South of Orlando's dazzle, hundreds of cattle ranches and a thriving beef and dairy industry prosper. The cowboy's own brand of excitement rears up twice a year (Feb and Oct) at Florida's largest and oldest professional rodeo, *Kissimmee's Silver Spurs;* (321) 697-3495 or (407) 677-6336.

In Kissimmee don't forget to visit the *Monument of States,* made of stones from every state in the Union. The 50-foot structure was built by Kissim-mee citizens in 1943 with 1,500 stones from every state and 21 foreign countries. The monument is located near the lakefront in downtown Kissimmee.

Kissimmee lies at the head of the 50-mile-long *Kissimmee Chain-of-Lakes,* and those who want to experience central Florida at its natural best should see it from the water. Far from the madding crowd are quiet lagoons and blue herons picking their way through water hyacinths. Besides being splendidly scenic, this is one of the country's best bass-fishing grounds. The sunset is in living color, the view is multidimensional, and the big sound is a night chorus of tree frogs and cicadas. Assorted watercraft may be rented at the marina on Big Lake Tohopekaliga, known more simply as Big Lake Toho. 101 Lakeshore Blvd.; (407) 846-2124; 5:30 a.m. to 5 p.m. weekdays and 5:30 a.m. to 4 p.m. weekends.

Originally founded in 1972 as a research center for the production and distribution of snake venoms, **_Reptile World Serpentarium_** now offers close-up views of poisonous snakes being milked. Time your visit to be on hand during one of the venom programs, given at noon and 3 p.m. daily except Mon. You'll see turtles and alligators as well as cobras, mambas, vipers, rattlesnakes, and nonvenomous giant pythons. The gift shop has an excellent selection of books on reptiles. Open 9 a.m. to 5 p.m. Tues through Sun. Closed Sept. Located 4 miles east of St. Cloud on US 192. Reptile World Serpentarium, 5705 E. Irlo Bronson Memorial Hwy., St. Cloud; (407) 892-6905.

Central Heartland

The central heartland of Florida seems, from certain view points, like a huge sprawling sea of orange trees. Tidy parallel rows of trees undulate off into the distance like dark-green waves. In the midst of citrus country are modern packing plants and frozen-juice processors well equipped to handle the huge harvest. Many highway fruit and juice stands cater to tourists intent on carrying some fresh Florida fruit home to their winter-bound northern friends. At **_Orange Ring_** you can sample a free glass of orange juice and purchase any number of goodies including orange butter and chocolate alligators. The packing plant, behind the gift shop, gives brief tours during the week. Open 8 a.m. to 5 p.m. Mon through Fri. Orange Ring, 35969 US 27 North (north of Haines City); (863) 422-1938; www.orangering.com.

Watch citrus candy being made in copper kettles at **_Davidson of Dundee Citrus Candy Factory_** on US 27 in Dundee. Open 8 a.m. to 6 p.m. daily, but candy is not made on weekends. Davidson of Dundee, 28421 US 27, Dundee; (800) 294-2266; www.dundeecitrus.com.

Chalet Suzanne Country Inn and Restaurant, in Lake Wales, opens itself up like the petals of a flower. First you discover a tiny, whimsical pastel village with each of its 26 rooms decorated in different combinations of Swedish tile, Spanish ironwork, and Moorish mosaics. Then you sample some of the Chalet's famous romaine soup in the intimate old-world dining room. (No wonder this soup was chosen to go to the moon with the crew of Apollo 15, Apollo 16, and even the Apollo-Soyuz dinner meeting.) Each place is set with fine china, perhaps German porcelain or elegant Limoges, and your view overlooks a small lake.

Then you come upon **_Chapel Antiques,_** where you can browse and enjoy all manner of fine glassware and antiques, the Wine Dungeon, the Wreck Room, the Soup Cannery, and a ceramic salon where Boz Birvis is turning out treasures. Chalet Suzanne is one surprise after another, and that, and the good taste with which everything is done, accounts for its success as well as its charm.

Gourmet magazine labeled Chalet Suzanne's food "glorious" and surely it is, but be warned that the prices are also glorious. If a glance at the lunch menu withers your wallet, ask for the soup and sandwich du jour (unlisted). That way you can treat yourself to a fine meal without taking out a new mortgage. Owned and operated by the Hinshaw family since 1931, Chalet Suzanne is between Cypress Gardens and Bok Tower Gardens just off US 27 and CR 17A. Or come by plane and land on the 2,380-foot private airstrip! Chalet Suzanne, 3800 Chalet Suzanne Dr., Lake Wales; (863) 676-6011 or (800) 433-6011; www.chaletsuzanne.com. Prices are expensive.

The 128-acre ***Bok Tower Gardens*** in Lake Wales have been devoted to peace and beauty since 1928. Listed on the National Register of Historic Places, the gardens and tower were dedicated to the American people by Edward Bok, a Dutch immigrant who wanted to make America "a bit more beautiful" because he had lived here. The hushed atmosphere of the surroundings is interrupted only by the bell serenade every half hour with daily concerts at 1 and 3 p.m. from the 205-foot "singing" tower, which has been called one of the world's great carillons. Enjoy the azaleas, camellias, magnolias, and many birds. Surrounded by citrus orchards, this is the place to come in the spring when the air is heavy with the scent of orange blossoms. The gardens are open 8 a.m. to 6 p.m. daily. Located 3 miles north of Lake Wales off CR 17A (Burns Avenue). Bok Tower Gardens, 1151 Tower Blvd., Lake Wales; (863) 676-1408; www.boktowergardens.org.

thesingingtower

After his visit to Historic Bok Sanctuary, carillonneur Daniel Robins wrote that the sanctuary "provides the most sympathetic setting for a carillon of any instrument which I have played here or in Europe and I think it entirely possible that it is the best setting which remains for an instrument anywhere. . . . What Mr. Bok intended as a sanctuary for wildlife has become . . . a sanctuary for the carillon as well."

Lake Kissimmee State Park is way off the beaten path, but worth it. The park consists of more than 5,000 acres bordered by Lakes Kissimmee, Tiger, and Rosalie. The lakes, floodplain prairies, marshes, and pine flatwoods are home to a variety of wildlife, including the rare Florida panther. (Don't count on seeing a panther; they're very shy.) This is a fine spot to boat, hike, picnic, and camp. For an excellent view of Lake Kissimmee, try the top of the observation platform.

One of the best features of the park is a reconstructed ***1876 Cow Camp*** with scrub cows and "cow hunters." (They will quickly tell you they do not care to be called cowboys.) Here you can learn firsthand about the bustling cattle business on the south Florida frontier and see one of the few remaining herds of scrub cows in existence.

As you walk down the trail to the camp, you travel back to the year 1876. The cow hunter may be having a cup of coffee near his campfire or perhaps is rounding up cows for the long cattle drive to the west coast of Florida. The cattlemen were paid in gold Spanish doubloons. The cow hunter welcomes your questions, but don't bother asking about anything that happened after 1876. He will just look very puzzled and won't know what you're talking about.

The Cow Camp is only open on weekends and holidays 9:30 a.m. to 4:30 p.m. The park is open 8 a.m. to sunset daily year-round. The park is 15 miles east of Lake Wales, off Camp Mack Road. Lake Kissimmee State Park, 14248 Camp Mack Rd., Lake Wales; (863) 696-1112; www.floridastateparks.org.

Follow nature trails and boardwalks through the jungles, cypress swamps, and tropical wilderness of **Highlands Hammock State Park.** Your stroll will be rewarded with glimpses of sunning alligators and rare orchids. You'll also want to visit the Civilian Conservation Corps (CCC) museum and ride the park's "trackless train" on regularly scheduled wildlife tours. It's a good place to bike (rentals available) and picnic. Highlands Hammock is open 8 a.m. until sunset daily. The park is located 6 miles west of Sebring, off US 27/CR 634 at 5931 Hammock Rd., Sebring; (863) 386-6094; www.floridastateparks.org.

Florida Southern College, in Lakeland, boasts the world's largest concentration of architecture by Frank Lloyd Wright. Wright's design for these 12 unconventional structures called for steel for strength, sand for Florida, and glass to bring the outdoors in. The steeple of the **Annie Pfeiffer Chapel,** designed as a chime resonator, casts shifting shadows into the interior. Tinted glass squares filter colored light in during the day. The low esplanade, a sheltered walkway, was obviously not designed with today's basketball players in mind; no ceiling or doorway is much over 6 feet tall! The Science Building, more than 400 feet long with a planetarium at the southern end, is the largest structure, and some say the most magnificent.

The lakeside campus is open to the public 8 a.m. to 5 p.m. weekdays. The "Child of the Sun" Visitors Center (863-680-4444) is open 10 a.m. to 4 p.m. Mon through Fri. From Orlando, go west on I-4 to the US 98 South exit 18. Turn left. Travel into town and turn left onto McDonald Street. The college is on the right. Florida Southern College, 111 Lake Hollingsworth Dr., Lakeland; (863) 680-4111 or (800) 274-4131; www.flsouthern.edu.

Kids go wild in **Dinosaur World,** and no wonder: It is truly a step back in time. This outdoor museum, with a half-mile trail among creatures of another time, is the world's largest dinosaur attraction. All you need is a little imagination as you wander through the subtropical jungle inhabited by more than 150 life-size dinosaurs. Ranging up to 80 feet in length, they are each labeled with their scientific name and a few fascinating facts. Kids can dig for real fossils (and take home a souvenir), uncover a skeleton at the Boneyard, and watch a movie on dinosaurs. Families are encouraged to picnic or celebrate a birthday with the realistic fiberglass replicas looking on. And you thought dinosaurs were extinct! Located in Plant City on I-4 between Disney and Busch Gardens, Dinosaur World is at 5145 Harvey Tew Rd., Plant City; (813) 717-9865; www.dinosaurworld.com.

Tampa–St. Petersburg Area

Spanish explorers discovered Tampa in the 16th century. They also discovered the resident Indians who resisted being converted to Catholicism and resented the European urge to conquer. The resulting clash of interests frequently led to bloodshed over the years.

One of those early Spanish explorers, Hernando de Soto, discovered the mineral springs of Safety Harbor, which he named the "Springs of the Holy Spirit," on May 18, 1539. He was not the first to be attracted by the springs. Various Indian tribes, inhabiting the area as long as 12,000 years ago, believed the springs had curative powers.

During a fight with the Seminoles, Colonel William J. Bailey captured a sick Indian who volunteered to be a guide if the colonel would take him to the healing springs. The colonel bought the springs and surrounding land from the government in the 1850s, the first person to own the springs after the US acquired Florida from the Spanish.

In the early 1900s five springs were identified that "cured" a variety of ailments from dropsy to psoriasis. Before long, Northerners were visiting the spa to "take the waters." In 1964 Safety Harbor Resort was officially listed as a historical landmark by the US Department of the Interior.

All well and good, but what's going on at the springs today? The answer is plenty, and in keeping with tradition, it's all very healthy and restorative to both body and spirit. The *Safety Harbor Resort and Spa* offers more than 50 rejuvenating, relaxing, and pampering spa and salon services ranging from deep-tissue sports massages, facials, loofah salt glows, and herbal wraps to aromatherapy. Lifestyle and fitness classes, tennis clinics, and golf on nearby courses are also featured. One of America's oldest spa resorts, Safety Harbor is the only one in Florida featuring natural mineral springs. On arrival, guests find a carafe of specially filtered mineral water in their rooms from the springs beneath the hotel.

Highlands Hammock State Park

Here thrives the Florida of old—the lush, swampy salad bar, which in prehistoric times quelled the hunger of huge mastodons. This is the jungle primeval, the primitive precondo Florida that enchants nature lovers and is today in such scarce supply. We could easily envision disillusioned Spanish explorers clanking through the dense undergrowth, steaming under the weight of their armor, as they uncovered only alligators, elegant birds, and exquisite natural beauty where they had hoped to find gold.

One of Florida's most valuable state parks, Highlands Hammock is a biologically rich mix of hammocks, pine flatwoods, sand pine scrub, cypress swamps, bayhead, and marsh. The great diversity of habitats—resulting from interaction of water level, soil, and climate—has created a fertile area for birders (177 species have been identified in the 2,800-acre park) as well as a marvelous maze of hiking trails.

After a looping drive through the park to get our bearings, we set out to explore. Surely these are some of the best trails in Florida. The US Champion Sabal palm appeared fairly regal at 90 feet, and on Big Oak Trail we admired 1,000-year-old oak trees. Wild fruit perfumed the air on Wild Orange Trail. Hickory Trail, Ancient Hammock Trail, and Fern Garden Trail all offered different versions of untamed beauty. But our favorite was Cypress Swamp Trail, a boardwalk meandering through the swamp and along Little Charley Bowlegs Creek.

The resort's spa menu offers nutritious, low-fat, low-calorie, gourmet cuisine. A full-fare menu is also offered, with emphasis on naturally grown fresh Florida fruits and vegetables and regional seafood specialties.

Located on the shores of Old Tampa Bay, Safety Harbor Resort is 20 minutes from two major international airports—Tampa International Airport and St. Petersburg/Clearwater International Airport—and is easily reached from I-75 and I-4. Call for directions. Safety Harbor Resort and Spa, 105 N. Bayshore Dr., Safety Harbor; (321) 332-7074; www.safetyharbor-resort.com.

Safety Harbor Museum of Regional History, a tiny gem of a museum featuring rare treasures of Native American tribes and other exhibits of local interest, is a short walk from the resort. Fascinating dioramas enlighten visitors to the rich history of this area as well as the evolution of the American Indian throughout the Southeast.

Located in Safety Harbor on Old Tampa Bay, the museum is on a Tocabaga shell mound site. Open 10 a.m. to 4 p.m. Thurs through Sat; 1 to 4 p.m. Sun; closed Mon through Wed. The Safety Harbor Museum of Regional History, 329 Bayshore Blvd. South, Safety Harbor; (727) 726-1668; www.safetyharbor museum.org.

All Photos © Shutterstock.

Page 1: Lighthouse.

Page 2: (clockwise from top left) Red flamingo in a park in Florida; Sunset on the pier; The American Riviera.

Page 3: (top) Beautiful living area in the Keys; (bottom left) Lush green Florida golf course aerial view; (bottom right, upper) Lifeguard stand, South Beach, Miami, Florida; (bottom right, lower) Shamu show.

Page 4: (clockwise from top left) Skyline view of downtown Miami and Biscayne Bay between two coconut trees; Architectural detail of the trolley stop building in the downtown Tampa area; Dock leading to beautiful water with sailboat in distance.

Tampa's real development began in 1883 when Henry B. Plant linked Tampa with Jacksonville by a combination of railroad and steamship connections. Henry Plant, competing with East Coast railroad tycoon Henry Flagler, erected the ostentatious Moorish-style *Tampa Bay Hotel* in 1891. Sporting silver Turkish minarets, the palatial hotel ushered in Tampa's era as a fashionable winter resort for well-heeled Northerners. Costing a cool $3.5 million, it was regarded in its day as the most elegant and most expensive hotel in the world.

Today it is a National Historic Landmark, considered the finest example of Moorish architecture in the western hemisphere, and is home to the *University of Tampa.* To see some of the furniture and art of the late Victorian era, visit the *Henry B. Plant Museum* in a wing of the main university building. Open 10 a.m. to 5 p.m. Tues through Sat and noon to 5 p.m. Sun. The museum/ university is at 401 W. Kennedy Blvd., Tampa, at the Hillsborough River; (813) 254-1891; www.plantmuseum.com.

Today Tampa is a major industrial metropolis and busy shipping center for a great variety of products including phosphates, citrus fruits, and cattle. At day's end you may be interested in watching shrimp boats unload their catch at the shrimp docks on the 22nd Street Causeway.

Citizens have worked hard to preserve Tampa's heritage. The Hispanic community centered in *Ybor City* has been largely returned to its late-19th-century appearance. Cigar makers demonstrate the art of hand rolling in restored *Ybor Square,* a complex of shops and restaurants. Ybor City, which is a National Historic District, is bounded by Columbus Drive, 5th Avenue, Nebraska Avenue, and 22nd Street.

Around the turn of the 20th century, the Ferlita Bakery flourished along with Ybor City and the cigar industry. In the "Cigar Capital of the World," workers lived very well indeed, and a boomtown atmosphere prevailed. The bakery (listed on the National Register of Historic Places) has now been transformed by the State of Florida into a museum where you can learn about Tampa's Latin community and see old photos, cigar industry artifacts, and the original 1896 bakery oven. The *Ybor City Museum State Park,* 1818 9th Ave., Tampa, is open 9 a.m. to 5 p.m. every day; (813) 247-6323; www.ybormuseum.org or www.floridastateparks.org.

Tampa's distinct Latin flavor is retained in its Spanish shops, restaurants, and the general ambience of the community. You may see long loaves of Cuban bread rolled out by hand at *La Segunda Central Bakery* if you arrive before 9 a.m. Go around to the back door and watch as bakers shape the dough and place a single strand of palmetto leaf on each yard-long loaf. The bakery is at 2512 N. 15th St. in Ybor City; www.lasegundabakery.com.

You may buy a fresh loaf from the store or order a Cuban sandwich (looking for all the world like a sub) for lunch at a number of Spanish restaurants on E. 7th Street in Ybor City. If you choose *La Tropicana,* you'll notice one table in the back that looks different from all the rest. It even has its own old-fashioned upright phone used to gather news for the local scandal sheet. If you have something to contribute, stop in at La Tropicana at 1822 E. 7th Ave.; (813) 247-4040. Those who don't go for subs might like the deviled crab or potato stuffed with meat. Open 7 a.m. to 3 p.m. Mon through Sat. Prices are inexpensive.

There's always a possibility you'll get caught in a hurricane, but then that's all part of the fun (and learning) going on at the *Museum of Science and Industry (MOSI).* The museum has tripled in size to become the largest science center in the Southeast, with Florida's only IMAX Dome Theatre. Take part in all kinds of fascinating experiments in this hands-on center, and be sure to see BioWorks Butterfly Garden and the planetarium. Exhibits and demonstrations explain the major scientific phenomena—energy, weather, electricity, water, flight and space, and the environment. Don't miss Amazing You, a tour of the human body from DNA cells to organs to individuals. The museum is in North Tampa, 3 miles east of I-275, and is open 9 a.m. to 5 p.m. Mon through Fri, 9 a.m. to 6 p.m. Sat and Sun. Museum of Science and Industry, 4801 E. Fowler Ave., Tampa; (813) 987-6000; www.mosi.org.

prehistoric florida

Once upon a time, gigantic sharks and whales, enormous mammoths and mastodons, vampire bats, giant sloths, and fierce saber-toothed cats made their home in Florida. Though they disappeared a very long time ago, they left a record of fossils, a calling card of sorts, to let us know they were here.

Get out your skateboard. Put on your jogging shoes or your roller skates. Tampa boasts nothing less than the longest continuous sidewalk in the world. The 6.5-mile sidewalk of *Bayshore Boulevard* is the focus of much activity as folks take advantage of this scenic stretch bordering one of the city's oldest and finest residential areas. During a hurricane, this is where the water comes ashore, and daring surfers replace joggers and skaters. You don't have to be quite that adventurous, but this just might be a good time to find out what it feels like to walk half a dozen miles.

You'll enjoy a "wild" safari on the *Serengeti Plain at Busch Gardens.* Four hundred head of exotic big game including giraffes, zebras, elephants, gazelles, and Cape buffalo roam at will as you cross the veldtlike plain via steam locomotive or skyride. Much more than an amusement park, Busch Gardens, with its African motif and more than 3,000 animals, is regarded as one of the top four zoos in the country. Be sure to pay your respects to the rare white Bengal tigers. The park is located at 1001 N. McKinley Dr., Tampa; Call (888) 800-5447 for current admission prices and hours, or visit www.busch gardens.com.

Bern's Steak House is as much an experience as it is a restaurant. The menu looks like an engineering spec sheet, the place is ornate (to put it mildly), and the emphasis is on doing things differently. Perhaps that explains why the gargantuan wine list is almost too heavy to lift. (To have your own copy, you'll have to part with more than $20.)

From their own organic farm to the world's largest wine cellar, the emphasis at Bern's is on putting together the perfect meal. Waiters train a minimum of one year working in every station in the restaurant before being permitted in the dining room. Cress seeds from London are sprouted right in the kitchen, and caviar is flown in daily. Your steak is cut, trimmed, and weighed only after you have placed your order. Coffee beans are roasted and hand-sorted, and the whole operation is coordinated by computer.

All this information (and much more) is on your menu, but is it all true? Yes. Bern's encourages tours of the kitchen and wine cellar throughout the evening. Between courses, diners take advantage of this offer to inspect the immaculate facilities and cavernous (and cold—take a sweater) wine cellar. They even get to see the sprouting cress seeds.

The final course of coffee and dessert is served in your own private room upstairs, which comes complete with numerous selections of music to choose from—including Bern's pianist, who will play favorites on request. You may dance if you wish, or simply spend the rest of the evening trying to select the perfect drink from a list of 1,000 dessert wines. The choice of dessert is not so overwhelming. Besides, you can't go wrong ordering the house specialty— Chocolate, Chocolate, Chocolate. Open 5 to 10 p.m. Sun through Thurs, 5 to 11 p.m. Fri and Sat. Bern's Steak House, 1208 S. Howard Ave., Tampa; (813) 251-2421; www.bernssteakhouse.com. Expensive.

Take the scenic drive on Dunedin Beach Causeway to *Honeymoon Island State Park* and notice the large pines on the island's northern loop trail. This is one of a very few virgin slash pine stands in south Florida, as well as an important nesting site for the threatened osprey. A wide variety of plants and birds, including several endangered species, call this lovely island home. You may want to picnic, swim, fish, or catch the ferry to Caladesi Island. Open 8 a.m. to sunset daily. Honeymoon Island is at No. 1 Causeway Blvd., Dunedin, west of US 19A; (727) 469-5942; www.floridastateparks.org.

Caladesi Island State Park, located off Dunedin, is one of Florida's few unspoiled barrier islands. Catch the ferry (which leaves hourly, weather permitting) from Dunedin Beach on Honeymoon Island and spend some time at this attractive state park. Accessible only by boat, this is a good place to swim, skin-dive, boat, picnic, or beachcomb for shells. The park has almost 3 miles of sandy beach, a ridge of virgin pine flatwoods, and a mangrove swamp. A 60-foot observation tower offers views of the area and of vessels in the Gulf. Open 8 a.m. to sunset daily. The island is north of Dunedin off US 19A. For information, call the ferry at (727) 734-1501 or the park at (727) 469-5918; www.floridastateparks.org.

world'slargest

Shuffle off to the world's largest shuffleboard courts—65 all told—complete with stadium seating. Ask a club member if someone will unlock the trailer housing the Shuffleboard Hall of Fame, which displays the world's most complete collection of shuffleboard irons. St. Petersburg Shuffleboard Club, 559 Mirror Lake Dr. North, St. Petersburg (www.shuffleboardclub.org).

Remember the old sugarcane mill, the railroad depot, and the bandstand in the middle of the park? Open-air *Heritage Village at Pinewood Cultural Park* has these and more. Travel back in time to the early days of Pinellas County while browsing the old barn, church, cottage, log house, and other structures. A guide in period dress will show you around, or you can poke about on your own. How did those early settlers manage? At least some of the answers are here in this pretty pine and palmetto park. Open 10 a.m. to 4 p.m. Tues through Sat, 1 to 4 p.m. Sun. Closed Mon. Heritage Village, 11909 125th St. North, Largo; (727) 582-2123; www.pinewoodculturalpark.org. Admission is free but donations are appreciated.

The *Suncoast Seabird Sanctuary* is dedicated to the rescue, repair, recuperation, and, hopefully, the release of rehabilitated wild birds. It all began when Ralph Heath nursed an injured cormorant back to health in 1971. Word spread and soon people were leaving injured birds on his doorstep. Today the sanctuary is home to more than 500 birds, and as many as 20 injured birds are brought in daily. Unfortunately, more than 90 percent of these injuries are directly or indirectly related to human beings, who seem adept at throwing the delicate balance of nature out of kilter.

This nonprofit organization (supported entirely by donations) has a full-time staff of 15, a hospital complete with intensive-care room, and an annual budget of $700,000. So far nearly 35,000 birds have been returned to the wild.

One success story involved the release of a Southern bald eagle. Some permanently injured birds become full-time residents. You may watch brown pelicans building nests with branches and rearing young in captivity. Notice the contingent of perfectly well birds perching on top of the aviary. Isn't it thoughtful of them to visit their hospitalized friends?

Bring a camera and leave a donation or, better yet, fill out an application to adopt a bird. The sanctuary is open 9 a.m. until dark daily. Suncoast Seabird Sanctuary, 18328 Gulf Blvd., Indian Shores; (727) 391-6211; www.seabird sanctuary.org. Free.

A couple of sea turtle hunters returning from the Gulf were the first to see *John's Pass* in Madeira Beach. (It didn't exist until the hurricane of 1848.) Juan Levique was the one who spotted the changed coastline, so naturally it came to be known as John's Pass. Today an early Florida fishing village atmosphere prevails. Boutiques and shops cater to tourists' whims. Choose from a large selection of beachwear, jewelry, stained glass, or handcrafted items. This is a fine place to fish, charter a boat, or just walk the boardwalk with an eye out for playful dolphins.

An excellent way to start the day is at the *Friendly Fisherman Seafood Restaurant* with a Boardwalk Breakfast. You can't miss with a basket of hot corn fritters. Later in the day you can stop in and munch on grouper cheeks (no bones!). The Friendly Fisherman is on the boardwalk at John's Pass in Madeira Beach. Inexpensive.

No wonder folks flock to St. Petersburg, with its exquisite beaches and 361 days of sunshine each year. Settled in the 1840s, St. Petersburg came to life in 1885 when Peter Demens extended his Orange Belt Railroad into the peninsula and named the settlement for his Russian birthplace. Imagine a place so confident of its sunshine that one of its newspapers gives away all the street editions if the weather remains cloudy for the entire day.

The world's most comprehensive collection of art by Spanish surrealist Salvador Dalí can be found in St. Petersburg. The $35 million collection features oil paintings, watercolors, drawings, graphics, and sculptures. The fascination here is to see Dalí's development from 1914 to 1980. The *Salvador Dalí*

st.petersburg

At an 1885 meeting of the American Medical Association in New Orleans, Dr. W. C. Van Bibber presented the results of a 10-year study on the establishment of a "world health city." He concluded that Point Pinellas (the St. Petersburg/Clearwater area) was the ideal location and cited a climate "unequaled anywhere." Few places enjoy as much sun as this area, where the sun shines an average of 361 days each year. The *Guinness Book of World Records* recognizes St. Petersburg as having the longest string of consecutive sunny days: The sun warmed the city for 768 consecutive days from February 9, 1967, to March 17, 1969.

Museum is open 10 a.m. to 5:30 p.m. Mon, Tues, Wed, Fri, and Sat; 10 a.m. to 8 p.m. Thurs; and noon to 5:30 p.m. Sun. It is located on the waterfront at 1 Dali Blvd., St. Petersburg; (727) 823-3767; www.thedali.org.

If you want a touch of history in your vacation itinerary, you will delight in the grand wedding cake of a hotel known as the *Don Ce Sar.* Take off your rose-colored glasses and it's still pink—really pink, as in flamingos, Easter eggs, and bubble gum.

Unfortunately, a glorious opening night in January 1928 was followed by the stock market crash of 1929. Despite the patronage of such prominent guests as Scott and Zelda Fitzgerald, Clarence Darrow, and Babe Ruth, the dismal days of the 1930s took their toll. Tourism had all but disappeared when the army bought it for a song during the war and turned it into a hospital. (The kitchen served as the morgue.) Deterioration and neglect pointed toward the Don's demise until a Save the Don committee worked a near miracle and rescued it during the 1970s.

The National Archives in Washington, D.C., lists the Don as a historical monument, and it is one of a few building landmarks used by the National Maritime Association on its maps and navigational aids for sailors. In April 1975 the Don was added to the National Register of Historic Places. An extensive renovation has been completed, and the palatial hotel glows throughout its 10 stories with all its original elegance. (It has received a AAA Four Diamond rating since 1978.)

The Don Ce Sar is at the southern end of the island of St. Pete Beach directly on the Gulf of Mexico. You can't miss it. It's the only thing around that is both huge and pink. The Don Ce Sar Beach Resort and Spa, 3400 Gulf Blvd., St. Pete Beach; (727) 360-1881; www.loewshotels.com.

flyinghigh

St. Petersburg was the birthplace of scheduled commercial aviation on New Year's Day 1915. Pilot Tony Jannus flew a Benoist airboat across the bay to Tampa with former mayor Abe Phiel along as the first passenger. The historic flight captured the world's attention, and the airline capitalized on the novelty during its brief, three-month term of operation. A replica of the Benoist is on exhibit at the St. Petersburg Museum of History.

Directly south of St. Pete Beach is sprawling *Fort DeSoto Park,* a great place to get away from it all and spend some quiet time with the pelicans and great white herons. Its 1,100 acres, with more than 7 miles of waterfront and almost 3 miles of fine swimming beaches, ramble over five islands: Madeline Key, St. Jean Key, St. Christopher Key, Bonne Fortune Key, and the main island, Mullet Key.

Ponce de León anchored off *Mullet Key* during the summer of 1513 to clean the barnacles off the bottom of his ship. He was interrupted by Indians who thought he had no business in their territory. In the skirmish that followed, the first white soldier known to be killed in North America died. Apparently Ponce de León didn't get the message that he was not welcome in the area. When he returned in 1521, he again fought with the native tribes, this time receiving the wound that later caused his death in Havana, Cuba.

Construction of Fort DeSoto began in 1898 and was completed two years later. Its eight 12-inch mortars never fired a single shot at any enemy. The remains of this old fort graphically illustrate the then-popular concept of harbor defense. Today it is an interesting relic of history and a good place to climb for a view of the surrounding sea.

Two islands provide a haven for campers, ancient oaks on the northern end of Mullet Key shade a lovely picnic area, and lifeguards are on duty at the swimming beaches during the summer. There are a boat-launching ramp, two fishing piers, and a small restaurant and gift shop near the fort.

By car you can get to Fort DeSoto Park only by two toll bridges. Pinellas County Park wants you to know, however, that the money goes to the State Road Department and not to the park. Fort DeSoto Park, 3500 Pinellas Bayway South, Tierra Verde; (727) 582-2267. Open 7 a.m. to dark daily. Boat ramp and two fishing piers open 7 a.m. to 11 p.m.

Western Interior

You'll get your exercise if you cover all 80 acres of canopies, stalls, and sheds at **Webster Flea Market,** one of the largest flea markets in the Southeast. Actually this flea market comprises four different markets: Sumter County Farmers' Market, a wholesale market, Webster Westside Market, and the Wee Flea (the gates between them are open for customers). It's hard to believe this all started in 1937 as a one-shed farmers' produce auction. More than 1,700 vendors await you and your spare change. It's all here—from fine antiques, clothes, fresh produce, and homemade sausage to just plain junk. You'll be exhausted if you try to see everything there is to see, but you'll surely find at least one item you cannot live another day without. Customers are welcome to camp overnight on Webster Westside's grounds. Some come on the first Sunday of each month for the car and motorcycle show and stay until Tuesday morning. Open every Mon at 5 a.m. in the winter and 6 a.m. in the summer. Webster Flea Market is located at 516 NW 3rd St., Webster (CR 478 and 3rd Street); (352) 793-9877 or (800) 832-7396; www.websterfleamarket.net.

The **Dade Battlefield Historic State Park** is the picture of serenity now, but it was once drenched in blood. Here Native Americans, who were

Sea Cows

The manatee has been hunted for centuries for its meat, bone, hide, and fat. Florida Indians regularly hunted manatees and sold excess meat to the Spanish. Hides were made into leather shields, cords, and shoes, and the ivorylike bones were believed to be of medicinal value. Pioneers arriving in the 19th century shot manatees for food. Cowpens Key in the Florida Keys is believed to be so named because manatees were once penned in a small cove there as a food supply.

The West Indian manatee, or sea cow, is Florida's official marine mammal. Only about 1,000 of these harmless, fascinating creatures now remain, living their peaceful lives in Florida waters. Manatees can live in fresh or salt water, but they apparently need to drink freshwater periodically. They are vegetarians subsisting entirely on aquatic plants. Huge, gentle, and slow-moving, manatees are distantly related to elephants and more closely to dugongs. An adult manatee averages between 10 and 12 feet long and may weigh from 1,000 to more than 2,000 pounds.

The species is listed as endangered by the US Fish & Wildlife Service. For nearly a decade, more than 100 manatees have died each year. Many manatee deaths are people related, and most of these occur from collisions with watercraft. Other problems include pollution, the ingestion of fish hooks and monofilament line, and their being crushed in canal locks and becoming tangled in crab-trap lines. Vandalism and harassment by boaters, divers, and anglers can force manatees to leave preferred habitats and lead to the separation of mothers and calves. Ultimately, loss of habitat is the most serious threat facing the manatee today.

not pleased at the prospect of being evicted from their land, ambushed more than 100 soldiers under the command of Major Francis L. Dade. The Dade Massacre, as it came to be known, touched off the Second Seminole War, a war that dragged on for seven years and became the country's costliest Indian war. While visiting the small museum and reading the markers along the battlefield trail, you'll have a chance to ponder the events of December 28, 1835. The park is open 8 a.m. to sunset daily. The visitor center is open 9 a.m. to 5 p.m. daily. Dade Battlefield Historic State Park, 7200 CR 603, Bushnell. Located southwest of Bushnell off US 301, exit 63 on I-75; (352) 793-4781; www.floridastateparks.org.

Gulf Coast

Every winter the largest congregation of West Indian manatees in the world, as many as 300, gathers in the transparent spring-fed ***Crystal River and Homosassa River*** near the Gulf of Mexico. This is the only place in North America offering carefully monitored interactions with manatees in the wild. *Rodale's*

Scuba Diving magazine survey has recognized the area as the "Best Place to see Large Animals" and ranked it high on its list of "Favorite Fresh Water Dives."

Divers come from all over the world to participate in these Manatee Encounters, which are offered throughout the year. You may view these endangered marine mammals from a boat or from the riverbanks, or you can actually snorkel and scuba dive among them. The best time for manatee viewing is from December through March when they migrate to the warm (72 degrees Fahrenheit) spring waters to feed on sea grasses. Despite their imposing size, manatees are gentle and curious and will swim right up to you. Even manatee mothers with babies seem to know you pose no danger.

Homosassa Riverside Resort offers a Manatee Awareness Program, with daily tours, boat (including pontoons, kayaks, and canoes) and equipment rental, day trips, and guides—everything you'll need to have a rare encounter with the manatees. The resort's accommodations are perfectly situated to enjoy waterfront activities, and **Riverside Crab House** next door serves up delicious crab-stuffed shrimp. Homosassa Riverside Resort is located at 5297 S. Cherokee Way, Homosassa. Call (352) 628-2474 or (800) 442-2040 to learn more or visit www.riversideresorts.com.

If you haven't looked a manatee in the eye lately, you'll never have a better opportunity than at **Homosassa Springs Wildlife State Park.** You may pay a visit to these gentle mammals while walking underwater (and staying nice and dry) in the underwater observatory.

Besides the lovable manatees, you'll see more than 34 varieties of fish, both saltwater and freshwater species. Educational programs—on alligators, manatees, and native Florida reptiles—are offered seven times daily. Be sure to take the nature cruise and stroll the trails. Open 9 a.m. to 5:30 p.m. daily. Located just west of US 19. Homosassa Springs, 4150 S. Suncoast Blvd., Homosassa; (352) 628-5343; www.floridastateparks.org or www.homosassasprings.org.

Withlacoochee State Trail, a linear state park, is part of the Florida Rails-to-Trails Program. This 46-mile former railroad track, from Citrus Springs south to Dade City, follows the former rail route to Inverness of the late 1800s. The trail, which features mileage markers, restrooms, picnic shelters, and benches, has been paved for hikers, cyclists, in-line skaters, and equestrians. Open sunrise to sunset daily. Bike rentals available nearby. Call Withlacoochee State Trail at (352) 726-2251 for more information or visit www.dep.state.fl.us.

A long time ago prehistoric people called Florida home, especially in the Crystal River area, where fresh seafood was abundant and the weather was warm. The **Crystal River Archaeological State Park** is considered one of the longest continually occupied sites (from 200 BC to AD 1400) in Florida. This six-mound complex on 14 acres is surely one of the most imposing prehistoric ceremonial centers on Florida's west coast. No one knows exactly what kind of ceremonies were conducted here, but it is clear that burials took place at some of the mounds. Take a leisurely stroll on the half-mile trail through temple mounds, burial mounds, and middens. Climb the stairs to the mound top for a view down the river. Knowledgeable park rangers are on hand to answer your questions. Be sure to see the collection of pottery and projectile points (in the visitor center) excavated on this site. The park is located 1 mile west of US 19, 2 miles north of Crystal River, on N. Museum Point. Open 8 a.m. to sunset daily year-round. For more information, write to Crystal River Archaeological State Park, 3400 N. Museum Point, Crystal River 34428-7724, or call (352) 795-3817.

Yulee Sugar Mill Ruins Historic State Park was once part of a thriving sugar plantation, the area's first known settlement made by a white man. David Yulee, a former US senator, operated the mill for 13 years beginning in 1851. He supplied the Confederate army with sugar products until 1864, when a Union naval force burned Yulee's home to the ground. Interpretive signs will guide you through the partially restored sugar mill, the only antebellum structure of its kind in the country. The ruins are located in Homosassa on SR 490 southwest of US 19. (352) 795-3817; www.floridastateparks.org.

Weeki Wachee Springs is home to live mermaids as well as more traditional denizens of the deep. The unusual theater is 16 feet below the surface of the spring (which is more than 137 feet deep) with glass windows for your viewing pleasure. Walk through lush tropical gardens and ride a *Wilderness River Cruise Boat.* Weeki Wachee Springs, 6131 Commercial Way, Weeki Wachee. The theme park is on US 19 south at the junction of SR 50; (352) 596-5656; www.weekiwachee.com.

The famous sponge industry of *Tarpon Springs* began in the 1890s when John K. Cheyney launched his first sponge-fishing boat and began hooking sponges. The diving techniques used to first harvest sponges in the

thebigscrub

Ocala National Forest, covering more than 430,000 acres, is known locally as the "Big Scrub." Ocala is the oldest national forest east of the Mississippi River as well as the southernmost in the country. This forest preserve, bounded by the St. Johns and Ocklawaha Rivers, contains central highlands, coastal lowlands, swamps, springs, and literally hundreds of lakes and ponds, as well as a great variety of vegetation and wildlife. Our only national forest with subtropical vegetation, Ocala boasts the world's largest stand of sand pine, the only tree capable of growing to usable size in dry sand. The forest is home to one of the state's largest deer herds, as well as such Florida rarities as the Southern bald eagle and black bear.

Mediterranean were introduced in 1905 by John Cocoris, an immigrant from Greece. The first Tarpon Springs sponger to try this method emerged after a 10-minute dive thoroughly convinced that these sponge beds could supply the whole world.

Word of the bountiful beds off Tarpon Springs spread to Greece, and soon whole families were packing up their lives and moving to the west coast of Florida. From their homeland they brought the colorful customs and traditional cuisine of the rich Hellenic culture. The village prospered during the first 40 years of the 20th century as sponging grew to be a multimillion-dollar business. Auctions held at the Sponge Exchange were lively affairs, and Tarpon Springs soon surpassed Key West as the country's main sponging center. But in the 1940s a mysterious disease known as the red tide decimated the sponge beds, and consumers began turning to synthetic sponges.

Today visitors fascinated by this Greek community stroll the sponge docks, which have been designated a National Historic Landmark. The Sponge Exchange has been taken over by boutiques and gift shops, but a few boats still return from sea with ropes of sponges drying in the rigging. Lining the docks are many Greek coffeehouses and restaurants where a meal of pastitso and baklava may be washed down with a glass of retsina wine.

The community still revolves around the church. **_St. Nicholas Greek Orthodox Cathedral,_** a fine example of neo-Byzantine architecture with icons, stained glass, and sculptured marble, was named for the patron saint of ships and seafaring men. The celebration of Epiphany, held each January 6, here is a study in pomp and pageantry. The archbishop leads the colorful procession from the church to Spring Bayou, the site of the original settlement. There he releases a dove and tosses a large gold cross into the water. Young men dive for the sacred trophy, and the successful one receives a blessing, which is supposed to bring him a year of good luck. The community then funnels all its energies into singing and dancing. Especially during this old-world festival, Tarpon Springs seems more like a Mediterranean community than a Floridian one. Open 10 a.m. to 4 p.m. Mon through Fri (possible to make advance arrangements for weekend tours of

a world of dinosaurs

Dinosaurs never roamed the Florida landscape . . . until now. Browse Dinosaur World, an outdoor display of 150 life-size dinosaurs in Plant City, between Orlando and Tampa. They aren't real, but you get the idea. Considering their size and appetite, it's probably a good thing they disappeared long before our first ancestors appeared on the planet.

the cathedral). The church is at 36 N. Pinellas Ave., Tarpon Springs; (727) 937-3540; www.epiphanycity.org.

Ocala Area

The Ocala area is a land of gently rolling hills, massive oaks bearded with Spanish moss, and sleek thoroughbreds gamboling in neatly fenced paddocks. This is the fastest-growing thoroughbred community in the world and is responsible for Florida's development, in less than half a century, as a major force in international racing and breeding.

The racing world sat up and took notice when Needles became the first Florida-bred horse to win the Kentucky Derby, in 1956. Since then what started as a few converted cattle farms has grown to nearly 500 thoroughbred facilities. Marion County is now second only to Lexington, Kentucky, in concentration of thoroughbred farms.

The English Shire Horse

The ancestors of the first horses appeared some 70 million years ago, give or take a few million. Those early terrier-size four-toed animals were a far cry from their regal descendants, but, genetically speaking, they were destined for greatness. From humble beginnings, two main types of horse evolved. One was a slender racing horse bred for speed, the other a sturdy workhorse—muscular and proud yet mild-mannered.

Descended from the Old English Black Horse, the Shire breed was firmly established more than 1,000 years ago. These horses had to be incredibly strong, not to mention courageous, to carry knights into the thick of battle in medieval times. After all, a full suit of armor for both horse and rider weighed more than 400 pounds. Later, Shires were used as coach horses, for hauling heavy loads, and farmwork.

The Shire horse is a magnificent breed—as gentle, intelligent, and hardworking as it is powerful. The largest of England's native horses, the massive Shires stand 16.2 to 18 hands high (17 hands equals 5½ feet) and normally weigh 2,000 to 2,500 pounds. No wonder they call them "gentle giants." Listed in the *Guinness Book of World Records* as the world's largest horse, a Shire named Samson (now deceased) stood just over 21 hands (7 feet 2 inches) high and weighed some 3,000 pounds.

Shires sport white feathery fetlocks (abundant hair beneath the knees) and are typically bay (reddish brown), brown, black, or gray. With their muscular, barrel-chested bodies and thick necks, they thrive on hard work.

This noble breed is threatened, as there are less than 4,000 purebred English Shires left in the world. But you can see dozens of these stalwart horses near Ocala at the New England Shire Centre.

Central Florida offers ideal conditions for raising superior thoroughbreds. Year-round sunshine, mineral-rich water, and fertile pastureland have turned out to be a winning combination. Mild weather, with cold snaps rarely lasting more than a few days, plays an important role. Central Florida's extended springs and autumns flank a long summer. The absence of a harsh winter means that, rather than standing idle in their stalls, horses run free all year. Unlike its northern counterpart, a new Florida foal is usually out romping with its dam within hours of its birth.

wildthings

Good news! Florida has the largest breeding population of bald eagles in the lower 48 states. Bad news! There are less than 100 Florida panthers left in the state. Mixed news! The Florida Everglades is the only place in the world where alligators and crocodiles live in the same habitat.

The area is wonderfully scenic and many horse farms welcome visitors for self-guided tours, but the hours vary. Visitors are encouraged to pick up information at the Ocala/Marion County Chamber of Commerce, 110 E. Silver Springs Blvd., Ocala, or call (352) 629-8051; www.ocalacc.com.

The **New England Shire Centre,** one of the world's largest Shire farms, is neither in New England nor in Merrie Old England. It's actually near Ocala, which claims to be the horse capital of the world. The central Florida location is no accident. The area boasts nearly ideal conditions, including mild winters and an abundance of limestone in the soil and water, which, as every horse breeder knows, builds strong bones. As for New England, that's where the owners began breeding and raising Shires.

On your tour of the Shire Centre, you will see dozens of Shires who, trust me, would love to see you. Shires are friendly, docile, well mannered, and as curious about you as you are about them.

The farm is a beauty—a 125-acre showplace owned by Candy and Carl Moulton, who are passionate about their Shires. Their lucky horses have the run of the place, including a two- to five-acre paddock for each mare-foal pair. To see this magnificent breed up close and personal, join a tour of the New England Shire Centre. Reservations are required. Open 9 a.m. to 6 p.m. daily. Call (352) 873- 3005; www.newenglandshirecentre.com.

Horse lovers congregate at the **Horse & Hounds Restaurant,** where jockeys and visitors alike enjoy the casual atmosphere and fine food. The walls are covered with equine memorabilia from polo and racing to dressage events. The specialty of the house is certified Angus beef in various tasty cuts; other favorites include pan-seared quail or macadamia-crusted shrimp. Be sure to try the spinach salad, a Horse & Hounds original, served with a marvelous emerald poppy-seed dressing. The restaurant is open 11 a.m. to 9:30 p.m. daily. Located at the corner of US 27 and 225A about 4.5 miles west of I-75. The address is 6998 NW US 27, Ocala. For reservations, call (352) 620-2500.

While you're in horse country, you really should take an **Ocala Horse Farm Tour.** Climb aboard a horse-drawn carriage or trolley and ride through some of the area's fabulous horse farms. You'll see all manner of gorgeous steeds from quarter horses to Tennessee walkers. Oh, the tales you will hear—tales of the privileged set galloping through the rarified thoroughbred world. Hollywood stars live on some of these magnificent estates along with heirs to some of America's great fortunes. The scenery is bucolic, the history of the area fascinating, and the tales range from funny to tragic. You'll need a reservation; call (352) 867-8717 or (877) 996-2252. Ocala Carriage & Tours is at 4776 NW 110th Ave.; www.ocalatours.com.

Just east of Ocala is the **Ocala National Forest,** with more than 300,000 acres of untamed springs, winding streams, and natural lakes. The southern-most national forest in the continental US, Ocala is a popular recreation area for canoeing, swimming, camping, hiking, picnicking, and hunting. Detailed maps of the forest may be obtained at the ranger station. Write USDA Forest Service, 325 John Knox Rd., Ste. F100, Tallahassee 32303. Call; (352) 236-0288; www.fs.usda.gov.

Although this is the largest area of sand pine in the world, with one of the largest deer herds in Florida, it is the clear, clean springs that steal the show. **Alexander Springs** pumps out 76 million gallons of 72-degree-Fahrenheit water each day of the year. The spring here is so large that local scuba experts use it for new-diver certification tests. Canoers use this run for an excursion into the unspoiled forest, and swimmers and sunbathers make good use of the large sand beach. Located in Ocala National Forest off CR 445; 49525 CR 445, Altoona; (352) 669-3522.

Another favorite, **Juniper Springs,** contributes 20 million gallons to the local water supply. Besides swimming, the most popular activity is canoeing the 7-mile spring run. Canoe rentals and pickup shuttle service are available. This campground is in such demand that reservations are not accepted, and accom-modations are handled on a first-come basis. Located in Ocala National Forest on SR 40 just west of SR 19; 26701 E. SR 40, Silver Springs; (352) 625-0546.

Salt Springs Recreation Area is on the shores of a beautiful natural spring that empties into Lake George, the state's second-largest lake. The 5-mile spring run is ideal for canoeing, boating, and fishing; the spring boil is a mecca for swimmers and snorkelers. Located in Ocala National Forest on SR 19 about 21 miles north of SR 40, Salt Springs has complete camping facilities; 14152 SR 19 North, Salt Springs; (352) 685-2048.

Bubbling Sands

Juniper Springs is a jewel. Rimmed by a circular stone wall and surrounded by dense semitropical forest, this swimming hole is a real stunner. For a while we watched as intrepid teenagers dropped from the limbs of a huge tree into the brilliant cobalt blue depths. Thunderous splashes as the kids cannonballed into the pool punctuated the rhythmic sounds of an undershot waterwheel almost hidden by foliage.

Two springs in this area, Juniper and nearby Fern Hammock, produce a combined flow of about 20 million gallons of 72-degree-Fahrenheit water every day of the year. But statistics don't even hint at their true beauty. Water boils up through clean white sand, creating ever-changing formations resembling creamy cumulus clouds. The billowing sand in this watery kaleidoscope never rests.

Water temperature may remain constant, but the weather changes with the season. According to the woman at the snack counter, Northerners enthusiastically plunge in year-round, but Floridians wouldn't dream of swimming during the winter. The local population shows up during the cooler months, but it is usually to camp, hike, and canoe. Temperatures in this national forest during the dry months between November and February range from 50 degrees to 72 degrees Fahrenheit. Summer is warmer, between 70 degrees and 95 degrees Fahrenheit, and wetter.

Passing close to Juniper Springs, the Ocala Trail (a portion of the Florida Trail) runs the 66-mile length of Ocala National Forest. We were content to stroll the lush ¾-mile nature trail, passing numerous small springs along the way. Our brief encounters with turtles and birds in this idyllic setting whetted our appetites for more. Exploring by canoe proved a satisfying answer. Because this is a one-way trip from Juniper Springs to the bridge on SR 19 (about 7 miles), an early start is recommended.

Juniper Creek begins as a swift, narrow stream almost completely hidden from the sun by dense foliage. After ducking overhanging branches and negotiating many twists and turns, we were glad to have the stream gradually widen and slow so we could relax and absorb some of the sights. A pair of otters followed us for about a mile, their heads popping up from time to time. Cormorants and ibises flew overhead, and herons stalked the shallows. After catching glimpses of both alligators and snakes, we understood why rafts, floats, and inner tubes aren't allowed on this pretty stretch of water. We stopped for a picnic along the way, felt eyes on us, and turned to find a deer watching.

Silver Glen Springs is a beautiful 1,000-acre area bordering a crystal-clear spring. It's a good place to hike, picnic, bird-watch, swim, boat, or fish. Located in Ocala National Forest off SR 19, 6 miles north of SR 40; 5271 N. SR 19, Salt Springs; (352) 685-2799.

Although Ocala's waterworks are impressive, they are literally just a drop in the region's overflowing bucket. Of the country's 78 major springs, 27 are

silversprings

"There is nothing on earth com-
parable to it. We seemed floating
through an immense cathedral
where white marble columns meet
in vast arches overhead and are
reflected in the grassy depths
below. The dusky plumes of palmetto . . . looked like fine tracery
of a wondrous sculptured roof. . . .
Clouds of fragrance were wafted
to us from orange groves along the
shore; and the transparent depth
of the water gave the impression
that our boat was moving through
the air."

—Harriet Beecher Stowe,
on her 1873 visit to Silver Springs

in Florida. Its central section is literally riddled with them. Springs are classified according to volume—a major spring, one of first magnitude, produces 100 cubic feet of water a second, or more than 64 million gallons daily. The combined output from all 300 of Florida's known springs is 8 billion gallons of water a day!

Silver Springs, near Ocala, is the largest limestone artesian spring formation in the world. With an average output of 550 million gallons a day, the springs have the greatest long-term measured average flow of any freshwater group in Florida. No wonder early Indians considered them sacred and paid homage to them with elaborate ceremonies. Scientists have discovered evidence of human activity dating back 100 centuries. Certainly this is one of Florida's oldest attractions.

Most of the earliest sightseers came by boat, although the 136-mile trip from Palatka involved several weeks of poling along the tortuous Ocklawaha River. By the 1880s steamboats began regular trips from Palatka to the springs carrying such notables as Mary Todd Lincoln, Harriet Beecher Stowe, and William Cullen Bryant. The expedition, a real breeze, took only two nights and a day.

florida'sfinest fossils

The **Center for Florida History** in the Museum of Arts and Sciences in Daytona Beach claims the most complete fossil record discovered in Florida, including a 13-foot-tall giant ground sloth skeleton that was excavated nearby. The Florida Museum of National History in Gainesville covers 65 million years of Florida history in its outstanding Evolution of Life & Land exhibit.

Visitors are rarely disappointed by this natural wonder. The limestone-filtered water in the deep-blue pool inspired one early journalist to describe the springs as shining "like an enormous jewel." Phillip Morrell, a young man living at Silver Springs, invented the glass-bottom boat to provide passengers their first fish-eye view of the aquatic world. Watching this ever-changing panorama while gliding over the pellucid springs is still a favorite activity. Numerous movies and television shows, attracted by the extraordinary clarity, have done underwater filming in this location.

The luxuriant gardens and subtropical scenery on the 350-acre site add to the viewing pleasure. Other diversions include a Jungle Cruise, Lost River Voyage, and a Jeep Safari. You'll see giraffes, ostriches, camels, and a colony of monkeys descended from those used in the old Tarzan movies. The springs are located just off I-75, 1 mile east of Ocala on SR 40. Open 10 a.m. to 5 p.m. daily. Silver Springs, 5656 E. Silver Springs Blvd., Silver Springs; (352) 236-2121; www.silversprings.com.

Eastern Interior

The endangered manatees have long made **Blue Spring State Park** their winter home. These large mammals congregate in Blue Spring Run between November and March because the year-round 72-degree-Fahrenheit water offers a refuge from the chilly St. Johns River. You may view these large "sea cows" (adults weigh about a ton) from observation platforms along Blue Spring Run. Once common from the Carolinas to Texas, these gentle giants now survive only in Florida, and this is one of the few places you may observe them in their native habitat. A 2-hour boat ride explores the St. Johns River and the area around Hontoon Island.

In 1872 the Thursby family built a big frame house on the top of an ancient snail-shell mound. The house and grounds have been restored to look as they did in the 1880s when oranges grew in the yard and the family sent their crops to Jacksonville by steamboat. The park is a fine place to camp (six family vacation cabins available), canoe, swim, fish, picnic, snorkel, and scuba dive. Located 2 miles west of Orange City off I-4 and US 17/92, the park opens at 8 a.m. and closes at sunset daily year-round. Blue Spring State Park, 2100 W. French Ave., Orange City; (386) 775-3663; www.floridastateparks.org.

The only way to reach **Hontoon Island State Park** is by boat. Luckily a daily ferry crosses the St. Johns River between the parking lot and the island. Of special interest is a 300-foot-long Timucuan Indian ceremonial mound. No vehicles are allowed. Besides being a sanctuary for the bald eagle, this is a good place to fish, picnic, and camp in either tents or cabins. The park is open 8 a.m. to sunset daily year-round. Six miles west of DeLand off SR 44; 2309 River Ridge Rd., DeLand; (386) 736-5309; www.floridastateparks.org. For camping reservations, call (800) 326-3521 or visit www.reserveamerica.com.

Between Sanford and Longwood, keep an eye out for the **Big Tree** marker. The country's largest bald cypress tree is less than a mile up the cutoff road. The "Senator" is 126 feet high with a diameter of 17½ feet and an estimated age of more than 3,000 years. Impressive! Big Tree Park is on General Hutchinson Parkway in Longwood. The park opens at 8 a.m. daily; the Seminole County Parks and Recreation Department closes the gates at sunset. Free.

You are not going to believe there are this many cacti in the world until you tour the greenhouses at *Florida Cactus Inc.* in Plymouth. Is your idea of a cactus green? Take a good long look at the endless rows of red, yellow, and pink cacti.

You may buy (or just admire) dish gardens, colorful grafted cacti, and cactus books. The mailing address is Florida Cactus Inc., PO Box 2900, Apopka 32704. The greenhouse, at 2542 Peterson Rd. in Plymouth, is located off US 441. From US 441, turn south onto Boy Scout Boulevard. Follow the Florida Cactus signs to S. Peterson Road. Open 7 a.m. to 5 p.m. Mon through Fri; closed weekends; (407) 886-1833. Free.

State Parks in Central Florida

State park information: (850) 245-2157 or www .floridastateparks.org. For camping reservations in any state park, call (800) 326-3521.

Anastasia State Park, (904) 461-2033

Anclote Key Preserve State Park, (727) 469-5942

Blue Spring State Park, (386) 775-3663

Bulow Creek State Park, (386) 676-4050

Bulow Plantation Ruins Historic State Park, (386) 517-2084

Caladesi Island State Park, (727) 469-5918

Crystal River Archaeological State Park, (352) 795-3817

Dade Battlefield Historic State Park, (352) 793-4781

DeLeon Springs State Park, (386) 985-4212

Faver-Dykes State Park, (904) 794-0997

Fort Cooper State Park, (352) 726-0315

Fort Pierce Inlet State Park/Avalon State Park, (772) 468-3985

Gamble Rogers Memorial State Recreation Area at Flagler Beach, (386) 517-2086

Highlands Hammock State Park, (863) 386-6094

Hillsborough River State Park, (813) 987-6771

Homosassa Springs Wildlife State Park, (352) 628-5343

Honeymoon Island State Park, (727) 469-5942

Hontoon Island State Park, (386) 736-5309

Kissimmee Prairie Preserve State Park, (863) 462-5360

Lake Griffin State Park, (352) 360-6760

Lake Kissimmee State Park, (863) 696-1112

Lake Louisa State Park, (352) 394-3969

Lake Manatee State Park, (941) 741-3028

Little Manatee River State Park, (813) 671-5005

Lower Wekiva River Preserve State Park, (407) 884-2008

Payne's Creek Historic State Park, (863) 375-4717

Ravine Gardens State Park, (386) 329-3721

Rock Springs Run State Reserve, (407) 884-2008

Savannas Preserve State Park, (772) 398-2779

Silver River State Park, (352) 236-7148

Tomoka State Park, (386) 676-4050

Washington Oaks Gardens State Park, (386) 446-6780

Wekiwa Springs State Park, (407) 884-2008

Ybor City Museum State Park, (813) 247-6323

Yulee Sugar Mill Ruins Historic State Park, (352) 795-3817

Places to Stay in Central Florida

CLEARWATER

Holiday Inn Select
3535 Ulmerton Rd.
(727) 577-9100 or
(888) 465-4329
www.ichotelsgroup.com

Residence Inn by Marriott
5050 Ulmerton Rd.
(727) 573-4444
www.marriott.com

Safety Harbor Resort and Spa
105 N. Bayshore Dr.,
Safety Harbor
(800) 447-4136
www.hotelreservations.com

CLEARWATER BEACH

Barefoot Bay Beach Resort and Marina
401 E. Shore Dr.
(727) 447-3316 or
(866) 447-3316
www.barefootbayresort.com

DAYTONA BEACH

Hilton–Daytona Beach Oceanfront Resort
100 N. Atlantic Ave.
(386) 254-8200
www.hilton.com

Holiday Inn–Indigo Lakes
2620 W. International Speedway Blvd.
(386) 258-6333
www.holidayinn.com

Super 8 Speedway
2992 W. International Speedway Blvd.
(386) 253-0643
www.super8daytonabeach.com

DELAND

Clarion Hotel
350 E. International Speedway Blvd.
(386) 738-5200
www.clarionhotel.com

DUNEDIN

Best Western Yacht Harbor Inn and Suites
150 Marina Plaza
(727) 733-4121
www.yachtharborinn.com

KISSIMMEE

Days Inn Maingate East
5480 W. Irlo Bronson Hwy.
(407) 396-7969
www.daysinnmaingate.com

LAKELAND

The Avenue Hotel
3405 S. Florida Ave.
(863) 646-5731
www.theavenuelakeland.com

Safar Inn
1817 E. Memorial Blvd.
(863) 688-9221
www.safarhotels.com

OCALA

Courtyard by Marriott
3712 SW 38th Ave.
(352) 237-8000
www.courtyard.com

ORLANDO

Courtyard at Lake Lucerne
211 N. Lucerne Circle East
(407) 648-5188
www.orlandohistoricinn.com

The Florida Hotel & Conference Center
1500 Sand Lake Rd.
(800) 916-8592
www.thefloridahotelorlando.com

Bradenton Area Convention & Visitors Bureau, PO Box 1000, Bradenton 34206, or 1 Haben Blvd., Palmetto 34221; (941) 729-9177 or www.visitflorida.com

Central Florida Visitors & Convention Bureau, 2701 Myrtle Park Dr., Auburndale; (800) 828-7655; www.visitcentralflorida.org

Citrus County Tourist Development Council, 9225 W. Fishbowl Dr., Homosassa; (800) 587-6667; www.visitcitrus.com

Clay County Chamber of Commerce, 1734 Kingsley Ave., Orange Park; (904) 264-2651; www.claychamber.org

Clearwater Regional Chamber of Commerce, 401 Cleveland St., Clearwater; (727) 461-0011; www.clearwaterflorida.org

Cocoa Beach Area Chamber of Commerce/Convention and Visitors Bureau, 400 Fortenberry Rd., Merritt Island; (321) 459-2200; www.cocoabeachchamber.com

Daytona Beach Area Convention & Visitors Bureau, 126 E. Orange Ave., Daytona Beach; (386) 255-5478; www.daytonabeachcvb.com

DeLand Area Chamber of Commerce, 336 N. Woodland Blvd., DeLand; (386) 734-4331; www.delandchamber.org

Dunnellon Area Chamber of Commerce, 20500 E. Pennsylvania Ave., Dunnellon; (352) 489-2320 or (800) 830-2087; www.dunnellonchamber.org

Florida's Space Coast Office of Tourism, 430 Brevard Ave., Ste. 150, Cocoa Village; (321) 433-4470 or (877) 572-3224; www.space-coast.com

Greater Hernando County Chamber of Commerce, 15588 Aviation Loop Dr., Brooksville; (352) 796-0697; www.hernandochamber.com

Greater Sebring Chamber of Commerce, 227 US 17 North, Sebring; (863) 385-8448; www.sebringflchamber.com

Greater Tarpon Springs Chamber of Commerce, 11 E. Orange St., Tarpon Springs; (727) 937-6109; www.tarponspringschamber.com

Hernando County Convention and Visitors Bureau, 30305 Cortez Blvd., Brooksville; (352) 754-4405 or (800) 601-4580; www.naturallyhernando.org

Indian River County Chamber of Commerce, 1216 21st St., Vero Beach; (772) 567-3491; www.indianriverchamber.com

Kissimmee Convention & Visitors Bureau, 1925 E. Irlo Bronson Memorial Hwy., Kissimmee; (407) 742-8200; www.visitkissimmee.com

Lake County Convention & Visitors Bureau, 20763 US 27, Groveland; (352) 429-3673; www.lakecountyfl.gov

Lakeland Area Chamber of Commerce, 35 Lake Morton Drive, Lakeland; (863) 688-8551; www.lakelandchamber.com

Lake Wales Area Chamber of Commerce, 340 W. Central Ave., Lake Wales; (863) 676-3445; www.lakewaleschamber.com

Melbourne/Palm Bay Area Chamber of Commerce, 1005 E. Strawbridge Ave., Melbourne; (321) 724-5400 or (800) 771-9922; www.melpb-chamber.org

New Smyrna Beach Area Visitors Bureau, 2238 SR 44, New Smyrna Beach; (800) 541-9621; www.nsbfla.com

Ocala/Marion County Chamber of Commerce, 310 SE 3rd St., Ocala; (352) 629-8051; www.ocalacc.com

Okeechobee County Tourist Development Council, 2800 NW 20th Trail, Okeechobee; (863) 763-3959; www.okeechobee-tdc.com

Orlando/Orange County Convention & Visitor Bureau, (407) 363-5872 or (800) 972-3304; www.visitorlando.com

Pasco County Office of Tourism, 7530 Little Rd., Ste. 340, New Port Richey; (727) 847-8990; www.visitpasco.net

St. Lucie County Chamber of Commerce, 1850 SW Fountainview Blvd., Ste. 201, Port St. Lucie; (772) 340-1333; www.stluciechamber.org

St. Lucie County Tourist Bureau, 2300 Virginia Ave., Fort Pierce; (800) 344-TGIF (8443); www.visitstluciefla.com

St. Petersburg/Clearwater Convention & Visitors Bureau, 13805 58th St. North, Ste. 2-200, Clearwater; (727) 464-7200 or (877) 352-3224; www.visitstpeteclearwater.com

Sanford County Chamber of Commerce, 400 E. 1st St., Sanford; (407) 322-2212; www.sanfordchamber.com

Sebastian River Area Chamber of Commerce, 700 Main St., Sebastian; (772) 589-5969; www.sebastianchamber.com

Seminole County Convention and Visitors Bureau, 1000 AAA Dr., Ste. 200, MS 14, Heathrow; (407) 665-2900 or (800) 800-7832; www.visitseminole.com

The Tampa Bay Beaches Chamber of Commerce, 6990 Gulf Blvd., St. Pete Beach; (727) 360-6957; www.tampabaybeaches.com

Tampa Bay Convention & Visitors Bureau, Tampa Bay & Company, 401 E. Jackson St., Ste. 2100, Tampa; (813) 223-111; www.visittampabay.com

Ybor City Visitor Information Center, 1600 E. 8th Ave., Ste. B104, Ybor City; (813) 241-8838; www.ybor.org

Hampton Inn at Universal
5621 Windhover Dr.
(407) 351-6716
www.hamptoninn.com

Peabody Orlando
9801 International Dr.
(407) 352-4000
www.peabodyorlando.com

SEBRING

Quality Inn
6525 US 27 North
(863) 385-4500
www.choicehotel.com

SILVER SPRINGS

Days Inn
5360 E. Silver Springs
Blvd.
(352) 236-2575
www.daysinn.com

Sun Plaza
5461 E. Silver Springs
Blvd.
(352) 236-2343

ST. PETE BEACH

**Tradewinds Sandpiper
Hotel and Suites**
6000 Gulf Blvd.
(727) 360-5551

Post Card Inn
6300 Gulf Blvd.
(727) 367-2711
www.postcardinn.com

ST. PETERSBURG

Comfort Inn Central
1400 34th St. North
(727) 323-3100

Hilton
333 1st St. South
(727) 894-5000
www.hilton.com

Magnuson Marina Cove
6800 Sunshine Skyway Ln.
(727) 867-1151
www.marinacoveresort
.com

**Renaissance Vinoy
Resort**
501 5th Ave. Northeast
(727) 894-1000
www.renaissancehotels
.com

TAMPA

Behind the Fence B&B
1400 Viola Dr., Brandon
(813) 685-8201
www.behindthefencebb
.com

Comfort Inn
820 E. Busch Blvd.
(813) 933-4011
www.choicehotels.com

Grand Hyatt Tampa Bay
2900 Bayport Dr.
(813) 874-1234
www.grandtampabay.hyatt
.com

La Quinta Inn
9202 N. 30th St.
(813) 930-6900
www.laquinta.com

Saddlebrook Resort
5700 Saddlebrook Way
Wesley Chapel
(813) 973-1111
www.saddlebrookresort
.com

Tahitian Inn
601 S. Dale Mabry Hwy.
(800) 876-1397
www.tahitianinn.com

TARPON SPRINGS

Tahitian Resort
2337 US 19
North Holiday
(727) 934-6357
www.tahitianresort.net

Tarpon Shores Inn
40346 US 19 North
(727) 938-2483
www.tarponshoresinn.com

**Innisbrook Resort and
Golf Club**
36750 US 19 North
Palm Harbor
(800) 492-6899
www.innisbrookgolfresort
.com

TITUSVILLE

La Cita Country Club
777 Country Club Dr.
(321) 383-2582
www.lacitacc.com

**Ramada Inn Kennedy
Space Center**
3500 Cheney Hwy.
(866) 700-4316
www.ramadaflorida.com

WINTER HAVEN

Florida Garden Motel
345 8th St. Northwest
(941) 294-3537

Places to Eat in Central Florida

CLEARWATER BEACH

Bob Heilman's Beachcomber
447 Mandalay Ave.
(727) 442-4144
www.bobheilmans.com

DAYTONA BEACH

Aunt Catfish's
4009 Halifax Dr.
(386) 767-4768
www.auntcatfishontheriver
.com

Down the Hatch Seafood Restaurant
4894 Front St.
Ponce Inlet
(386) 761-4831
www.down-the-hatch-
seafood.com

Park's Seafood
951 N. Beach St.
(386) 258-7272

DUNEDIN

Bon Appetit
150 Marina Plaza
(727) 733-2151

KISSIMMEE

Charley's Steak House
2901 Parkway Blvd.
(407) 239-1270

Pacino's (Italian)
5795 W. Irlo Bronson
Memorial Hwy.
(407) 396-8022
www.pacinos.com

OCALA

Aunt Fannie's Restaurant
1031 S. Pine Ave.
(352) 732-4497

ORLANDO

The Crab House
8291 International Dr.
(407) 352-6140
www.crabhouseseafood
.com

Dux
Peabody Orlando Hotel
9801 International Dr.
(407) 345-4550
www.peabodyorlando.com

Passage to India
6129 Westwood Blvd.
(407) 351-3456
www.passageto.com

ST. PETE BEACH

The Lobster Pot
17814 Gulf Blvd.
Redington Shores
(727) 391-8592
www.lobsterpotrestaurant
.com

Maritana Grille
Don Ce Sar Beach Resort
3400 Gulf Blvd.
(727) 360-1882
www.doncesar.com

The Wine Cellar Restaurant & Fine Catering
17307 Gulf Blvd.
North Redington Beach
(727) 393-3491
www.thewinecellar.com

ST. PETERSBURG

Basta's
1625 4th St. South
(727) 894-7880
www.bastas.net

TAMPA

Columbia
800 2nd Ave. Northeast
(727) 822-8000
www.columbiarestaurant
.com

Donatello
232 N. Dale Mabry Hwy.
(813) 875-6660
www.donatellorestaurant
.com

Mise En Place
442 W. Kennedy Blvd., Ste. 110
(813) 254-5373
www.miseonline.com

Sidebern's
2208 W. Morrison Ave.
(813) 258-2233
www.sideberns.com

TARPON SPRINGS

Louis Pappas Market & Cafe (Greek/American)
731 Wesley Ave.
(727) 937-1770

WINTER HAVEN

Sundown Restaurant & Cocktails
1100 3rd St. Southwest
US 17 South at Avenue K
(863) 293-0069

SOUTHWEST FLORIDA

We will never forget canoeing on the Peace River—to step back in time 10,000 years or so—collecting fossilized shark teeth and pitching our tent on the riverbank. During another memorable canoe trip we watched in awe as a huge sun slipped silently into the sea. Good night, sun.

If you want to move around southwest Florida in a hurry, then I-75 is the way to go. A more pleasurable route for your wanderings is US 41, which tries to get as close to the Gulf as it can. It often succeeds, with glorious sunset-over-the-water views.

To access the tempting islands just offshore, you'll have to cross a bridge (often complete with toll) or arrange for boat transportation. Be patient with both options, and remember that getting off the beaten path has its own built-in rewards.

To reach the Peace River, head inland to Arcadia either by SR 70, SR 72, or US 17. The bonus for using SR 72 is that it takes you through the heart of verdant Myakka River State Park.

You'll find Corkscrew Swamp by heading east of Naples on CR 846. To explore Big Cypress Swamp, take either Alligator Alley (I-75) or Tamiami Trail (US 41), routes connected by

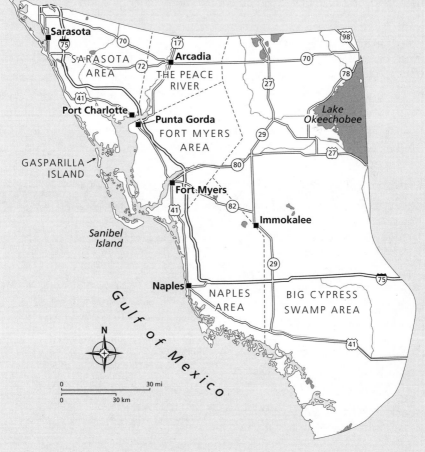

Sarasota

70

17

75

SARASOTA
AREA

72

Arcadia

70

98

78

27

THE PEACE
RIVER

41

Port Charlotte

Punta Gorda

FORT MYERS
AREA

Lake
Okeechobee

29

27

GASPARILLA
ISLAND

80

29

Fort Myers

82

Immokalee

41

Sanibel
Island

29

75

Naples

NAPLES
AREA

BIG CYPRESS
SWAMP AREA

Gulf of Mexico

41

N

0   30 mi

0   30 km

SR 29 that will eventually take you to Fort Lauderdale or Miami if you stay on them long enough.

Big Cypress Swamp is a vast wilderness area featuring a range of habitats including sandy islands of slash pine, wet and dry prairies, hardwood hammocks, and dense forests of cypress trees. You would do well to exercise caution when driving in this undeveloped area, especially on unpaved roads.

Thirty miles south of Naples are the Ten Thousand Islands, a maze of mangrove islands teeming with wildlife. Stick with conducted tours, or, at the very least, have a guide with you.

Everglades City is quite literally the jumping-off place. Access to the wilderness is strictly by water from here on in. Take mosquito repellent and a guide, then discover a haunting environment like none other on Earth.

Sarasota Area

Aficionados of the arts feel right at home in Sarasota, which offers the appealing combination of sandy beaches and sophistication. Settled in 1842, the city's attributes were not really appreciated until it was "discovered" by a Chicago socialite in 1910. Wealthy and influential Northerners followed, and in 1927

TOP EVENTS IN SOUTHWEST FLORIDA

Mullet Festival & Craft Fair, Goodland, January, (239) 394-3041

Southwest Florida Lee County Fair, North Fort Myers, February, (239) 543-8368

Swamp Cabbage Festival, LaBelle, February, (863) 675-2995, www.swampcabbagefestival.com

Annual Sanibel Shell Show, Sanibel Island, March, (941) 472-3151

Desoto County Fair, Arcadia, March, (863) 494-5678, www.desotocountyfair.org

Marco Spring Arts and Crafts Festival, Marco Island, March, (239) 394-4221

Sarasota Jazz Festival, Sarasota, April, (941) 366-1552, www.jazzclubsarasota.org

Suncoast Super Boat Grand Prix, Sarasota, June/July, (941) 371-8820, ext. 1800, www.suncoastoffshore.org

Fifth Avenue South Oktoberfest, Naples, October, (239) 262-6141, www.octoberfest-fifth-avenue-south.com

Sarasota Medieval Fair, Sarasota, November, (888) 303-3247, www.sarasotamedievalfair.com

John Ringling decided this would be the ideal winter quarters for his circus. John and Mable Ringling were instrumental in making Sarasota what it is today.

"The Greatest Show on Earth" made a fortune for Ringling, who knew just what he wanted to do with his money. He built his dream mansion, poured millions into his art collections, and invested heavily in civic improvements for Sarasota. The Ringling enthusiasm was contagious, and the city became known as a mecca for the arts.

Today's proliferating art galleries and theaters are direct descendants of the circus king's munificence. The *John and Mable Ringling Museum of Art* gives visitors a chance to see a cultural complex that puts Florida on the fine-arts map. Included are a museum of art with one of the most distinguished collections of baroque art in the hemisphere, the *Museum of the Circus,* and *John Ringling's Home.*

To call Ca'd'Zan (meaning House of John) simply Ringling's home doesn't quite do it justice. The thirty-two-room mansion on Sarasota Bay, patterned after the Doge's Palace on the Grand Canal in Venice, is one of America's great historic houses. Built in the 1920s at a cost of millions of dollars and since restored, this stately residence features a huge crystal chandelier from the lobby of New York's Waldorf Astoria Hotel and is elaborately furnished with art objects from around the world.

circusking's mansion

"Chandeliers with crystals the size of oranges hang in the galleries. Painted panels of Arcadia adorn one room. There are antique columns of every size and description, and gold galore—gold tables, gold Madonnas, gold reliquaries, enough to put King Tut to shame. John Ringling didn't think big; he thought tremendous."

—*Saturday Review* magazine

Although the home is officially known as the House of John, Mable Ringling had a lot to say about the design. She insisted on including the tower of the old Madison Square Garden (where the circus regularly appeared) in the plans. The architects had some problems with the tower in combination with the Venetian palace idea, but they gave in when Mable declared, "It is my house. I know what I want and that is that."

The Ringling Complex is open 10 a.m. to 5 p.m. daily except Thanksgiving, Christmas, and New Year's Day. A restaurant is located near the Museum of the Circus. The complex is located on US 41, 3 miles north of downtown Sarasota. The John and Mable Ringling Museum of Art, The State Art Museum of Florida, 5401 Bay Shore Rd., Sarasota; (941) 359-5700; recording of weekly events at (941) 351-1660; www.ringling.org.

Did you know that at least 27 species of sharks inhabit the Gulf of Mexico off Sarasota? Were you aware that more than 600 species of fish and even more invertebrates live in Sarasota's Gulf and bay waters? If you'd like to know more about these creatures of the deep, stop in at the **Mote Marine Science Center.** Guides will introduce you to the residents of 36 aquaria, including "Nibbles" the nurse shark and 2 West Indian manatees. The sea horses and sea turtles are especially popular, as is the extensive shell collection. The Research Exhibits provide the inside scoop on current scientific projects and explain how this research applies to our lives. Board the **Sarasota Bay Explorers** for an ecotour of Sarasota's waterways. A marine biologist on board will help you get firsthand experience with the fascinating creatures living in local grass flats. From downtown Sarasota, follow CR 780 to St. Armands Circle, continue to New Pass Bridge Area, and look for directional signs. Open 10 a.m. to 5 p.m. daily. Mote Marine Science Center, 1600 Ken Thompson Pkwy., Sarasota; (941) 388-4441 or (800) 691-MOTE (6683); www.mote.org.

Orchid lovers should spend some time browsing the extensive collection of tropical plants at the **Marie Selby Botanical Gardens.** This is the only public garden in the US focusing on epiphytes, which are plants that grow on other plants. The research done here is vitally important because the tropical forests and jungles of the world are fast disappearing, and with them are going many rare and beautiful plants.

Eight and a half bay-front acres on the slender peninsula between Sarasota Bay and Hudson Bayou contain more than 20,000 colorful plants, including more than 6,000 orchids. Besides being a magnificent floral display, Selby is an internationally recognized center for botanical research and plant identification.

Don't miss any of the 20 garden areas, especially the Tropical Display House, the Bamboo Pavilion, the Banyan Grove, the Cactus and Succulent Garden, the Shoreline Restoration Garden, the award-winning Hibiscus Garden, and the Palm Grove. Also, be sure to visit the former Christy Payne Mansion, a unique example of eclectic Southern colonial architecture, now serving as the gardens' Museum of Botany and the Arts, with its ever-changing exhibit of botanical art and photographs.

You'll enjoy strolling through the waterfront gardens and seeing the greenhouse abloom with elegant air plants. The plant store has tropical plants for sale and the gift/bookshop has books on everything you ever wanted to know about gardening, plus accessories. The gardens are located at US 41 and South Palm Avenue, 4.5 miles south of the Sarasota-Bradenton Airport. Open 10 a.m. to 5 p.m. every day of the year except Christmas. The Marie Selby Botanical Gardens, 811 S. Palm Ave., Sarasota. If you wish to have a guided tour, be sure to call ahead: (941) 366-5731; www.selby.org.

Spanish Point

Historic **Spanish Point** is one of those hidden gems you'll want to share with everyone, even those who aren't used to thinking beyond the beach. This sprawling 30-acre museum in Osprey, Florida, preserves and interprets no less than 5,000 years of history. And that's just the beginning. Whether you're interested in ancient history (3000 BC to AD 1000), in the pioneer life of early homesteaders (1867–1910), or just wish to stroll this peaceful peninsula overlooking Little Sarasota Bay, your time here will be richly rewarded.

Spanish Point is one of the largest intact prehistoric sites along Florida's west coast. It's the only place in the US where visitors can sit and contemplate the past surrounded on three sides by prehistoric shell middens, mounds of shells where Native Americans threw the remains of many a seafood feast.

If your idea of Florida is row upon row of high-rise condos, then you're in luck, because they seem to be everywhere. But if you'd like to stay in a bungalow on the beach, then you'll have to do a little investigating. ***Bungalow Beach Resort*** on Anna Maria Island, tucked neatly in among coconut palms and tropical blossoms, is our kind of place. This beautifully restored 1930s-style island resort is directly on the beach. Walk out the door and in half a dozen steps, you're admiring glistening white sand and the shimmering aqua waters of the Gulf of Mexico as far as the eye can see. Gaze at the water, read a book, walk the beach, and doze in the sun. Bungalow Beach Resort on Anna Maria Island, 2000 Gulf Dr. North, Bradenton Beach; (941) 778-3600 or (800) 779-3601; www.bungalowbeach.com.

A little chitchat with the friendly folks in the bungalow next door at the Bungalow Beach Resort resulted in a good suggestion for breakfast. Is ***Ginney's & Jane E's*** at the Old IGA an antiques shop, a bakery, a coffeehouse, a gourmet grocery, or an Internet cafe? Fortunately, it is all of those things, but lucky for us and our appetites, there were fresh-from-the-oven warm scones, a cup of coffee (daily grinds are posted on the blackboard), and a corner with a computer to check e-mail. Then we retreated back to our bungalow by the

greatestshow onearth

Born to a poor German immigrant family, John Ringling and his brothers toured the Midwest countryside as musicians. They billed their act as the "Ringling Brothers Moral, Elevating, Instructive & Fascinating Concert and Variety Performance." Over the years this eventually evolved into the "Greatest Show on Earth," and John became the vastly rich king of the circus.

Gulf and another soul-satisfying day in the Florida sunshine. Ginney's and Jane E's at the Old IGA is open daily in season from 8 a.m. to 5 p.m. and off-season from 8 a.m. to 3 p.m. Mon through Thurs and 8 a.m. to 5 p.m. Fri through Sun. 9807 Gulf Dr., Anna Maria; (941) 778-3170.

Take time to enjoy the luxuriant landscape from the jungle walk and aqueduct to the sunken garden, fern walk, and butterfly garden. Listed on the National Register of Historic Places, Historic Spanish Point is fully accredited by the American Association of Museums. Open Mon through Sat 9 a.m. to 5 p.m. and Sun noon to 5 p.m. Guided tours daily. Call for the schedule: (941) 966-5214; www.historicspanishpoint.org.

Myakka River State Park—28,000 acres of river, lakes, marsh, hammocks, and prairies—is one of the country's outstanding wildlife sanctuaries and breeding grounds. A 7-mile drive through this scenic park will acquaint you with the overall features of the area, but to really experience its incredible diversity, why not rent a bike or, better yet, a canoe? Camping opportunities range from rustic cabins to a backpack trail that leads to six primitive camping areas.

Birders will feel that their time on the lakeshore birdwalk and observation platform has been well spent when they catch sight of a majestic bald eagle, great blue heron, sandhill crane, egret, or ibis. Some 200 species of birds have been spotted in the park, and there are large rookeries. Board *Gator Gal,* the world's largest airboat, or the special *Safari Tram* (open December through June) for a scenic cruise. Both excursions are narrated by knowledgeable guides. Open 8 a.m. to sunset daily. The park is 14 miles east of Sarasota on SR

AUTHORS' FAVORITE ATTRACTIONS IN SOUTHWEST FLORIDA

Corkscrew Swamp Sanctuary, near Naples; http://corkscrew.audubon .org

J. N. "Ding" Darling National Wildlife Refuge, Sanibel Island; www.fws.gov/ dingdarling

Gasparilla Island

The John and Mable Ringling Museum of Art, Sarasota; www.ringling .org

John Ringling's Home, Sarasota

Peace River

Ten Thousand Islands, Everglades National Park; www.florida-everglades.com

Thomas Edison's winter residence, Fort Myers; www .edisonfordwinterestates.org

72; 13207 SR 72, Sarasota; (941) 361-6511; www.floridastateparks.org or www
.myakkariver.org.

Because they are near the longest sloping continental shelf in the world,
the beaches around Venice are a fertile fossil-hunting area, especially for shark
teeth. Some of the teeth being washed ashore belong to creatures that have
been extinct for millions of years. Put on your swimsuit and start scooping up
sand in the shallow water. Keep a sharp eye out: Some teeth are very tiny.
Access to these beaches is free.

Gasparilla Island

Pristine shell-strewn beaches, fragrant tropical flowers, and not a single traffic
light on the entire island. Year-round sunshine tempered by breezes from the
Gulf. Best tarpon fishing in the world. Streets that make a statement: Damn if
I know, damn if I care, and damn if I will. Welcome to Gasparilla Island or, as
it is better known (for its main community), *Boca Grande.*

Gasparilla, approximately an hour's drive south of Sarasota, is one of a
string of barrier islands scattered along southwest Florida's coast between
Tampa and Fort Myers. Bordered on the west by the Gulf of Mexico, on the
north by Little Gasparilla Pass, on the east by Charlotte Harbor, and on the
south by Boca Grande Pass, the island is accessible by toll bridge or boat.

Boca Grande (Spanish for "big mouth") Pass, one of Florida's deepest
natural inlets, accounts for its early history. Calusa Indians were drawn to its
rich fishing grounds. Railroads that once carried phosphate mined in central
Florida to the island's deep-water harbor later transported distinguished guests
for the winter season.

Today Boca Grande's population of nearly 800 more than triples during
winter and spring. Visitors come for their own reasons, which range from
exhilarating angling to somnolent afternoons under a palm tree.

No wonder Katharine Hepburn adored the ice cream in Boca Grande. At
one time a handwritten note of hers posted in the *Loose Caboose* (433 W.
4th St., Boca Grande) declared: "That ice cream is perfect. Wow!" Of course,
you might not see it amid the general accumulation of stuff—the fuzzy alligator wearing sunglasses, the antique vacuum cleaner on the wall, or the sign:
STOP—LOOK—LISTEN—PROCEED WHEN TRAIN IS COMING.

Not to worry. There hasn't been a train here in years. The preferred transportation is by bicycle, and the bike path extends the length of this lush, 7-mile
sliver of land. Lots of folks prefer parking their cars and relying solely on pedal
power. Better for the blood pressure. Come to think of it, the entire island of
Gasparilla is good for the blood pressure. Stash the alarm clock. You'll know

when the sun emerges and when it slips into the Gulf. If you must know how long it takes to reach tournament-size tarpon, the answer is "not long." Listen up: The major sounds on this tranquil island are gulls calling or maybe the soft whisper of a dolphin breathing.

The Boca Grande Chamber of Commerce consists of one person in the chamber of commerce office who'll give you a map and offer to "tell you anything you want to know." Where can you get the best breakfast in town? *Third Street Cafe* (310 E. Railroad Ave., Boca Grande; 941-964-0155; closed July 5 to October).

Apparently the folks staying in the grand old *Gasparilla Inn* are quite happy with their fare, or they wouldn't return with such astonishing regularity. In 1911, when the 20-room inn was newly opened and so empty it echoed, the first inquiry came from a socially prominent Bostonian. Before granting a reservation, the manager asked her to wire both a social and a bank reference. When the word got around that this hostelry catered to the "right" people, the right people appeared and stayed the season.

There are two seasons on the island: the social season from mid-October to July and the tarpon season from mid-April to July. The Gasparilla Inn, open from mid-December to June, has expanded to 139 rooms (with the addition of cottages) and boasts the only golf course (private) on the island. (877) 403-0599; www.gasparillainn.com.

What to do on Boca Grande? True beach lovers don't need anything more than dazzling white sand, a view of the distant horizon, and the gently lapping, Perrier-clear Gulf. Others enjoy shelling, birding, and all manner of water sports from fishing to sailboarding.

Grab your bike (rentals available) and wander the back roads. Island architecture, blessedly free of high-rises and time-shares, is an eclectic mix of Spanish-style stucco (note the community center and the Catholic church), elegant walled mansions of the rich and famous, and the more humble dwellings of fisherfolk.

Explore at your own pace. If you're looking for local color, *Whidden's Marina* offers a double dose. Stop in *Our Lady of Mercy Chapel* to see the 16th-century icon of Our Lady of Perpetual Help and other old-world treasures. Stroll down lanes canopied by banyans or hedged by scarlet hibiscus, and pause to admire a century-old gumbo-limbo tree. Breathe deeply of air perfumed by plumeria blossoms.

At day's end saunter down to Miller's Marina and watch the fishing boats unload their catch, or head for the restored 1890 lighthouse on the island's southern tip for a show that's always in season: a luminous bronze sun slipping into the Gulf of Mexico.

The Peace River

Shark teeth, some as large as your hand, can be found in the Peace River. In fact, a canoe trip down the pristine Peace can provide you with one of your very best off-the-beaten-track experiences in the entire state. Florida's most uninhabited waterway, which is too shallow for motorboats, winds its tranquil way from a source in central Florida's Green Swamp to the Gulf of Mexico. The Peace once marked the boundary between Indian territory to the east and white settlers' land to the west.

Every bend in the river is a movie set of palmettos, pine, cypress knees, and long strands of gray Spanish moss hanging from the gnarled limbs of live oaks. Wildflowers line the banks, and large waterbirds stand in the shallows. You may spot armadillos, alligators, and deer. You will surely see cows that belong to the cattle ranches you paddle past. The perfectly clear water makes fossil finding easy, and there are many lovely spots to camp along the riverbanks.

Tailor your trip length to your own whims. Half-day trips are fun, but to really get in tune with this beautiful river, plan to spend several days. Put your canoe in at the bridge in Fort Meade, Bowling Green, Wauchula, Zolfo Springs, Gardner, Brownsville, Arcadia, or Nocatee.

The friendly folks at *Canoe Outpost* will help select the right trip for you, answer all your questions, and provide whatever you need to be comfortable and safe. They can furnish transportation upstream, canoes, paddles, life jackets and cushions, all camping gear, coolers, and ice. Downstream enjoy picnicking or camping and hiking on the Outpost trails. The Canoe Outpost is located a mile northwest of Arcadia, at 2816 NW CR 661, Arcadia. Open 8 a.m. to 4:30 p.m. daily except Christmas Day. Call (863) 494-1215 or visit www.canoeout post.com.

Punta Gorda Area

At *Babcock Wilderness Adventures* you'll see wildlife—alligators, deer, wild turkey, an assortment of birds, even the highly endangered Florida panther (caged), and other native wildlife—on this swamp-buggy adventure through vast *Crescent B Ranch.* Your 90-minute nature tour explores a variety of habitats, including dense woods, freshwater marsh, open range, and a 10,000-acre cypress swamp. Horses and Cracker cows, descendants of early cattle, roam the ranch. Southwest Florida was once an open range that supported great herds of wild scrub cattle.

Cuban buyers would pay as much as $15 in gold doubloons per head. Hustling cow hunters soon became cattle barons. This changed when local ranchers began fencing their land in the early 1900s and cattle could no longer run free. Nature tours are available by reservation only 10 a.m. to 3 p.m. Nov through May and in the morning only June through Oct. For more information on the tours or the museum, seasonal restaurants, and the country store at the Crescent B Ranch, write Babcock Wilderness Adventures, 8000 SR 31, Punta Gorda 33982, or call (800) 500-5583. You can also visit their website at www .babcockwilderness.com.

crackercattle

What are Cracker cattle? This hardy breed, named after the sound created by the cracking whip of the cow hunters, was brought from Spain by Juan Ponce de León. When the Spanish attempts to establish a colony in the New World failed, the cattle ran wild. After a few hundred years surviving on their own, the feral cattle evolved into a smaller version of the Texas longhorn cattle with shorter horns. After 1850 this wild strain crossbred with European cattle to produce the Cracker cows visitors see today on Babcock Wilderness Adventures.

Take a leisurely scenic *King Fisher Fleet Harbor Cruise* of the pristine 270-square-mile Charlotte Harbor Aquatic Preserve, Florida's second-largest estuarine system. Watch for dolphins from the bow of a comfortable double-deck yacht. Choose from full-day sightseeing, half-day, out-island, ecotours, fishing trips, and sunset cruises. Contact King Fisher Cruise Lines Inc. at Fishermen's Village Marina, 1200 W. Retta Esplanade, Punta Gorda. They can also be reached by phone at (941) 639-0969 or found online at www .kingfisherfleet.com.

Fishermen's Village, built on the site of the old city docks, is a bustling harbor-front mall and marina with an attractive mix of boutiques, galleries, specialty shops, restaurants, and a small but inspiring military museum. There are vacation-rental villas on the mall's second floor, a marina with cruise boats, fishing boats, rental speed boats, Jet Skis, and bikes. The sunsets are fabulous. Fishermen's Village is located at 1200 W. Retta Esplanade, Punta Gorda. Open 10 a.m. to 8 p.m. Mon through Sat and noon to 6 p.m. Sun. Call (800) 639-0020 or visit www .fishville.com. Call the harbormaster at (941) 575-3000 for marina information.

Proud to be an American? You'll be even more proud after your visit to the tiny *Florida Military Heritage & Aviation Museum,* featuring an impressive display of military artifacts and memorabilia. Staffed by veterans, this nonprofit museum is dedicated to educating the public, especially children, about our country's rich military heritage. The museum is open 10 a.m. to 8 p.m. Mon through Sat and from noon to 6 p.m. Sun. Located in Fishermen's Village at 1200 W. Retta Esplanade, Ste. P 48, Punta Gorda; (941) 575-9002; www .freedomisntfree.org.

The *Peace River Wildlife Center,* in Ponce de Leon Park, rehabilitates injured or orphaned animals and birds, and, whenever possible, returns them to the wild. Severely injured wildlife are given a permanent home here. This small, well-kept facility is a fine place for a close-up look at American bald eagles, brown pelicans, great blue herons, great horned owls, red-tailed hawks, snowy egrets, and a host of other birds, not to mention a variety of animals. Take a guided tour (offered regularly throughout the day from 11 a.m. to 3 p.m.) or wander on your own. A volunteer will get you started and gladly answer questions. Be sure to check out the gift shop. The center and the gift shop are open year-round 8 a.m. to 5 p.m. except Christmas Day. The Peace River Wildlife Center is located at 3400 Ponce de Leon Pkwy., Punta Gorda; (941) 6373830.

Fort Myers Area

It's hard to resist such a huge collection of shells and coral. Pick out your own oyster (complete with pearl), examine rare shells from the seven seas, or select just the right piece of precious black coral. The *Shell Factory and Nature Park* has more than 70,000 square feet of temptations, which include a year-round Christmas shop, imported gifts, beachwear, and handmade moccasins. Quite a display! The Shell Factory is open daily 10 a.m. to 6 p.m., the Nature Park from 10 a.m. to 5 p.m. daily. Located on US 41 (N. Tamiami Trail) 4 miles north of Fort Myers at 2787 N. Tamiami Trail, North Fort Myers; (239) 995-2141 or (800) 282-5805; www.shellfactory.com.

The fortunate location of *Sanibel Island* enables it to snare some of the ocean's most beautiful treasures. This pretty island has a well-deserved reputation as one of the three best shelling beaches on Earth. (The others are in Africa and the southwest Pacific.) Beachcombers take their hobby very seriously, pacing the shoreline with bodies bent in a position known locally as the "Sanibel Stoop."

Nearly half of the land on Sanibel and the adjoining island of Captiva has been preserved in its natural state. The most frequented sanctuary is the *J. N. "Ding" Darling National Wildlife Refuge,* named for a Pulitzer Prize–winning political cartoonist. Darling was an ardent conservationist before anyone ever heard the word "ecology." This mangrove wilderness at the southern end of the Atlantic flyway is a way station for migrating birds, and it shelters more than 200 varieties, including the endangered wood stork. Viewing is best at sunrise or sunset. Visitors can drive, bike, or paddle winding canoe trails through the 6,000-acre refuge, which is laced with estuaries for fishing and trails for hiking. The visitor center is open 9 a.m. to 5 p.m. daily. The wildlife

Mammoth Pleasures of the Peace River

I looked downriver where my husband had been wading a few moments before. A few bubbles. Nothing more.

Alligators! My mind somersaulted. There are alligators in this river.

He had been walking in waist-deep water. I started wading toward him but the river slowed me. He surfaced, grabbed a breath, and submerged, obviously not in the clutches of a reptilian wrestler.

Still, the man does not usually go underwater without provocation. Just then he exploded from the water.

"They aren't tires," he shouted jubilantly between gasps. Sloshing toward me, he proclaimed, "They're teeth!" He held two large rocks out for us to see. "They looked like tires underwater. See the tread." It did indeed look like tread. "So I kicked one and almost broke my toe," he explained cheerfully.

Later, we verified his find with a museum expert. Sure enough, he was holding the molars of some prehistoric elephant that had tromped Florida's steaming jungles many thousands of years before. The "tread" turned out to be the grinding surface this huge vegetarian used to chew up his dinner. Each tooth weighed in at 14 pounds.

Bill had begun thinking in terms of teeth after we stopped in a tiny one-room museum near our canoe launch site at Zolfo Springs. There we'd seen a mammoth tooth still attached to the jaw and studied a series of photographs of a dig conducted by the Smithsonian Institution. A Boy Scout troop canoeing down the river had come upon a tusk sticking out of the bank. Some exploratory probing revealed the tusk was still very much attached to a complete mammoth skeleton that was later exhumed by geologists.

Central Florida's Peace River is a fertile bed for fossil collectors. Each of our kids came away with a pocketful of shark teeth, some as large as their palms. But Bill, with his two mammoth teeth, was the clear winner.

drive is open 7:30 a.m. to 7 p.m. Sat to Thurs. Closed Fri. For information, contact the US Fish and Wildlife Service, 1 Wildlife Dr., Sanibel; (239) 472-1100; www.dingdarling.org.

Useppa Island has a beach that looks like it was yanked from the South Pacific, as well as a swimming pool, tennis court, three-hole golf course, and deepwater marina. Best of all, it has a profusion of lush tropical vegetation—palms, royal poinciana, and massive banyans.

Useppa is considered the most beautiful island in the chain of islands in Pine Island Sound, but its air of serenity hides a tempestuous past. The Calusa Indians apparently found it appealing. Archaeologists claim this is the oldest continuously occupied landmass on the western Florida coast. (Native tribes started piling up oyster shell mounds in 3500 BC.)

For a while the notorious pirate Jose Gaspar held his favorite female captive here. (The run-of-the-mill ladies were kept in a group on the nearby island named for these unsavory goings on—Isla de las Captivas, now known as Captiva Island.) Joseffa was a headstrong 16-year-old who never did take to Gaspar. He found this so withering to his ego that he chopped off her head. As you can imagine, this place has its share of ghost stories. (Local dialect changed "Joseffa" to "Useppa.")

Streetcar tycoon John Roach bought Useppa in 1894, and publisher Barron Collier purchased it in 1912. Lots of rich and famous folks liked the combination of beauty and privacy that this tiny half-mile-long island afforded. Theodore Roosevelt, the Vanderbilts, the Rockefellers, Zane Grey, and Mae West stopped in from time to time, and the Izaak Walton Fishing Club was founded here. More recently Useppa served as the training ground for the Bay of Pigs invasion.

Neglect and deterioration threatened to scuttle the island's charm, but Gar Beckstead arrived just in time. In 1976 he purchased Useppa, moved his family there, and started the long process of restoration. In his mission to recapture the past, Gar uncovered one historic treasure after another, including a bathtub full of signed tarpon scales. To stroll the east ridge's pink pathway to the old *Collier Inn* is to return to the era of the 1920s. Architecture is strictly controlled; new cottages are all white frame with latticework and wide, screened porches to match their restored counterparts. No cars intrude on the quiet.

Today Useppa Island is run as a private club, but nonmembers are welcome to stay as long as a week on an "investigatory" visit. (Members arrive by boat or seaplane.) A wide range of rental accommodations are available; (239) 283-1061.

If you prefer a day trip, sign up to cruise on the **Lady Chadwick.** This 150-passenger, double-decked excursion boat takes passengers through scenic Pine Island Sound while the

captivenomore

With their beautiful beaches and delightful seaside setting, both Sanibel and Captiva seem ideal island havens for the peace-and-quiet crowd. In fact, it was from Captiva Island that Anne Morrow Lindbergh drew inspiration to write her best-selling book, *A Gift from the Sea.*

Actually, these serene islands have seen their share of violence. Seafaring Indians, rampaging pirates, saltwater floods, and hurricanes all have left their marks on these sandy isles. According to legend, pirates once imprisoned a band of women on Isla de las Captivas, which explains why it is now known as Captiva Island.

OTHER ATTRACTIONS WORTH SEEING IN SOUTHWEST FLORIDA

Bailey-Matthews Shell Museum, Sanibel Island, www.shellmuseum.org

Broadway Palm Dinner Theatre, Fort Myers, www.broadwaypalm.com

Naples CityDock, Naples, www .naplesgov.com

Naples Trolley Tours, Naples, www .naplestrolleytours.com

Naples Zoo at Caribbean Gardens, Naples, www.napleszoo.com

captain points out leaping dolphins and baby ospreys peering from nests on the channel markers. Choose from a variety of cruises; (239) 472-5300; www .captivacruises.com.

If your yacht is less than 100 feet, the marina can accommodate it. Useppa Island lies just 2 miles south of Boca Grande Pass at Marker 63 on the Intra-coastal Waterway, midway between Naples and Sarasota on the southwest coast of Florida. Useppa Island Club, PO Box 640, Useppa Island 33922; (239) 283-1061; www.useppa.com.

Cabbage Key was once home of playwright and mystery novelist Mary Roberts Reinhart. Her house, built in 1938 on the highest point of the island, has been converted into *Cabbage Key Inn and Restaurant.* One memorable feature of the inn is its "wallpaper" worth more than $22,000. Somewhere along the way, the guests started tacking one dollar bills to the walls, and signing them. Today these bills cover the ceilings, walls, and beams. Visitors get a kick out of locating "their" dollar when returning to Cabbage Key.

Cabbage Key is a popular watering hole with excellent docking facilities. You might want to explore the nature trails before dining on one of the out-door porches. Accessible only by boat or seaplane, Cabbage Key is 5 miles south of Charlotte Harbor on the Intracoastal Waterway at Channel Marker 60. Boats from three areas make the run to Cabbage Key. Breakfast is served 7:30 to 9 a.m. Mon through Sat and 7:30 to 10 a.m. Sun; lunch 11:15 a.m. to 3 p.m. Mon through Fri and 11:15 a.m. to 4 p.m. Sat and Sun; dinner 6 to 8:30 p.m. daily. Cabbage Key Inn and Restaurant, PO Box 200, Pineland 33945. Call for reservations 9:30 a.m. to 3:30 p.m. 7 days a week, (239) 283-2278; www.cabbage key.com.

Fort Myers got its start as a military post during the Seminole Indian wars. Abandoned after a brief occupation by federal troops during the Civil War, the fort became the center of a tiny village reached, in those days, by boat. Majestic palm-lined avenues and a profusion of exotic flowers and fruit trees contribute to Fort Myers's tropical good looks.

Thomas Edison, who made his winter home here, imported 200 royal palms from Cuba in 1900, starting Fort Myers on its way to being known as a "City of Palms." Edison was a great promoter of Fort Myers and wanted to bestow the fruits of his genius on the local citizenry. Soon after perfecting the electric lamp, he offered to provide the entire city with electric streetlights. The town voted against the proposal when many expressed fear that the lights would keep the cows from getting a good night's sleep.

Thomas Edison's winter residence is a must-see, especially if there are aspiring inventors in the family. Edison held 1,093 patents, and many of his inventions are on display in the adjoining museum. You cannot help being impressed and inspired by this inventor's philosophy and achievements. Unusual plants and trees from the far corners of the globe flourish on his 14-acre homesite on the Caloosahatchee River. The residence is open daily 9 a.m. to 5:30 p.m. Closed Thanksgiving and Christmas. Edison's home is located at 2350 McGregor Blvd., Fort Myers; (239) 334-7419.

The ***Calusa Nature Center and Planetarium*** lures visitors with more than 100 live animals native to Florida, a re-created Calusa Indian Village, and

Enlightenment

Since southwest Florida is blessed with a fine year-round climate, it makes sense that **Thomas Edison** came to Fort Myers on his doctor's orders. At 38 he was seriously ill, his health suffering from years of overwork. If he wanted to live, his doctor warned him, he would have to escape the brutal northern winters.

Edison investigated Fort Myers, liked its warm tropical climate and Gulf breezes, and proceeded to lead an enormously productive life to the age of 84. The annual trip was not an easy matter in those days. It involved, among other things, a 10-hour sail from Punta Gorda 52 miles to the north. The prescient inventor, who obviously believed the area's attributes far outweighed these inconveniences, declared, "There is only one Fort Myers and ninety million people are going to find it out."

Edison, who spent nearly 50 winters in Fort Myers, is considered the most inventive man who ever lived, but he was also an accomplished horticulturist. His riverfront garden contains more than 1,000 varieties of plants imported from all over the world.

Edison's genius is evident throughout his 14-acre Caloosahatchee River estate. Here the visitor will find Florida's first modern swimming pool, the couch where Edison took his famous catnaps, the inventor's unique Model-T Ford, and Florida's largest banyan tree.

daily snake and alligator demonstrations. Stroll 3 miles of trails and boardwalk through a cypress and pine swamp, or join a tour guided by an expert on the natural history of southwest Florida. Be sure to visit the hawks, eagles, and owls at the Audubon Aviary, and let the fluttery residents of the Butterfly Aviary rest on your shoulder. Enjoy a laser light show at the planetarium, or just sit back and admire the heavens. The gift shop is excellent. The Nature Center and Planetarium (open 9 a.m. to 5 p.m. Mon to Sat and 11 a.m. to 5 p.m. Sun) is located just north of Colonial Boulevard, west off I-75, exit 22 (the entrance is on the west side of Ortiz Avenue). Call (239) 275-3435 for schedule and show information or write to Calusa Nature Center and Planetarium, 3450 Ortiz Ave., Fort Myers 33906. You can also visit their website at www.calusanature.com.

If you want to be a short drive from the beach, need a pet-friendly place to stay, and you're on a budget, consider *Rock Lake Resort.* Just half a mile from downtown Fort Myers, these cottages, complete with kitchenettes, encircle a small, private lake. You can canoe, swim in the pool, and play tennis on the lighted court. Wheelchair-accessible and rooms for the hearing-impaired are available. Rock Lake Resort is at 2930 Palm Beach Blvd., Fort Myers. Call (239) 332-4080 for more information or visit www.bestlodgingswflorida.com.

The world is not flat, but round. Columbus proved it, and you're sure, right? But can you really be sure that the earth isn't hollow, that life doesn't cover its inner walls, and that the sun isn't actually in the center of this round sphere? If you find these thoughts intriguing, you should stop in at the *Koreshan State Historic Site.*

Dr. Teed, a physician from Chicago, founded a *utopian commune,* which he called Koreshan Unity, here in the later 1800s. The doctor brought a group with him from Chicago, but the movement never caught on, though some of

Swamp Buggy Races

Hunters originally designed swamp buggies to provide access to the boggy Everglades. In fact, these races were first run in 1949 to signal the opening of the Everglades hunting season. Racing these souped-up buggies is the local version of a tractor pull but, they claim, a lot more fun. The racecourse is flooded with water for two weeks before the race to ensure it is in the worst possible condition. If you want to see these hardy vehicles tackle the celebrated "Mile o' Mud" and the perilous "Sippy Hole," don't miss the Swamp Buggy Races each March, May, and October. Contestants compete in various classes, and at the end of the races, the Swamp Buggy Queen is taken for a victory ride around the track and given a royal dunking. The races are held at the Florida Sports Park off SR 951 near Rattlesnake Hammock Road in Golden Gate, Naples; (941) 774-2701; www.swampbuggy.com.

his followers still publish a newspaper and magazine. For one thing, there were no children to carry the banner for Dr. Teed because he insisted everyone practice celibacy. You may visit the tropical garden and restored village of this pioneer settlement and learn how Dr. Teed went about proving his theories in the museum. This is also a good place to camp and canoe. Open 8 a.m. to sunset daily. Guided tours are given according to seasonal demand. Take I-75, exit 19. Go 2 miles on Corkscrew Road to Junction 41 in Estero. Call (239) 992-0311 or visit the website at www.floridastateparks.org for more information. Camping reservations can be made online at www.reserveamerica.com or by calling (800) 326-3521.

Naples Area

The city of Naples caters to the upper crust with all the amenities money can buy, but it has not forgotten the less well-heeled folk who have the run of its splendid 7-mile public beach and *1,000-foot fishing pier.* Shoppers will look a long time before finding such a marvelous assortment of shops. If your credit cards are suffering from lack of use, don't worry. Shopping in Naples is guaranteed to get them back in the swing of things.

Browsers are more than welcome at the **Old Marine Market Place,** better known as Tin City. A carefully preserved part of Naples's past, now restored, awaits you on Naples Bay at 1200 5th Ave. South. This old-fashioned shopping bazaar was created from historic boat buildings connected by cobbled and planked river walks and comes complete with waterfront dining and open-air markets. Don't miss the chic stores on 3rd Street and those marvelously posh emporiums on 5th Avenue.

Longtime Naples resident Michael Watkins, general manager of the landmark **Naples Beach Hotel and Golf Club,** contends that the best way to see this attractive area is by bike. His suggested route includes stops at Lowdermilk Park, the Conservancy Nature Center, Tin City, the restored historic Naples Depot, Cambier Park, Naples Fishing Pier, and the shops on 5th Avenue and 3rd Street. In the process you'll pass through some gorgeous residential real estate. Bikes are available for rent at the hotel's front desk, along with complimentary bicycle maps. For information or reservations, contact the Naples Beach Hotel and Golf Club, 851 Gulf Shore Blvd. North, Naples; (239) 261-2222 or (800) 455-1546; www.naplesbeachhotel.com.

The **Conservancy of Southwest Florida's Naples Nature Center** is, surprisingly, on a wooded 21-acre site right in the middle of Naples. The Conservancy Museum of Natural History contains natural history, animal and marine displays, and interactive exhibits. Visitors can touch a snake, count an

Done in by Donna

First inhabited 1,000 years ago by Calusa Indians, Everglades City became a hideout for outlaws, gun and rum runners, and those seeking a simpler life. Unlivable conditions, hordes of mosquitoes, and the threat of attacks from Seminole and Miccosukee Indians thwarted the pioneering spirit of the first American settlers. However, Everglades City experienced economic rebirth when the city was named Collier County seat in 1923. Seen as a center of commerce and possible rival to Miami, Everglades City dominated the financial life of lower southwest Florida. That hopeful period came to an end in 1960 when Hurricane Donna swept away the community's chances for a golden future, and the government seat was moved to higher ground.

alligator's teeth, and explore southwest Florida's underwater world through different marine aquariums. Be sure to stroll the two nature trails and visit the recuperating animals and birds (mostly eagles, hawks, and owls) in the *Wildlife Rehabilitation Center.* Most are successfully released back into the wild. Naturalist-guided trail walks are offered daily. Guided electric boat trips run from November through March.

This private, nonprofit organization is dedicated to environmental protection, conservation, wildlife rehabilitation, nature education, and ecological research. Open 8:30 a.m. to 5 p.m. Mon through Fri. The Conservancy of Southwest Florida's Naples Nature Center is located at 1450 Merrihue Dr. (1 block east of Goodlette Road), Naples; (239) 262-0304; www.conservancy.org.

For casual waterfront dining (on outdoor picnic tables, if you wish), you should seek out *Buzz's Lighthouse Restaurant.* While peeling your shrimp and sipping a cold beer, you can watch the dolphins leap and the seagulls hover. (Please, heed the sign that asks you not to feed the birds. There's a very good reason for it.) The atmosphere is relaxed, the service friendly, and the jumbo sandwiches excellent. The prices are inexpensive to moderate. The restaurant is open 11:30 a.m. to 9 p.m. Tues through Sun; closed Mon. Lighthouse Restaurant, 9180 Gulf Shore Dr., Naples; (239) 597-2551.

Thirty miles to the south of Naples are the *Ten Thousand Islands.* This maze of mangrove islands teeming with fish and bird life is best approached with a guide. Guided tours leave from the ranger station at the entrance to the western portion of Everglades National Park. This is literally the jumping-off place because the only access to the wilderness is by water.

One of the most satisfying ways to explore these islands, if you have insect repellent on hand, is by canoe. To glide quietly by an egret rookery, to listen to the beat of many wings as flocks pass overhead, and to watch the evening sun beam a path of orange across a silent sea is to know Florida at its very best.

Sightseeing tours into the Ten Thousand Islands region and the mangrove swamps of the northwestern Everglades leave from the Gulf Coast Ranger Station every 30 minutes. For information about boat tours (available year-round) and boat rentals at the Gulf Coast Ranger Station, write the concessionaire at Everglades National Park Boat Tours, PO Box 119, Everglades City 34139, or call Everglades National Park at (305) 242-7700. Open 8:30 a.m. to 5 p.m. daily.

Big Cypress Swamp Area

Corkscrew Swamp Sanctuary, maintained by the National Audubon Society, is an 11,000-acre preserve with a dwindling population of wood storks. These rare large birds, dangerously close to extinction, are definitely worth the trip. The most interesting time to visit is from December through March, when the storks nest and breed. Their breeding is timed so that young storks are raised when food is plentiful (which depends entirely on receding water levels to concentrate the fish). An unexpected rainstorm at the wrong time of year can mess up the whole process. (A single family of wood storks requires 440 pounds of food per breeding season!) The frantic activity of the nesting season is something to see. The male gathers the sticks for the nest, the female arranges them, and young storks kick up quite a racket.

The sanctuary also protects the largest stand of virgin bald cypress trees in the country. A boardwalk trail (2.25 miles long) winds through this primeval forest of huge trees, some more than 700 years old! An illustrated self-guiding tour booklet describes plants and animals, and there are members of the staff along the way to answer questions. You'll see lots of birds, turtles, and alligators along with a variety of lush plant life.

Visit Corkscrew's Blair Audubon Center and Swamp Theatre, a multimedia exhibit depicting daily and seasonal changes in the swamp. Shop in the nature store or have a snack in the tearoom. No pets are admitted, and overnight camping is not permitted within sanctuary boundaries or in the parking area. The swamp is open 7 a.m. to 7:30 p.m. daily, April 11 through September 30, and 7 a.m. to 5:30 p.m. October 1 through April 10. The Corkscrew Swamp Sanctuary and Blair Audubon Center are located at 375 Sanctuary Rd., Naples. Call (239) 348-9151 or visit www.corkscrew.audubon.org for more information.

Corkscrew Swamp Sanctuary is at the northern end of *Big Cypress Swamp,* a vast wilderness area administered by the National Park Service. You may explore this swamp by car on Alligator Alley (I-75) and Tamiami Trail (US 41), which are connected by SR 29. The fascinating Loop Road (CR

94) from 40-Mile Bend to Monroe Station is only paved for 8 miles. Be careful on unpaved roads, as they can be dusty and rough or, worse, muddy—as in stuck-in-the-mud.

Approximately one-third of Big Cypress is covered by cypress and the rest is given over to prairies of saw grass, mixed hardwood hammocks, marshes, and estuarine mangrove forests. You may also see alligators, wild turkeys, deer, minks, bald eagles, ibises, herons, egrets, and wood storks. The Big Cypress Visitor Center is 55 miles east of Naples on US 41 in the sanctuary. Open 9 a.m. to 4:30 p.m. daily except Christmas. For information, contact the Park Superintendent, Big Cypress National Preserve, 33100 Tamiami Trail East, Ochopee; (239) 695-2000; (239) 695-1201 for visitor information; www.nps.gov/bicy.

State Parks in Southwest Florida

State parks information: (850) 245-2157 or www.floridastateparks.org. For camping reservations in any state park, call (800) 326-3521.

Alafia River State Park, (813) 672-5320

Cayo Costa State Park, (941) 964-0375

Charlotte Harbor State Park, (941) 575-5861

Collier-Seminole State Park, (239) 394-3397

Delnor–Wiggins Pass State Park, (239) 597-6196

Don Pedro Island State Park, (941) 964-0375

Egmont Key, (727) 893-2627 Central or southwest

Estero Bay Preserve, (239) 992-0311

Fakahatchee Strand Preserve State Park, (239) 695-4593

Fort Cooper State Park, (352) 726-0315

Gasparilla Island State Park, (941) 964-0375

Highlands Hammock State Park, (863) 386-6094

Hillsborough River State Park, (813) 987-6771

Judah P. Benjamin Confederate Memorial at Gamble Plantation State Historic Site, (941) 723-4536

Koreshan State Historic Site, (239) 992-0311

Lake June-in-Winter Scrub State Park, (863) 386-6099

Lovers Key State Park, (239) 463-4588

Myakka River State Park, (941) 361-6511

Oscar Scherer State Park, (941) 483-5956

Skyway Fishing Pier State Park, (727) 865-0668

Stump Pass Beach State Park, (941) 964-0375

Werner-Boyce Salt Springs State Park, (727) 816-1890

Ybor City Museum State Park, (813) 247-6323

Places to Stay in Southwest Florida

EVERGLADES CITY

Everglades Spa-fari and Lodge
201 W. Broadway
(239) 695-3151 or
(239) 695-1006
www.evergladesspa.com

FORT MYERS

Howard Johnson Inn
4811 Cleveland Ave.
(239) 936-3229
www.hojo.com

Sanibel Harbor
17260 Harbour Pointe Dr.
(866) 283-3273
www.sanibel-resort.com

FORT MYERS BEACH

Pink Shell Beach Resort & Spa
275 Estero Blvd.
(239) 463-6181 or
(888) 222-7465
www.pinkshell.com

Sandpiper Gulf Resort
5550 Estero Blvd.
(239) 463-5721 or
(800) 584-1449
www.sandpipergulfresort.com

MARCO ISLAND

The Boathouse Motel
1180 Edington Place
(239) 642-2400
www.theboathousemotel.com

Eagle's Nest Resort
410 S. Collier Blvd.
(239) 394-5167
www.eaglesnestmarco.com

Hilton Marco Island Beach Resort
560 S. Collier Blvd.
(239) 394-5000
www.marcoisland.hilton.com

NAPLES

La Playa Beach Resort
9891 Gulf Shore Dr.
(239) 597-3123
www.laplayaresort.com

Naples Grande Resort and Club
475 Seagate Dr.
(239) 597-3232
www.naplesgranderesort.com

Red Roof
1925 Davis Blvd.
(239) 774-3117
www.redroof.com

The Ritz-Carlton, Naples
280 Vanderbilt Beach Rd.
(239) 598-3300
www.ritzcarlton.com

SANIBEL & CAPTIVA ISLANDS

South Seas Island Resort
5400 Plantation Rd.
Captiva Island
(239) 472-5111
www.southseas.com

Sundial Beach & Golf Resort
1451 Middle Gulf Dr.
Sanibel Island
(239) 472-4151 or
(866) 565-5093
www.sundialresort.com

'Tween Waters Inn
15951 Captiva Dr.
Captiva Island
(239) 472-5161 or
(800) 223-5865
www.tween-waters.com

West Wind Inn
3345 W. Gulf Dr.
Sanibel Island
(239) 472-1541
www.westwindinn.com

SARASOTA

Best Western Midtown
1425 S. Tamiami Trail
(941) 955-9841
www.bwmidtown.com

The Cypress B&B
621 Gulfstream Ave. South
(941) 955-4683
www.cypressbb.com

Holiday Inn Express
6600 S. Tamiami Trail
(941) 924-4900 or
(800) 449-1460
www.hiexpress.com

Hyatt Regency Sarasota
1000 Boulevard of the Arts
(941) 953-1234
www.sarasota.hyatt.com

Timberwoods Vacation Villas
8378 S. Tamiami Trail
(941) 312-5934
www.timberwoods.com

La Quinta Inn & Suites
1803 N. Tamiami Trail
(941) 366-5128

VENICE

Holiday Inn
380 Commercial Ct.
(941) 584-6800
www.holidayinn.com

Inn at the Beach Resort
725 W. Venice Ave.
(941) 484-8471
www.innatthebeach.com

Places to Eat in Southwest Florida

FORT MYERS

The Veranda
2122 2nd Street and Broadway
(239) 334-8634
www.verandarestaurant.com

VISITOR INFORMATION FOR SOUTHWEST FLORIDA

Best of Naples, 4044 W. Lake Mary Blvd., #104–275, Lake Mary; (407) 688-7998; www.bestof.net/naples

Boca Grande Chamber of Commerce, 480 E. Railroad Ave., Boca Grande; (941) 964-0568; www.bocagrandechamber.com

Charlotte Harbor & Gulf Islands Visitors Bureau, 18501 Murdock Circle, Ste. 502, Port Charlotte; (941) 743-1900 or (800) 652-6090; www.charlotteharbortravel.com

Lee County Visitor and Convention Bureau, 12800 University Dr., Ste. 550, Fort Myers; (800) 237-6444 or (239) 338-3500; www.fortmyers-sanibel.com

Marco Island Area Chamber of Commerce, 1102 N. Collier Blvd., Marco Island; (239) 394-7549 or (800) 788-6272; www.marcoislandchamber.org

The Greater Naples Area Chamber of Commerce, 900 5th Ave. South, Naples; (239) 262-6141; www.napleschamber.org

Sanibel and Captiva Islands Chamber of Commerce, 1159 Causeway Rd., Sanibel 33957; (239) 472-1080; www.sanibel-captiva.org

Sarasota Convention & Visitors Bureau, 701 N. Tamiami Trail, Sarasota; (941) 957-1877 or (800) 800-3906; www.sarasotafl.org

FORT MYERS BEACH

Anthony's on the Gulf
3040 Estero Blvd.
(239) 463-6139
www.fortmeyersbeach
restaurants.com

NAPLES

The Chardonnay
2331 9th St. North
(239) 261-3111
www.chardonnaynaples
.com

SANIBEL & CAPTIVA ISLANDS

The Bubble Room
15001 Captiva Dr.
Captiva Island
(239) 472-5558
www.bubbleroomrestaurant
.com

South Seas Island Resort
5400 Plantation Rd.
(239) 472-7696 or
(866) 565-5089
www.southseas.com

SARASOTA

Michael's on East
1212 East Ave. South
(941) 955-1945
www.michaelsoneast.com

VENICE

Sharky's on the Pier
1600 Harbor Dr.
(941) 488-1456
www.sharkysonthepier.com

SOUTHEAST FLORIDA

Think of Florida and your mind is likely to wander to Miami Beach, with its sandy beaches, Latin music and warm winter weather. Those who crave off the beaten path adventures will eventually discover another kind of Florida—the Florida Everglades. The amazing thing is that these two completely different faces of Florida are in such close proximity. Miami, with its gleaming towers, stands in stark contrast to the beautiful wild birds of the glades, with their colorful plumage. The question is how to best reach these unique destinations and make best use of your time there.

It's not easy to get off the beaten path in southeast Florida, but here and there you can do it by seeking out SR A1A (the closest road to the ocean) rather than I-95, the Florida Turnpike, or, heaven forbid, US 1. Try to avoid traveling on major roads in this congested area during rush hours (7:30 to 9:30 a.m. and 4:30 to 7 p.m. weekdays). SR A1A will present wonderful seascapes from time to time and is less crowded than US 1. You would be wise to avoid US 1 entirely, as it is neither swift nor scenic—merely frustrating.

To reach the Everglades and its grand expanse of saw grass, either US 41, better known locally as Tamiami Trail (for

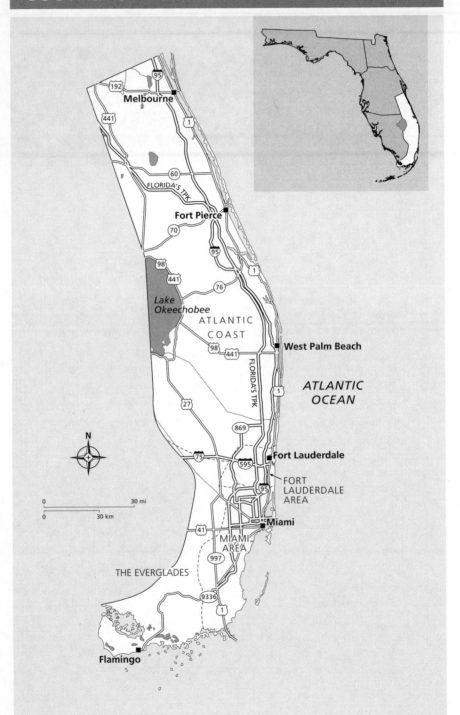

northern access via Shark Valley), or SR 9336 (the road to Flamingo in the south) will take you into the wilderness. Vast prairies of sedge are punctuated by hammocks, stands of pine and palmetto, and freshwater sloughs. *Note:* If you continue on Tamiami Trail, you'll end up in Tampa. The name is a combination of Tampa and Miami, a historic route completed in 1928 that opened the Everglades to travelers.

Atlantic Coast

Sebastian Inlet State Park is now an ocean playground, but you would have a hard time telling that to the survivors of the fleet of ships that went down here in 1715. Spanish galleons, loaded with gold and silver, were pummeled by a terrible storm before they sank to the bottom of the sea. At the *McLarty Treasure Museum,* you'll see artifacts of the Ais Indians, as well as exhibits and dioramas on the Spanish treasure. The salvage efforts, both historic and recent, are a story in themselves.

Located in Sebastian Inlet on SR A1A about midway between Melbourne and Vero Beach, the area offers outstanding fishing, camping, and hiking. The time to comb the beach for ancient pieces of eight is right after a storm. You'll need a lot of luck, but it's not impossible. Sebastian Inlet State Park is located at 9700 S. SR A1A, Melbourne Beach. Call (321) 984-4852 or visit the website at www.floridastateparks.org. For camping reservations, call Reserve America at (800) 326-3521 or visit www.reserveamerica.com. The museum is open 10 a.m. to 4 p.m. daily year-round.

The *Gilbert's Bar House of Refuge* (1876) is the last of 10 lifesaving stations built by the US Treasury Department in 1876 along the east coast of Florida. Listed on the National Register of Historic Places, the house is furnished with antiques from the 1890s. The site was one of the first living-history museums in south Florida. From Stuart, take E. Ocean Boulevard and turn right at the first stop light on Hutchinson Island. Follow the road through the Indian River Plantation, Marriott Resort, 1.3 miles to the entrance. Open 10 a.m. to 4 p.m. Mon through Sat and 1 to 4 p.m. Sun. The house is located at 301 SE MacArthur, Stuart. Call (772) 225-1875 for more information.

If you'd like to view water traffic negotiating the 14-foot St. Lucie Locks, drive 8 miles southwest of Stuart on SR 76 for a look.

Bass fishermen should head for *Lake Okeechobee,* about 40 miles inland, which is the second-largest lake wholly within the US. It might encourage you to know that more than 3.5 million pounds of fish (including both sport and commercial catches) are caught here every year. Take your pick of fishing camps—they are all over the place.

TOP EVENTS IN SOUTHEAST FLORIDA

Art Deco Weekend Festival, Miami Beach, January, (305) 672-2014, www .mdpl.org

Carnaval Miami and Calle Ocho, Miami, February/March, (305) 644-8888, www.carnavalmiami.com

Sunfest, West Palm Beach, April/May, (561) 659-5980, www.sunfest.com

Coconut Grove Goombay Festival, Miami, June, (305) 448-9501, www .goombayfestivalcoconutgrove.com

Bon Festival, Delray Beach, August, (561) 495-0233

Orange Bowl Parade, Miami, December, (305) 341-4777, www .orangebowl.org

Been frog gigging lately? Fox hunting? Bass fishing? How about joining a swamp buggy tour?

The Old South awaits. Maybe you've been up to your neck in frogs before and feel it's time to get back to the time-honored ways of the Old South. *Seminole Inn* (also known as Seminole Country Inn) is the answer. Smack-dab in the heart of cattle-and-citrus country, this mission revival–style historic hotel is 30 miles northwest of West Palm Beach in Indiantown. The owners of the inn maintain a herd of Florida cattle, descended from those imported by the Spanish in the 15th century, and they arrange outings to their farm, High Horse Ranch. They serve tempting dishes featuring their home-grown vegetables in their restaurant. Fried green tomatoes are a local favorite. Built in the 1920s by S. Davies Warfield, president of the Seaboard Air Line Railroad, the Seminole Inn is a charming alternative to the usual back-to-basics hunting lodge. Warfield's niece, Wallis Warfield Simpson, who would become the Duchess of Windsor a decade later, attended the inn's grand opening. With high cypress ceilings, pine floors, solid brass wall fixtures, and winding staircases, the inn is quite elegant enough for the best of the frog giggers. In 2006 Seminole Inn was added to the National Register of Historic Places. P.S.: There's a rocking chair on the porch for you. Seminole Inn, 5885 SW Warfield Blvd., Indiantown; (772) 597-3777; www .seminoleinn.com.

Back on the coast, *Blowing Rock Preserve* on Jupiter Island is worth a 10-minute walk through a pine forest. When a stiff wind is coming out of the northeast, the surf surges through holes in the rocks to create spectacular geysers.

It's only 85 feet high, but in Florida they call it a mountain even if it is only an overgrown sand dune. Add a 25-foot observation tower to Hobe Mountain in *Jonathan Dickinson State Park,* and you have a good view of the ocean and surrounding woodlands. The park was named for a Quaker who was shipwrecked nearby in 1696, discovered by Indians, and survived all sorts of traumas before getting his wife and baby safely home to Philadelphia. His journal provides valuable insight into early Florida.

An exciting way to see the park is a trip down the Loxahatchee River to Trapper Nelson's camp. The Loxahatchee is the only National Wild and Scenic River in the state of Florida, and you really ought to experience it. Take the 44-passenger pontoon boat, **Loxahatchee Queen** (772-546-2771; www .floridaparktours.com), or rent a canoe and paddle past the alligators and bald eagles to Trapper Nelson's. The boat ride takes almost 2 hours; if you paddle yourself, count on 3 hours. Alas, the legendary Trapper Nelson is no longer with us, but a ranger will fill you in on some of his eccentricities.

A wide range of activities includes fishing (both saltwater and freshwater), boating, camping, and bicycling. The park, on US 1 just 6 miles north of Jupiter, is open 8 a.m. to sunset daily year-round, but call if you're interested in the boat trip, because it does not go every day. Contact Jonathan Dickinson State Park, 16450 SE Federal Hwy., Hobe Sound; (772) 546-2771; www.floridastate parks.org. For camping reservations, call (800) 326-3521.

In Jupiter the 105-foot redbrick *Jupiter Lighthouse* is one of the oldest (1860) lighthouses on the Atlantic coast. Still functioning, it is operated by the Coast Guard as a navigational aid. The lighthouse, beside Jupiter Inlet, provides a fine view of the Gulf Stream. Open 10 a.m. to 5 p.m. Tues through Sun. Jupiter Lighthouse is at 500 Captain Armour Way; (561) 747-8380; www .jupiterlighthouse.org.

AUTHORS' FAVORITE ATTRACTIONS IN SOUTHEAST FLORIDA

Biscayne National Park, Homestead; www.nps.gov/bisc

Everglades National Park, near Homestead; www.nps.gov/ever

Flagler Museum, Palm Beach; www .flaglermuseum.us

Miami Beach Historic Architectural District, Miami Beach

Morikami Museum and Japanese Gardens, Delray Beach; www.morikami .org

Shark Valley, Everglades National Park; www.sharkvalleytramtours.com

Vizcaya Museum and Gardens, Miami; www.vizcayamuseum.org

The Palm Beach area was developing slowly until Henry Flagler pushed his famous railroad south. With the railroad's arrival in 1894 and the grand hotels that Flagler built, Palm Beach quickly established and still holds a reputation as an enclave for the ultra-wealthy. When Flagler planned his own Palm Beach home, he chose the architectural firm that had built the New York Public Library and the US Senate Office Building. Described in the press as "more wonderful than any palace in Europe" and costing $5 million to build and furnish in 1901, Whitehall is a showcase that has been marvelously refurbished as the *Flagler Museum.* The multimillionaire's private railroad car is on display, as are treasures collected from all over the world. The mansion provides a glimpse into the era before income taxes and sets a new standard for the term "opulent." Open 10 a.m. to 5 p.m. Tues through Sat and noon to 5 p.m. Sun, the museum is on Whitehall Way, off Coconut Row, in Palm Beach. The Flagler Museum, 1 Whitehall Way, Palm Beach; (561) 655-2833; www.flagler.org.

The *Norton Museum of Art* has a reputation as one of the foremost museums in the US. The museum features a world-renowned permanent collection of European, American, Chinese, and contemporary art, with works by Monet, Picasso, Gauguin, Stuart Davis, and Georgia O'Keeffe, as well as an ever-changing schedule of special traveling exhibitions. Enjoy lunch in the cafe and shop in the museum store. Open 10 a.m. to 5 p.m. Tues, Wed, Fri, and Sat; 10 a.m. to 9 p.m. Thurs; and 11 a.m. to 5 p.m. Sun. Closed Mon. The museum is at 1451 S. Olive Ave., West Palm Beach; (561) 832-5196; www.norton.org.

You may never have heard of George Morikami, but you will be impressed with his life story and the *Morikami Museum and Japanese Gardens.* This humble pineapple farmer lived in a modest trailer and never stopped working his fields even though he amassed considerable wealth. The museum depicts a unique chapter in Florida's history. Enter the "Yamato-kan," and remove your shoes (paper slippers provided) before stepping into tatami-matted rooms celebrating both traditional and modern Japanese life. The Morikami is the only museum in the US dedicated exclusively to the living culture of Japan. Here you'll browse photographs of George Morikami and his 20th-century Japanese farming community. The museum grounds include a 200-acre park with an authentic teahouse, extensive Japanese gardens, scenic vistas, tropical bonsai, and a koi pond. Nature trails and picnic areas are available in the outlying park grounds. Visit the museum store and enjoy an Asian repast at the Cornell Cafe. Schedule your visit to coincide with seasonal festivals: Oshogatsu (Jan), Hatsume (Feb), Children's Day (Apr), and Obon (Aug). The museum is open 10 a.m. to 5 p.m. Tues through Sun. Contact the Morikami Museum and Japanese Gardens at 4000 Morikami Park Rd., Delray Beach; (561) 495-0233; www .morikami.org.

Did architect Addison Mizner ever leave his mark on Boca Raton! In 1918 the 45-year-old, suffering from heart and lung ailments, came to Florida to die. As restless as he was eccentric, he became bored with dying and began designing homes for the super-rich. He parlayed his profits into a fortune by wheeling and dealing in real estate and then tackled his real ambition: building a dream city.

He designed **The Cloister** to be a hotel worthy of being the centerpiece for this splendid project and held a grand opening in February 1926. At the time it was the most expensive hundred-room hotel ever built. The style of architecture has been summed up as "Bastard-Spanish-Moorish-Romanesque-Gothic-Renaissance-Bull-Market-Damn-the-Expense." But Florida went quickly from boom to bust, and the hotel closed after a single season. Mizner's extravagant vision fizzled, but his pink wedding-cake hotel was destined to play many roles over the years, including one as a World War II barracks.

bocaratonhotel

Construction crews working on the Boca Raton Hotel were appalled at architect Addison Mizner's instant-aging techniques. He stomped on beautiful wood floors in hobnailed boots and broke new tiles, then cemented them back together. Frank Lloyd Wright once remarked that many architects had imagination but only Mizner had the courage to let it out of the cage.

Today the **Boca Raton Resort and Club,** its original splendor intact, thrives in its reincarnation as a premier resort. The hotel is on Camino Real between US 1 and SR A1A and is on the Intracoastal Waterway across from its seaside extension, the Boca Beach Club. Boca Raton Resort and Club, 501 E. Camino Real, Boca Raton; (561) 447-3000 or (888) 543-1277; www.bocaresort.com.

Care to eat where Winston Churchill, Franklin D. Roosevelt, and the Vanderbilts once dined? If that list doesn't impress you, how about Casey Stengel and Jack Dempsey? Both notables and non-notables have been flocking to **Cap's Place** for a long time because of its excellent fresh fish.

Back in the 1920s, this group of wooden shacks attached to an old barge was floated up the Intracoastal Waterway from Miami to its present location on Cap's Island. Once a center for rum-running and gambling, the restaurant has cleaned up its act, if not its ramshackle appearance.

The trick is knowing how to get there. In Lighthouse Point follow NE 24th Street toward the ocean. Soon you'll see official-looking signs leading the way to Cap's Place. You'll end up in a parking lot. If the boat isn't there, don't worry. It'll arrive soon. After a brief boat ride to the island, a welcome to cap's sign comes into view. The building looks pretty run-down, but say hello to the pelicans roosting in the nearby trees and press on.

Inside you'll find a rattlesnake skin on the wall measuring more than 6 feet and a sign that says help preserve wildlife, throw a party at cap's. The floors are uneven, but the food is good. You can't miss with a stone-crab appetizer (in season), hearts-of-palm salad, the catch of the day, and key lime pie. Entrees range from moderate to expensive. The boat ride is free, but tips are appreciated on the return trip. Open 7 days a week Jan through Apr and 6 days May through Dec from 4:30 p.m. Call (954) 941-0418 or go to www.capsplace.com. Cap's Place, 2765 NE 28th Ct., Lighthouse Point.

Fort Lauderdale Area

Pompano Beach Air Park is the winter home of the *Stars and Stripes,* one of five touring dirigibles in the world. The airship is 192 feet long, 55 feet wide, and 59 feet high. Powered by small engines, it has a cruising speed of 35 miles per hour and can operate 8 hours a day for a week on the same amount of fuel it takes to taxi a big jet out to the runway for takeoff. The visitor center is open to the public Nov through May; hours are 9 a.m. to 5 p.m. Mon through Fri, 10 a.m. to 6 p.m. Sat and Sun. Sorry, you can't take a ride, but you can get a good close-up look at this huge flying machine at 1500 NE 5th Ave. (on the west side of Pompano Air Park). Call (954) 946-8300 or visit www.goodyear blimp.com for more information.

One way to glimpse Fort Lauderdale's glittering waterways is by cruising on the **Jungle Queen** *riverboat.* Daily 3-hour sightseeing cruises at 10 a.m. and 2 p.m. (dinner cruise at 7 p.m.) go up New River and by Millionaires Row with a stop-off at Indian Village to see birds, monkeys, and a real live alligator show. You'll learn something about the history of the area, where the cruise liners in Port Everglades are heading, who lives where, and how they made their money. The riverboat leaves from Bahia Mar Yachting Center, 801 Seabreeze Blvd., Fort Lauderdale; (954) 462-5596; www.junglequeen.com.

Speaking of cruises, thousands of people cruise to exotic ports of call from **Port Everglades.** More than 20 cruise lines depart from six ultramodern terminals. This is the deepest port between Norfolk and New Orleans and serves more five-star cruise ships than any other port in the nation. You'll get a good view of Port Everglades activity from the SE 17th Street Causeway Bridge.

One of Fort Lauderdale's worst-kept secrets is a restaurant that doesn't advertise and is appropriately named **By Word of Mouth.** Before you are seated, you are shown all the evening's selections, and the host or hostess describes the ingredients and methods of preparation. You may select sun-dried tomato and pesto pâté, a salad of smoked turkey with dried cherries and hazelnuts, New Mexican cornbread salad, Key West lobster with amaretto cream, and then top the whole thing off with chocolate raspberry cake, a house favorite.

By Word of Mouth is at 3200 NE 12th Ave., Oakland Park. The word is out. (Being featured in *Gourmet* magazine took care of that.) Lunch starts at 11 a.m. Mon through Fri; dinner starts at 5 p.m. Wed through Sat. Prices are expensive, and you'll need a reservation: (954) 564-3663.

The ***Stranahan House*** is a gem. When Frank Stranahan came to take charge of the New River overnight camp in 1893, it was the only outpost on a road between Lake Worth and Lemon City (now North Miami). By the late 1890s, Stranahan's trade with the Seminole Indians was at its peak, and winter tourism was in its infancy.

Love and marriage entered his life when the first teacher arrived at the new settlement. The couple's restored store/home of classic Florida frontier design is the oldest existing structure in Broward County. The Stranahan House (off Las Olas Boulevard, at the New River tunnel) is at 335 SE 6th Ave., Fort Lauderdale. It's open daily with tours at 1, 2, and 3 p.m. Closed Sept. Call (954) 524-4736; www.stranahanhouse.org.

Ever dream of becoming an astronaut or a musical genius? The ***Museum of Discovery and Science*** provides the opportunity to explore these notions along with many other mysteries of science. Exhibit areas are displayed over two floors including Florida EcoScapes, a bilevel ecology mountain complete with live animal and plant species; Space Base, a simulation of the weightlessness of space on a Manned Maneuvering Unit; KidScience, featuring its own whimsical musical staircase; and Choose Health, an interactive examination of how nutrition and controlled substances affect the human body.

OTHER ATTRACTIONS WORTH SEEING IN SOUTHEAST FLORIDA

Butterfly World, Coconut Creek, www .butterflyworld.com

Everglades Alligator Farm, Homestead, www.everglades.com

Fairchild Tropical Garden, Miami, www.fairchildgarden.org

Lion Country Safari, Loxahatchee, www.lioncountrysafari.com

Miami Metro Zoo, Miami, www.zoo miami.org

Miami Seaquarium, Miami, www.miami seaquarium.com

Museums of Science and Planetarium, Miami, www.miamisci.org

Worth Avenue, Palm Beach, www .worth-avenue.com

Play a game of virtual volleyball. Spin like a "human hurricane." Lift a 500-pound weight with a giant lever. Program a robot. You can do it all at Gizmo City, one of the museum's exciting permanent exhibits. One of the museum's most popular attractions is the 5-story AutoNation *IMAX 3-D Theatre* with a larger-than-life technique that allows viewers to "feel" the momentum of high-flying special effects. Exhibit hours are 10 a.m. to 5 p.m. Mon through Sat and noon to 6 p.m. Sun. The Museum of Discovery and Science is located on downtown Fort Lauderdale's historic Riverwalk and is the northern anchor of Broward County's Arts and Science District across from the Broward Center for the Performing Arts; 401 SW 2nd St., Fort Lauderdale; (954) 467-6637; www .mods.org.

The *Bonnet House Museum and Gardens,* a charming 35-acre ocean-front estate, was once the winter home of artists Frederick and Evelyn Bartlett. Named for the bonnet water lily that thrives in its tropical lagoons, this tranquil slice of Old Fort Lauderdale is surrounded by lush gardens, fruit trees, and a mangrove jungle. Frederick built his plantation-style home in the 1920s, and the couple spent their lives embellishing it with myriad creative touches including murals and hand-painted ceilings. Enjoy a self-guided tour of the grounds and a guided tour of the museum house. Take time to admire the orchid garden, shell museum, lacy wrought-iron balconies, the Barletts' porcelain collection from their world travels, and treasures carried home from their beachcombing expeditions. The Bonnet House is at 900 N. Birch Rd., Fort Lauderdale, just south of Sunrise Boulevard, between the Atlantic Ocean and the Intracoastal Waterway. Open 10 a.m. to 4 p.m. Tues through Sat, and 11 a.m. to 4 p.m. Sun. Closed Mon, Thanksgiving, Christmas, and New Year's Day. Call (954) 563-5393 or check out the website at www .bonnethouse.org.

Fort Lauderdale's multimillion-dollar *Museum of Art* is a real prize. Some have called its astonishing 20th-century collection "unsettling" and "disturbing," but none has denied its vitality. The

artdecodreaming

The Art Deco style became wildly popular during the decade following the 1925 Exposition Internationale des Arts Décoratifs et Industriels Modernes in Paris. The Art Deco hotels, along and near Ocean Drive in South Beach, were slated to be demolished to make way for modern high-rises when Barbara Capitman, vowing to protect them, founded the Miami Design Preservation League. Three years of intense effort resulted in a square mile of these architectural treasures being included on the National Register of Historic Places, the first 20th-century district to qualify. Today visitors throng to the district, thanks to a revival of interest in this unique style of architecture and publicity generated by Gloria Estefan and other celebrities.

impressive fan-shaped museum and new wing feature distinctive exhibition spaces, a sculpture terrace, gift shop, and art library. It contains the largest collection of ethnographic material in Florida encompassing Oceanic, West African, pre-Columbian, and American Indian art.

The museum is at 1 E. Las Olas Blvd., Fort Lauderdale; (954) 525-5500; www.moafl.org. Open 11 a.m. to 6 p.m. daily except Thurs (11 a.m. to 8 p.m.). The museum is closed on all national holidays. Parking is available at the municipal parking facility on SE 1st Avenue that borders the museum on the east. Ask for hours of free public tours.

The largest tree in Florida, a cluster fig that is 49 feet in circumference and 108 feet tall, keeps right on growing at *Flamingo Gardens.* That's just the beginning. There are also 60 acres of botanical gardens, an Everglades wildlife sanctuary, a tram ride through citrus groves, alligators, and peacocks. This is your chance to see a sausage tree, an African tulip tree, and a gumbo limbo, along with other exotic plants and trees. Open 9:30 a.m. to 5 p.m. daily; closed Mon from June through Nov, Thanksgiving, and Christmas. The gardens are located west of Hollywood off SR 84 at 3750 S. Flamingo Rd., Davie; (954) 473-2955; www.flamingogardens.org.

Everglades Holiday Park is a gateway to the largest subtropical wilderness in the continental US. One way to get acquainted with the Everglades is by a guided hour-long airboat ride. You'll see alligators, exotic birds, and an endless expanse of saw grass. The park is at the end of Griffin Road west of US 27, about 30 minutes from Fort Lauderdale and Miami; 21940 Griffin Rd., Fort Lauderdale. Call (954) 434-8111 or (800) 226-2244; www.evergladesholiday park.com.

In Fort Lauderdale when they refer to Davie, Florida, as "out west," they aren't just kidding. Davie is an authentic Western town full of real live cowboys and cowgirls. If you'd like to look like they do, stop in at *Grifs Western Store* (6211 Orange Dr., Davie; 954-587-9000; www.grifswestern.com; 10 a.m. to 9 p.m. Mon through Sat, 11 a.m. to 5 p.m. Sun), which smells very leathery and sells all manner of boots, hats, shirts, jeans, and saddles. Even the McDonald's in Davie sports a corral with salt licks, watering troughs, and hitching posts for your steed.

Miami Area

It's amazing what money can do. Publisher William Randolph Hearst wanted a Spanish monastery at his San Simeon castle in California, so he bought the *Cloisters of the Monastery of St. Bernard de Clairvaux* and had it shipped from Europe—only it wasn't quite as simple as it sounds. The monastery arrived in this country in 10,751 crates, but Florida customs officers wouldn't release them because they were worried about hoof-and-mouth bacteria in the packing hay. The monastery was finally reassembled, one piece of stone at a time, after Hearst's death. Built in 1141, this is the oldest building in this hemisphere. You can still see the marks early stonemasons carved in the rock. Open 11 a.m. to 4 p.m. Sun and 10 a.m. to 4 p.m. Mon through Fri; sometimes closed for special events. Located at 16711 W. Dixie Hwy. in North Miami Beach; (305) 945-1461; www.spanishmonastery.com.

Some of the smaller hotels at the south end of Miami Beach have been getting face-lifts, and the heritage of old Miami Beach is being preserved in the process. A square-mile area featuring the distinctive resort atmosphere of the late 1920s to the 1940s is being restored. Officially known as the *Miami Beach Historic Architectural District* (fondly called the "Art Deco District"), this section contains the nation's largest collection of historically designated Art Deco structures. The buildings, totaling more than 800, are the first 20th-century structures to be included on the National Register of Historic Places. The Art Deco District stretches from 6th to 23rd Streets between Alton Road and the ocean in Miami Beach. The *Art Deco District Welcome Center,* located at 1001 Ocean Dr. in Miami Beach, provides walking tours of the district at 10:30 a.m. every day but Thurs, when the tour is at 6:30 p.m. Call (305) 531-3484 for more information or visit www.mdpl.org.

South Beach, a unique blend of glitz, glamour, and old-fashioned neighborhood, has become the trendy place to be. Young, old, black, white, straight, gay, Jewish, Christian, rich, and poor—they're all here and proud of it. At the south end of Miami Beach and barely a square mile in size, our very own "American Riviera" has become much more than an international playground. This world-class film and entertainment center, known for its ideal weather and fascinating mix of people, is home to a world-class ballet, symphony, opera, theaters, art galleries, dance clubs, jazz cafes, outdoor concerts, and an impressive collection of museums.

If you have time for only one South Beach museum, make it *The Wolfsonian.* This 70,000-piece, mixed-media museum showcasing the propaganda arts of the 19th and 20th centuries is housed in an excellent example of Mediterranean revival architecture. You will be intrigued by this investigation into the ways in which graphic design shapes and reflects human experience. Open noon to 6 p.m. Mon, Tues, Sat, and Sun, noon to 9 p.m. Thurs and Fri. Closed Wed and major holidays. Summer hours (Memorial Day to Labor Day): noon to 9 p.m. Thurs and Fri; noon to 6 p.m. Sat and Sun; closed Mon, Tues, and Wed. Free admission after 6 p.m. on Fri all year. The Wolfsonian, Florida International University, 1001 Washington Ave., Miami Beach; (305) 531-1001; www.wolfsonian.org.

Known for innovative New World cuisine, South Beach offers a variety of culinary adventures. The quintessential South Beach experience, however, is still alfresco dining at one of the popular outdoor cafes. The **News Cafe,** facing the great Atlantic Ocean, is a clear favorite. The idea was to create a pleasant environment where folks could hang out, read a paper over a leisurely cup of coffee, people-watch, and listen to good music. Since its beginning in 1988, News Cafe has provided patrons with a variety of newspapers and magazines.

The original eight-seat ice cream parlor has evolved into a 350-seat cafe, and the newsstand has grown into a well-stocked news store. The food is excellent. Try the fried calamari, a cold cup of gazpacho, bruschetta (Italian bread, tomato, and herbs), or perhaps a tabbouleh salad of parsley and bulgur wheat. Enjoy watching the world Rollerblade by? If so, you might want to linger over a cappuccino with Frangelico. Open 24 hours a day, News Cafe is located in South Beach at 800 Ocean Dr., Miami Beach; (305) 538-6397; www .newscafe.com.

Let's say you're a rock climber and find yourself in Florida. Poor choice of a place to be, you say? Not at all. You should head straight for **Eden Roc, a Renaissance Resort & Spa** on Miami Beach and check out the latest trend in fitness challenges: a rock-climbing wall. This is the first such wall in the entire state. Here you can climb to your heart's content with other rock-climbing buffs and enjoy the facilities of a first-class hotel in the process.

A distinctly Latin flavor permeates Miami, but it is most highly concentrated in its Cuban community. The Hispanic heart of the city is found in the colorful section of southwestern Miami known as **Little Havana.** This cluster of restaurants, nightclubs, cigar factories, fruit stands, and shops pulses with the energy of these lively, voluble people. Lingering over an aromatic cup of Cuban coffee and listening to Spanish may make you forget what country you're in. Little Havana is a 30-block strip on SW 8th Street (known here as Calle Ocho) in Miami.

dreamcityof opa-locka

Arabian-style architecture complete with pink minarets and golden domes marks Opa-Locka. Consisting of more than 90 Moorish buildings constructed during the 1920s boom, this was once the dream city of aviator Glenn Curtiss. Inspired by the tales of *The Arabian Nights,* Curtiss financed the construction of this modern-day "Baghdad of Dade County," but the area is now depressed. Visitors are cautioned not to wander far from the restored City Hall at Opa-Locka and Sharasad Boulevards. Opa-Locka is at the junction of NW 27th and NW 135th Streets, 10 miles northwest of downtown Miami.

American Police Hall of Fame and Museum

The morbidly curious may want to experience being strapped into an electric chair, without, of course, a jolt of the juice. Or maybe you'd like to inspect a gas chamber and imagine what it must be like to breathe deeply of lethal fumes. If you're into weapons and aren't allergic to gore, this may be a fine attraction for you. We hasten to add that not all the exhibits are gruesome, and it's hard not to be moved by the huge memorial to more than 5,000 American police officers killed in the line of duty. Let's just say that the **American Police Hall of Fame and Museum** is not everyone's cup of tea. Open 10 a.m. to 6 p.m. daily; closed Thanksgiving. Located at 6350 Horizon Dr., Titusville; (321) 264-0911; www.aphf.org.

Vizcaya Museum and Gardens is a must-see. Vizcaya is James Deering's Italian Renaissance palace, one of the finest homes ever built in America. Deering, vice president of International Harvester, spent 20 years collecting priceless treasures from around the world before beginning to build a home for them in 1914. After a global search, he selected Biscayne Bay as the ideal location for his winter retreat. The 70-room villa was finished in 1916 and the formal gardens took five years to complete, with as many as a thousand artisans working at a time. The result is a magnificent achievement featuring an extraordinary collection of furnishings and art objects as well as gardens that have been called "the finest in the western hemisphere." Open daily 9:30 a.m. to 4:30 p.m. except Tues, Thanksgiving Day, and Christmas Day. Guided tours are available. Vizcaya Museum and Gardens is located at 3251 S. Miami Ave., Miami; (305) 250-9133; www.vizcayamuseum.org.

Be sure to take a leisurely drive through *Coral Gables,* one of the country's richest neighborhoods, to admire live oaks, Spanish-style homes, the baroque-style Coral Gables Congregational Church, and the beautifully restored Biltmore Hotel.

If you overnight at the *Mayfair Hotel and Spa,* you'll be in the heart of Miami's trendy Coconut Grove shopping and dining village, an enclave of exclusive boutiques, restaurants, and entertainment. A brief stroll in one direction takes you to *CocoWalk,* a lively open-air mall; walk the other way for the upscale shops and cafes of the Streets of Mayfair.

The Mayfair Hotel is as much an experience as it is a place to spend the night. Each of 179 individually named suites has its own character and design and comes with a Japanese hot tub or marble Roman whirlpool bath, hand-carved mahogany furniture, and private terrace. Several rooms harbor antique British pianos!

And that's not all. In the midst of the largest orchid garden of any hotel in south Florida is the romantic, open-air Orchids Champagne Court. Ask someone to point out the Mayfair orchid, specially developed and named for the hotel's gardens. If weather is inclement, you may sip your bubbly indoors in romantic alcoves or at the marble Champagne and Wine Bar. The Mayfair Hotel and Spa, a Mobil Four-Star, AAA Four Diamond Hotel, is at 3000 Florida Ave., Coconut Grove; (305) 441-0000 or (800) 433-4555; www.mayfairhotelandspa.com.

The historic pioneer home known as *The Barnacle* (1891) once belonged to one of Coconut Grove's earliest settlers, Ralph Middleton Munroe. This photographer and naval architect named the tiny village "Coconut Grove" and helped the settlement grow by encouraging his influential northern friends to visit. The resourceful Mr. Munroe first built a 1-story building of wood salvaged from shipwrecks. Later, he jacked the house up on stilts and added a new first floor to make room for his growing family. Take note of Munroe's ingenious "air-conditioning" system and enjoy the lushly landscaped grounds. The park is open 9 a.m. to 5 p.m. Fri through Mon with guided 1-hour tours at 10 a.m., 11:30 a.m., 1 p.m., and 2:30 p.m. Open Wed and Thurs for group tours with advance reservations. Closed Tues, Thanksgiving, Christmas, and New Year's Day. Barnacle Historic State Park, 3485 Main Hwy., Coconut Grove; (305) 442-6866; www.floridastateparks.org.

In 1895 early settlers to Coconut Grove built *Plymouth Congregational Church,* which is considered south Florida's finest example of Spanish Mission architecture. Vines cover the twin belfry towers, a peacock saunters about the grounds, and the church is surrounded by native flora. No wonder this is the most sought-after wedding chapel in Miami. It is located at Main Highway and Devon Road at 3400 Devon Rd., Coconut Grove; (305) 444-6521; www.plymouthmiami.com.

The amazing thing about *Hotel St. Michel,* with its vaulted ceilings, graceful arches, Spanish tiles, and antique furnishings, is that you don't need a passport to get there. This small, European-style inn has mastered the little touches that mean so much to the traveler—a basket of fruit on arrival, a newspaper delivered to your door each morning, and a hearty continental breakfast (included in the price of the room) to get you going. (Their warm, flaky croissants are immense!)

The hotel (built in 1926) has been beautifully restored, and each of the 28 rooms has its own distinct personality. Along with all the charm, it's nice to have air-conditioning, a phone, a television, and a friendly face at the desk eager to help.

Hotel St. Michel is on the corner of Ponce de Leon Boulevard and Alcazar Avenue at 162 Alcazar Ave., Coral Gables. To contact the hotel, call (305) 444-1666. Their website is www.hotelstmichel.com.

Here's a switch. At ***Monkey Jungle*** you're in the cage, and the monkeys run free. Hundreds of monkeys, gorillas, baboons, and trained chimpanzees swinging freely through a Florida rain forest obviously get a kick out of seeing you confined. Visitors enjoy performances daily in this unusual attraction that boasts the most complete collection of simians in the US. Be sure to see the Wild Monkey Swimming Pool, the orangutan family, "King" the lowland gorilla, and the chimpanzee twins.

Monkey Jungle is also the site of one of the richest fossil deposits in southern Florida, including evidence linking the 10,000-year-old Paleo Indians to south Florida. More than 5,000 specimens have been unearthed from the limestone pit housing Florida alligators. Open 9:30 a.m. to 5 p.m. daily. Take Florida Turnpike's Homestead Extension (SR 821) south to exit 11 (Cutler Ridge Boulevard/SW 216th Street). Once on 216th Street, go west 5 miles. Or take US 1 south to 216th Street and go west 3 miles. Contact the Monkey Jungle at 14805 SW 216th St., Miami; (305) 235-1611; www.monkeyjungle.com.

You shouldn't leave south Florida without spending some tranquil time amidst its lush foliage. ***Fairchild Tropical Botanic Garden,*** with its renowned collection of palms, cycads, and other plants, will fill the bill nicely. Tram tours, leaving from the Garden Shop on the hour weekdays and on the half hour weekends, follow a path through informal groupings of plants and beside peaceful meadows and lakes. This 83-acre garden's offerings include a rain forest, an endangered species garden, a Mayan fruit garden, and a palmetum housing a collection of some 900 of the world's 2,600 known species of palms. Guided walking tours of the palmetum, the arboretum, and the conservatory are offered seasonally. The garden is open 9:30 a.m. to 4:30 p.m. every day except Christmas. Fairchild Tropical Botanic Garden, 10901 Old Cutler Rd., Coral Gables; (305) 667-1651; www.fairchildgarden.org.

a park is born

In 1960 two developments were planned for the area that Biscayne National Park now protects. Opposition to these development proposals led to the establishment of Biscayne National Monument in 1968. In 1980 Congress enlarged the boundaries and declared Biscayne the 47th national park in the US.

Is there such a thing as a strawberryaholic? If you're one (you know who you are), better hunker down beside ***Burr's Strawberry Farm,*** because you'll never want to leave. Fresh strawberries are the main item here, but there are also tomatoes, pecans, strawberry ice, and ice-cream sundaes featuring pineapple, mango, coconut, and—surprise—strawberry. A strawberry milkshake is a must. Burr's is at 12741 SW 216th St. (near Homestead on the road to the Monkey Jungle), Miami; www.burrsberryfarm.com. Open daily December to early May.

The folks at the **Knaus Berry Farm** make the best black-bottom cake on the entire earth—not to mention outstanding cinnamon rolls, homemade breads (try the dilly bread), herb bread sticks, cookies, berry ice cream, and berry jellies. These folks know how to grow a strawberry.

The families who run this vegetable stand/bakery/ice-cream stand may look Amish with their long beards, black hats, bonnets, and shawls, but they're German Baptists. They believe in peace, brotherhood, temperance, and simple living. Because they are baptized by triple immersion, they are sometimes called Dunkers, which comes from the German *tunken,* meaning to immerse.

Their stand is open 8 a.m. to 5:30 p.m. (closed Sun) from mid-Nov to late Apr. Knaus Berry Farm, 15980 SW 248th St., Homestead; (305) 247-0668; www .knausberryfarm.com.

Brilliantly colored tropical fish dart among the reefs, and dense forests of exotic trees, ferns, vines, shrubs, and flowers cover the low-lying land of **Biscayne National Park,** a marine park and sanctuary for marine life, water-birds, boaters, snorkelers, and divers. Since most of Biscayne National Park is underwater, the only way to really tour it is by boat. The water portion of the park is open 24 hours. This, by the way, is the largest marine sanctuary administered by the National Park Service. Certainly the tiny Convoy Point Visitor Center exhibit and few nearby picnic tables are, in themselves, hardly worth the trip. However, a park concessionaire at Convoy Point offers **glass-bottom-boat tours** and **snorkeling trips** to the reefs, as well as island excursions for picnicking, camping, and hiking.

Biscayne has a subtropical climate that is warm and wet from May through October and mild and dry from November through April. Temperatures hover in the high 80s Fahrenheit and low 90s in summer and range from the 60s to the low 80s in winter. High humidity and abundant sunshine are year-round features. Summer, the peak season for tropical storms and hurricanes, typically brings brief, torrential afternoon thunderstorms, but this is also the best time for diving and snorkeling because of the warmth and clarity of the water.

Convoy Point Visitor Center, open 7 a.m. to 5:30 p.m., is 9 miles east of Homestead on N. Canal Drive (SW 328th Street) adjacent to Homestead Bay-front Park. Access to park islands and most of the marine sanctuary is by boat only. Biscayne National Underwater Park, 9710 SW 328th St., Homestead; (305) 230-7275; www.nps.gov/bisc.

Perched on the southwestern edge of Lake Okeechobee (the Seminole word for "big water"), Clewiston is deep in the heart of sugarcane country. No wonder it calls itself "America's Sweetest Town." **Clewiston Inn,** handsome in its neoclassical-revival style, is one of those lucky finds we stumbled on after a long day on the road. The oldest (1938) hotel in the Lake Okeechobee area, it was originally built by US Sugar Corporation to host visiting executives. Even if you can't stay for dinner or overnight in one of the 52 rooms, take time to sit back and sip a tall cool one in the Everglades Lounge. The wraparound mural here was painted by J. Clinton Shepherd and depicts life in the Everglades. Be sure to check out the old photographs showing the art-

howthealligator gotitsname

Early Spanish settlers called this reptile "el largarto," the lizard. Alligator is the corruption by English settlers of the Spanish name.

Crocodiles, much less common than alligators, are distinguished by their narrow snouts and greenish-gray color. The only crocodiles in the US are found in southern Florida.

ist's accomplishment in various stages of completion. He stayed in the inn for several months in the early 1940s while painting the mural. Sweet!

You might want to ask the bartender what the chipmunk is doing there. On second thought, maybe you'd better indulge the artist's whim and order up a fresh drink. The inn is 60 miles west of West Palm Beach and 60 miles east of Fort Myers. The Clewiston Inn, 108 Royal Palm Ave., Clewiston; (863) 983-8151 or (800) 749-4466; www .clewistoninn.com.

Our day with the Seminoles was both fun and educational. Billie Swamp Safari and Ah-Tah-Thi-Ki museum, both located deep in the Everglades on the Big Cypress Seminole Reservation, are close enough to each other to be done in one day and far enough away to qualify as way, way, way off the beaten path.

On **Billie's Swamp Buggy Eco-Tour,** we saw an array of exotic creatures ranging from monster alligators to water buffalo wandering free in the wild. We also recommend the Everglades Airboat Ride and the Snake, Alligator, and Swamp Critter Shows. To experience the real Florida, as it was before the Europeans arrived, plan to overnight in a traditional Seminole-style chickee. Surrounded by 2,200 acres teeming with wildlife, you will gain an appreciation for the survival skills of these Native Americans.

If it sounds too much like roughing it, don't worry. Someone else is doing the cooking. The **Swamp Water Cafe** serves both American fare and such Seminole delicacies as catfish, frog legs, gator tail nuggets, and traditional Seminole fry bread.

Less than 10 minutes away, **Ah-Tah-Thi-Ki,** a fascinating modern museum, tells the story of the life and culture of the Florida Seminoles. A five-screen film on Seminole history gave us an understanding of the trials these Native Americans have endured over the years. A life-size tableau of the sacred Green Corn dance, collections of rare artifacts of the past and a boardwalk nature trail though the Big Cypress Swamp complete the riveting tribute to this unconquered tribe.

The museum (863-902-1113; www.ahtahthiki.com) and Billie's Swamp Safari are located on Big Cypress Seminole Reservation, midway between Fort Lauderdale and Naples. Take I-75 (Alligator Alley) to exit 49. Drive north 19 miles. Billie Swamp Safari, (800) GO-SAFARI; www.swampsafari.com.

The Everglades

There is no place like the Everglades anywhere on the planet. The Indians named it well. They called it Pa-hay-okee, which means grassy waters. Much of this unique wilderness consists of a shallow river percolating slowly toward the sea through a vast expanse of grass. Unlike any other river on earth, this one is 50 miles wide and a mere 6 inches deep. The water drops ever so gradually, only 15 feet over its entire 100-mile course. This is the country's largest remaining subtropical wilderness.

The river of grass seeps southward from Lake Okeechobee to the mangrove-lined rivers along the Gulf Coast through a transition zone where temperate climate blends with subtropic. The many different habitats along the way teem with life. Some plants and animals are tropical species native to the Caribbean Islands. Others are from the temperate zone.

panthercountry

The endangered Florida panthers, also known as cougars, are among North America's rarest mammals. The remnant south Florida population is all that remains of a great number of panthers that thrived in the Eastern US 100 years ago.

Today the Everglades has generally come to mean all the various environments in the approximately 1.5 million acres encompassed by *Everglades National Park.* Visitors reach the park by taking SR 9336 to the main park entrance, approximately 10.5 miles southwest of Homestead. The park road ends at Flamingo on the southern tip of the Florida mainland, a distance of 38 miles from the entrance.

The first thing a visitor will be aware of on the drive from the main entrance are vast prairies of 10-foot-high sedge, which make up the greatest concentration of saw grass in the world. But just as vital to the intricate balance of life are mounded islands called hammocks rising above the river of grass, stands of pine and palmetto, and freshwater sloughs.

Labyrinthian mangrove forests, shallow offshore bays, and the many dollops of land known as the Ten Thousand Islands also are vital parts of this complex Everglades picture. Ten thousand is really just an approximation because new islands are being formed all the time, some consisting of only

everglades

Everglades National Park encompasses 1.4 million acres, making it larger than the state of Delaware. The highest point in Everglades National Park is 10 feet above sea level.

a few salt-tolerant mangrove trees. The area has a reputation as a fertile fishing ground, and the bird activity, especially at sunset, is impressive. This watery wilderness is easy to become lost in; it's a good idea to arrange for a guide or join a boat tour in Everglades City.

In the past, few comprehended the true value of the Glades in terms of sheer food production. This natural nursery ground supplies much of the Gulf with shrimp and the entire eastern seaboard, including New England, with fish. As a spawning ground, it is irreplaceable.

The value of the Everglades reaches far beyond a multimillion-dollar fishing industry. Few places anywhere offer greater variety of beautiful, rare, and interesting birds. About 300 species have been identified in the park, with large waterbirds—herons, egrets, ibises, and spoonbills—getting the greatest share of attention. The sprawling mangrove wilderness, one of the world's most unusual plant communities, is refuge for panthers, bobcats, deer, raccoons, diamondback terrapins, alligators, dolphins, and manatees as well as a wide variety of fish.

Visitors to the park who expect grand scenery in the tradition of soaring mountains or great canyons will be disappointed. Getting to know the Glades is like any worthwhile relationship. It takes time. The trick to appreciating this wilderness is to be able to absorb its subtleties, and that cannot be done from behind the windows of a car. Trails range from easy walks of less than half a mile to more strenuous 14-mile hikes. There is as much life per square inch as anywhere else on earth, but this is not the kind of environment that overwhelms. This is a place that whispers.

Park officials recommend that you begin your visit with a stop at the main visitor center near the main park entrance on SR 9336. There you may view a short film explaining the interrelationships of people and nature in the Everglades and pick up information that will help you understand the environment and plan your time wisely. Naturalists give hikes, talks, canoe trips, tram tours, and demonstrations throughout the year. Activities change daily. Campfire programs are offered during the winter months. One day there may be a sunrise

Everglades Birthday

We were houseboating in the Everglades to escape irritating interruptions that had been running roughshod over our lives. How was I to know it would be a week of constant interruptions? The first morning out I was drying a dish when Suzi squealed from the front deck. I raced through the houseboat like someone who had never seen a dolphin run and leap before the bow. (Which I hadn't.) The 15-minute dolphin show was, I hasten to add, well worth the run.

I was stowing blankets and pillows when a tarpon showed his golden back not 5 feet from the boat. The fish cooperatively repeated his performance for me, to the extreme frustration of our son, who was casting right over it.

I was making up the beds for the night when they called me to the sundeck to watch the pelicans make their awkward landings on a nearby island.

Even the interruptions had interruptions. I was trying to photograph an osprey flying by with a fish in its talons when the dolphins popped up right in front of me.

If I had to be reminded of the passage of time by a birthday, a houseboat meandering through the Everglades proved a fine place for such a reminder. There were so many gifts—the sight of a bald eagle regally surveying its domain from atop a dead tree, hugs and kisses from everyone, a glimpse of a great blue heron making its way along the shoreline, and fresh trout for dinner.

Sitting on the deck thinking of the time going by, I felt that here it was easier. Here there was not so much emphasis on the accumulation of years as there was on the pleasure of being alive.

And isn't this the way life should be lived more of the time? Routine chores interrupted by the glimpse of a sunning alligator, a roseate spoonbill, or a spectacular sunset. A white ibis to watch while drying the dishes, a dolphin to guide the way.

And time . . . time to open oneself to the lure of the Everglades.

bird walk or a paddle out into Florida Bay or a cross-country slough slog or a moonlight tram tour. Ask at the visitor center for schedules. Other entrances to the park are at Shark Valley on the Tamiami Trail (US 41) and at Everglades City in the northwest corner of the park.

Whether you choose to canoe through the Ten Thousand Islands, cruise the **Wilderness Waterway** by outboard, take a swamp tromp with a naturalist, or explore the various trails on your own, you will be well rewarded. You'll soon discover that the Everglades is as much an experience as it is a place. It is the incomparable pleasure of watching a great blue heron make its dainty-footed way along the shoreline, of coming upon a flock of roseate spoonbills feeding, or of listening to a dolphin take a long, deep breath. To see egrets

packtherepellent

The Everglades' subtropical climate governs its life. The nearly uniform warm, sunny weather makes the park a year-round attraction, but there are two distinct seasons. Winter is dry, and summer is very wet. Heavy rains fall during intense storms from May through October. Rainfall can exceed 50 inches a year. Warm, humid conditions bring out hordes of mosquitoes, sand flies, and other biting insects that are an important part of intricate food chains.

streaming across a sinking orange sun is to glimpse but a sliver of the abundant beauty in this mysterious, ancient land.

Park campgrounds—located at Long Pine Key, Flamingo, and Chekika—provide drinking water, picnic tables, grills, tent and trailer pads, and restrooms. Flamingo has cold-water showers. Recreation vehicles are permitted, but there are no electrical, water, or sewage hookups. Campground stays are limited to 14 days from December 1 to March 31. You may camp at other designated sites, on beaches, or in the backcountry. Access is either on foot or by boat, and you must first obtain a backcountry use permit.

You may explore well-marked canoe trails or chart your own course. Choose livery service or a complete camping outfit that meets the special requirements for canoeing in the Everglades.

The Wilderness Waterway, a well-marked inland water route, runs from Flamingo to Everglades City. Sequentially numbered markers guide you over its 99 miles. Boats more than 18 feet long or with high cabins and windshields should not attempt the route because of narrow channels and overhanging foliage in some areas. The route requires a minimum of 6 hours with outboard motor or 7 days by canoe. One-day round-trips are not recommended.

Campsites are available along the route. Be sure to notify a park ranger at either Flamingo or Everglades City both at the start and the end of your trip. The Flamingo marina, which can accommodate boats up to 60 feet long, rents houseboats, small powered skiffs, and canoes. Year-round boat tours at Flamingo travel through the mangrove wilderness and into Florida Bay.

thecuttingedge

Saw grass is one of the oldest sedges known. Unlike regular grass, which has a hollow stem, sedge has a solid triangular stem. Blades of this plant are edged with razor-sharp, sawlike teeth.

Sightseeing boats go into the Ten Thousand Islands region and the mangrove swamps of the northwestern Everglades. These concession-operated tours leave from the Gulf Coast Ranger Station every 30 minutes. Open 9 a.m. to 5 p.m. daily. For information about boat tours and canoe rentals at the Gulf Coast

Ranger Station, write the concessionaire at Everglades National Park Boat Tours, 815 Copeland Ave., Everglades City 34139; (239) 695-2591; www.everglades nationalparkboattoursgulfcoast.com.

Shark Valley lies off US 41, the Tamiami Trail. Here, along the 15-mile loop road, you may see a variety of wildlife that inhabits the wide, shallow waterway, which eventually empties into Shark River. Alligators, otters, snakes, turtles, and birds, including rare wood storks and the snail kite, are native to this watery expanse. Hardwood hammocks and other tree islands dot the landscape. The loop road is used for tram rides, biking, and walking. An observation tower along the road provides a spectacular view. Reservations are recommended for tram rides during the busy winter season. For further information contact the Everglades Park Superintendent, 40001 SR 9336, Homestead 33034-6733. For visitor information, call (305) 242-7700; www.nps.gov/ever.

It's hard to believe the **Miccosukee Indian Village** in the Florida Everglades is just 25 miles west of the gleaming towers of downtown Miami. Approximately 600 contemporary Miccosukees are descendants of some 50 tribespeople who escaped deportation from the US during the Indian wars of the 19th century.

Guided tours include the village of chickee huts where tribal members lived in traditional fashion. You may watch Indians wrestle alligators, take an adventurous airboat ride through the Everglades, or visit the Indian Museum, which features artifacts from various tribes.

Members of the Miccosukee tribe create and sell handmade dolls, wood carvings, beadwork, basketry, jewelry, and other crafts. The restaurant features authentic Miccosukee dishes along with standard American fare. Open 9 a.m. to 5 p.m. daily. The Miccosukee Indian Village is located 25 miles west of Miami at Mile Marker 70, US 41 Tamiami Trail, Miami; (305) 552-8365; www.miccosukee resort.com/indian_village.htm.

State Parks in Southeast Florida

State park information: (850) 245-2157 or www .floridastateparks.org. For camping reservations in any state park, call (800) 326-3521.

Avalon State Park, (772) 468-3985

Barnacle Historic State Park, (305) 442-6866

Bill Baggs Cape Florida State Park, (305) 361-5811

Curry Hammock State Park, (305) 289-2690

Fort Pierce Inlet State Park, (772) 468-3985

Fort Zachary Taylor Historic State Park, (305) 292-6713

Hugh Taylor Birch State Park, (954) 564-4521

John D. MacArthur Beach State Park, (561) 624-6950

John U. Lloyd Beach State Park, (954) 923-2833

Jonathan Dickinson State Park, (772) 546-2771

Key Largo Hammocks Botanical State Park, (305) 451-1202

Oleta River State Park, (305) 919-1844

St. Lucie Inlet Preserve State Park, (772) 219-1880

San Pedro Underwater Archaeological Preserve State Park, (305) 664-2540

Seabranch Preserve State Park, (772) 219-1880

Sebastian Inlet State Park, (321) 984-4852

Places to Stay in Southeast Florida

BOCA RATON

Best Western University Inn
2700 N. Federal Hwy.
(561) 395-5225
www.bestwestern.com

Marriott
5150 Town Center Circle
(561) 392-4600
www.marriott.com

CORAL GABLES

Biltmore Hotel
1200 Anastasia Ave.
(305) 445-1926 or
(866) 925-0857
www.biltmorehotel.com

Hyatt Regency
50 Alhambra Plaza
(305) 441-1234
www.hyatt.com

Westin Colonnade
180 Aragon Ave.
(305) 441-2600
www. starwoodhotels.com

FORT LAUDERDALE

Hyatt Regency Pier 66
2301 SE 17th St.
(954) 525-6666
www.pier66.hyatt.com

La Quinta Inn and Suites
13600 NW 2nd St.
Sunrise
(954) 845-9929
www.lq.com

Riverside Hotel
620 E. Las Olas Blvd.
(954) 467-0671
www.riversidehotel.com

HOLLYWOOD

Holiday Inn Airport
2905 Sheridan St.
(954) 925-9100 or
(800) 315-2621
www.holidayinn.com

HOMESTEAD

Best Western
411 S. Krome Ave.
Florida City
(305) 246-5100
www.bestwestern.com

Floridian
990 N. Homestead Blvd.
(800) 371-9232

MIAMI

Hampton Inn
2800 SW 28th Terr.
(305) 448-2800
www.hamptoninncoconut
grove.com

Doral Golf Resort and Spa
4400 NW 87th Ave.
(305) 592-2000
www.doralresort.com

Fairfield Inn Miami Airport West by Marriott
3959 NW 79th Ave.
(305) 599-5200
www.marriott.com

La Quinta Inn and Suites
7925 NW 154th St.
Miami Lakes
(305) 821-8274
www.lq.com

Quality Inn South
14501 S. Dixie Hwy.
(305) 251-2000
www.qisouth.com

Turnberry Isle Resort & Club
19999 W. Country Club Dr.
Aventura
(305) 932-6200
www.fairmont.com/
turnberryisle

MIAMI BEACH

Fontainebleau Hilton Resort and Towers
4441 Collins Ave.
(800) 548-8886
www.fontainebleau.com

PALM BEACH

Fairfield Inn and Suites
2870 S. Ocean Blvd.
(561) 582-2585
www.marriott.com

The Four Seasons
2800 S. Ocean Blvd.
(561) 582-2800
www.fourseasons.com

POMPANO BEACH

Super 8
2300 NE 10th St.
(954) 943-3500
www.super8.com

STUART

Best Western–Downtown
1209 S. Federal Hwy.
(772) 287-6200
www.bestwindernstuart
.com

Stuart Inn
950 S. Federal Hwy.
(772) 287-3171

WEST PALM BEACH

Days Inn West Palm Beach
2300 45th St.
(561) 689-0450
www.daysinn.com

VISITOR INFORMATION FOR SOUTHEAST FLORIDA

Bal Harbour Village, 655 96th St., Bal Harbour; (305) 573-5177 or (800) 847-9222; www.balharbourflorida.com

Greater Boca Raton Chamber of Commerce, 1800 N. Dixie Hwy., Boca Raton; (561) 395-4433; www .bocaratonchamber.com

Greater Fort Lauderdale Convention & Visitors Bureau, 100 E. Broward Blvd., Ste. 200, Fort Lauderdale; (954) 765-4466 or (800) 22-SUNNY (227-8669); www.sunny.org

Greater Hollywood Chamber of Commerce, 330 N. Federal Hwy., Hollywood; (954) 923-4000 or (800) 231-5562; www.hollywoodchamber.org

Greater Miami Convention & Visitors Bureau, 701 Brickell Ave., Ste. 2700, Miami; (305) 539-3000 or (800) 933-8448; www.gmcvb.com

Greater Pompano Beach Chamber of Commerce, 2200 E. Atlantic Blvd., Pompano Beach; (954) 941-2940; www .pompanobeachchamber.com

Indian River Chamber of Commerce, 1216 21st St., Vero Beach; (772) 567-3491; www.indianriverchamber.com

Jensen Beach Chamber of Commerce, 1900 Ricou Terr., Jensen Beach; (772) 334-3444; www .jensenbeachchamber.biz

Miami Beach Latin Chamber of Commerce, 510 Lincoln Rd., Miami Beach; (305) 674-1414; www .miamibeach.org

Palm Beach County Convention & Visitors Bureau, 1555 Palm Beach Lakes Blvd., Ste. 800, West Palm Beach; (800) 554-7256; www .palmbeachfl.com

Stuart/Martin County Chamber of Commerce, 1650 S. Kanner Hwy., Stuart; (772) 287-1088; www .goodnature.org

Tropical Everglades Visitor Center, 160 US 1, Florida City; (305) 245-9180 or (800) 388-9669; www .tropicaleverglades.com

PGA National Resort & Spa
400 Avenue of the Champions
Palm Beach Gardens
(877) 422-5608
www.pgaresorts.com

Places to Eat in Southeast Florida

BOCA RATON

City Fish Market
7940 Glades Rd.
(561) 487-1600
www.buckheadrestaurant.com

CORAL GABLES

Bangkok Bangkok II
157 Giralda Ave.
(305) 444-2397

Caffe Abbracci
318 Aragon Ave.
(305) 441-0700
www.cafeabbracci.com

John Martin's Irish Pub & Restaurant
253 Miracle Mile
(305) 445-3777
www.johnmartins.com

FORT LAUDERDALE

Mango's
904 E. Las Olas Blvd.
(954) 523-5001
www.mangosonlasolas.com

HOMESTEAD

The Capri Restaurant
935 N. Krome Ave.
Florida City
(305) 247-1542
www.dinecapri.com

MIAMI

Brisa Bistro Hilton Hotel
1601 Biscayne Blvd.
(305) 714-3680

Chef Allen's
19088 NE 29th Ave.
Aventura
(305) 935-2900
www.chefallens.com

Shula's Steak House
7601 Miami Lakes Dr.
Hialeah
(305) 820-8136
www.donshula.com

MIAMI BEACH

Blue Door, Delano Hotel
1685 Collins Ave.
(305) 674-6400

Joe's Stone Crab
11 Washington Ave.
(305) 673-0365
www.joesstonecrab.com

Lemon Twist (French)
908 71st St.
(305) 865-6465
www.lemontwist-miami.com

Yuca (Cuban)
501 Lincoln Rd.
(305) 532-9822
www.yuca.com

L'Escalier, The Breakers Resort
1 S. County Rd.
(888) 273-2537
www.thebreakers.com

THE FLORIDA KEYS

Introduction to the Florida Keys: The whole place is off the beaten path, so just slow down and bask in the sunshine. This incredible engineering feat—128 miles of Overseas Highway—113 miles of roadway and 43 bridges—is yours to enjoy, from sunrise (look left) to sunset (look right). Who wouldn't want to go to the end of this intriguing road?

The Overseas Highway (US 1) begins at Florida City, but the Card Sound Road (SR 997) is a more scenic and less congested way to connect to it. Since there is only one road to Key West, you aren't in any danger of getting lost. Also, keeping track of your progress is a cinch. Small green mile markers on the right side of the road begin with number 126 a mile past Florida City on US 1 and end with Mile Marker 0 in Key West. These markers, used instead of addresses, make it easy to locate places.

The Overseas Highway is really spectacular, especially after the Seven-Mile Bridge, where the islands are less developed. In fact, the seascapes on both sides of the highway seem to blossom and expand as you drive south. Pines, palms, and mangroves frame ocean views of every conceivable shade of blue. Great whipped-cream clouds are

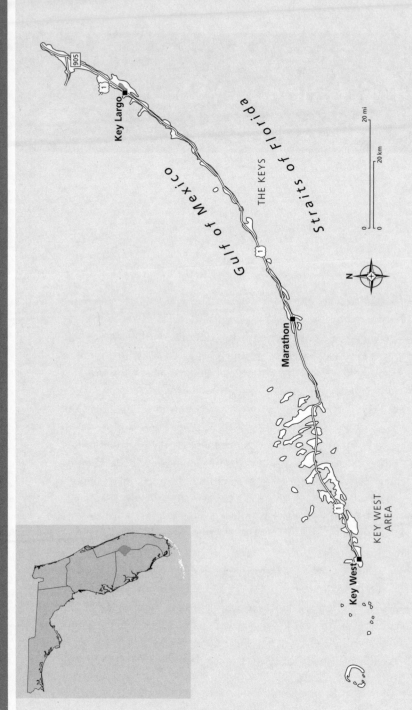

THE FLORIDA KEYS

backdropped by an immense sky, and you are cruising, albeit by car, toward the end of the road.

The Keys Leading to Key West

The Keys gleam like gems set in a sea that dazzles from transparent turquoise and milky emerald to deep sapphire. Strung on a ribbon of concrete and steel better known as the ***Overseas Highway,*** this archipelago curves 100 miles from Biscayne Bay to Key West. Nearly 70 miles west of the highway's end in Key West are a few leftover jewels, which Ponce de León christened the Tortugas (Spanish for "turtles").

These frost-free islands, warmed by the Gulf Stream in winter and cooled by the trade winds in summer, appear to be an uncomplicated antidote for the winter weary. Nothing in their swaying palms or glistening sandy beaches offers the slightest hint of a tempestuous past.

Yet early history of the Keys is peppered with both drama and tragedy. Ponce de León, who claimed Florida for Spain in 1513, charted the Keys and named them Los Martires (The Martyrs), because from a distance they looked like men who were suffering. The name proved to be prophetic. Spanish ships, laden with gold and treasures from Central America, were routinely plundered as they passed the islands. Such famous pirates as Black Caesar, Blackbeard, and Lafitte found the Keys' many inlets and coves ideal for concealing their ships and stashing their booty.

By the turn of the 20th century, the Keys were more than ready for tycoon Henry Flagler's incredible scheme to link them to the mainland by rail. His idea was to extend his famous Florida East Coast Railway across 100 miles of water and 29 islands. As one of the founders of Standard Oil, Flagler had plenty of wealth to devote to this grand project popularly known as Flagler's Folly. At age 75, having spent a lifetime responding to improbable challenges, he could afford to ignore those who said it couldn't be done. Besides, it didn't seem like such a big deal. "All you have to do," he said, "is to build one concrete arch, and then another, and pretty soon you will find yourself in Key West."

TOP EVENTS IN THE FLORIDA KEYS

Underwater Music Festival, Big Pine Key, July, (305) 872-2411, www.flakeys.com

Fantasy Fest, Key West, October, (305) 296-1817, www.keywestchamber.org

Unfortunately, the railroad turned out to be an economic failure. To make matters worse, a horrendous hurricane tore through the Keys in 1935, destroying embankments and even sweeping a train into the sea. After nearly 2.5 years of relative isolation, the impoverished people of the Keys were delighted when the State of Florida built the 128-mile Overseas Highway. The highway, a continuation of US 1, is an incredible engineering feat consisting of 113 miles of roadway and 43 bridges.

Residents of the Keys, buoyed by their new accessibility, placed their hope for the future in tourism, a hope that has become reality. More than 1 million tourists each year seek out the Keys' subtropical climate and easygoing island lifestyle. They are usually in quest of an off-the-beaten-path experience, and they are rarely disappointed with what they find. You can traverse the highway in less than 3 hours; but then, you can also see the Mona Lisa in less than a minute. The point is to take your time and enjoy. There are lots of things to see and do, but you will need to slow down to fully absorb and appreciate the natural beauty that surrounds you.

The Upper Keys, those nearest the mainland, stretch from Key Largo through Long Key. Key Largo is the base for the nation's first underwater park. *John Pennekamp Coral Reef State Park,* 21 miles long and approximately 4 miles wide, protects 40 species of coral and 650 species of fish on the only

Flagler's Folly

Henry Flagler's dream railroad was finally completed on January 21, 1912. The next day, when Flagler arrived aboard the first official train, Key West staged the largest celebration the island had ever seen. Schoolchildren turned out to welcome the railroad's mastermind. Flagler walked on a thick carpet of roses gathered from local gardens to receive accolades from an excited citizenry. It was an emotional moment for the 83-year-old visionary, whose last great dream had finally become reality. His life's work completed, Flagler was to die the following year.

Despite early rave reviews, the railroad proved to be an economic disaster. Cargoes fell well below optimistic projections, and too few wealthy visitors could be lured so far from the mainland. The Great Depression dealt a lethal blow to the staggering enterprise, but it was violent weather that finally finished it off.

The worst hurricane the area had ever known devastated the Keys on Labor Day in 1935. A 20-foot wall of water smashed the islands, and the barometer registered 26.35, the lowest reading ever recorded in the western hemisphere. The storm swept a train into the sea and washed away many miles of track along with most of the embankments. The death toll, estimated at about 500 people, also included one railroad, a magnificent achievement whose moment in the sun was over.

The Conch Republic

The friendly freewheeling community of the Keys once seceded from the Union, established the Conch Republic, and demanded foreign aid from the US government. Natives are called Conchs (pronounced "konks") after the mollusk that thrives in local waters, but transients abound. When we asked one waiter how long he'd been in the Keys, he checked his watch (for the time, not the date) before replying. All agree the attitude here is different. These mellow folks measure time by watching the sun rise over the Atlantic then strolling to the other side of the island to watch it slide into the Gulf of Mexico.

living reef along the Atlantic coast. The reef, which was severely damaged by commercial souvenir hunters in the 1930s and 1940s, has recovered under the park's protection. These spectacular coral gardens were saved by a conservation movement spearheaded by John Pennekamp, an associate editor at the *Miami Herald,* whose stories fired up public interest in this national treasure.

Dive shops abound in Key Largo, as do scuba-diving courses culminating in certification. Skin divers, snorkelers, and passengers on glass-bottom boats revel in the park's clear-water views to 60 feet, which include colorful coral formations, exotic fish, turtles, and old sailing wrecks. *Christ of the Deep,* a replica of Guido Galletti's *Christ of the Abyss* in the Mediterranean Sea, highlights one of the reef's natural underwater valleys.

A glass-bottom boat leaves three times daily (9:15 a.m., 12:15 p.m., and 3 p.m.) for a guided tour of **Molasses Reef.** You'll see high coral ridges, tunnels, and a variety of formations including elkhorn, staghorn, star, and brain coral without ever getting wet. Certified scuba divers may board a boat that leaves daily at 8:30 a.m. and 1 p.m. for trips to Molasses Reef, French Reef, or Benwood Wreck (depending on conditions). Snorkelers take advantage of a convenient dive platform on *El Capitan,* which leaves three times daily on 2.5-hour reef trips. Usually the excursion heads for Grecian Rocks, where you'll see colorful angelfish, parrotfish, and some harmless nurse sharks. Captain Slate's Atlantis Dive Center, 51 Garden Cove Dr., Key Largo; (800) 331-DIVE (3483); www.the floridakeys.com/captslate. For boat tour information, call (305) 451-1325.

John Pennekamp Coral Reef State Park also has canoe and kayak rentals as well as beaches and nature trails. The campsites are much in demand, so be sure to make reservations well ahead or get there early. Contact the park at PO Box 487, Key Largo 33037; boating reservations: (305) 451-6300; camping reservations: (800) 326-3521; park number: (305) 451-1202; www.floridastate parks.org.

What do you know about ethnobotanic gardens? First we'd better define ethnobotany: the exploration of how a region's indigenous plants are used as food, shelter, clothing, or medicine. As you can see, it's a terribly important field of study. What we're talking about is sheer survival. Those early cave men and cave women had to keep each other alive. Without the women they didn't have much of a chance to keep the population going from one century to the next. Babies are small and fragile. Someone had to keep the wolf from the door. Someone had to gather the food, store the food, cook the food—don't worry, someone always showed up when it was time to eat the food. The Little Red Hen knew all about sharing the workload. Registered guests at Key Largo's **Kona Kai Resort and Gallery** are welcome to enjoy a complimentary self-guided tour through the property's new botanic gardens. Kona Kai has partnered with a resident botanist to conduct formal tours, presentations, and events within the gardens. All are designed to showcase the elegant, unusual plants that help people become more in tune with nature and perceive plants and the natural world as a whole. This, by the way, is one of the first ethnobotanic gardens in the US Southeast. Guided appointment-only tours for the general public are available as well, weather permitting. Tours are 90 minutes long and limited to six adults. Tour times are Tues and Sat at 9:30 a.m. and Thurs at 4:30 p.m. A $15 donation is required. www.konakairesort.com.

At the **Holiday Inn Key Largo Resort and Marina,** you may see the **African Queen,** an old river freighter that Humphrey Bogart and Katharine Hepburn made famous in the 1951 film classic. The remodeled inn, located at

AUTHORS' FAVORITE ATTRACTIONS IN THE FLORIDA KEYS

Audubon House and Tropical Gardens, Key West; www .audubonhouse.com

Bahia Honda State Park, Big Pine Key; www.bahiahondapark.com

Ernest Hemingway Home and Museum, Key West; www .hemingwayhome.com

Fort Jefferson, Dry Tortugas National Park; www .fortjefferson.com

John Pennekamp Coral Reef State Park, Key Largo; www.pennekamppark .com

Mallory Docks, Key West

Mel Fisher Maritime Heritage Society Museum, Key West; www.melfisher.org

National Key Deer Refuge; www.fws .gov/nationalkeydeer

Mile Marker 100 (99701 Overseas Hwy., Key Largo), now has a tiki bar and Bogey's Cafe. To take a tour on the freighter, call (305) 451-2121; www.holiday innkeylargo.com.

Theatre of the Sea in Islamorada (Spanish for Purple Isle) is the second-oldest marine-life park in the world. A 2-hour tour includes a look at an extensive shark and ray collection and a dolphin show in a natural coral grotto. Who knows? This may be your only chance to be kissed by an affectionate sea lion or touch a shark (and come away with all your fingers intact). For information and reservations on the "Swim with a Dolphin" program, call (305) 664-2431. Open 9:30 a.m. to 4 p.m. daily. Theatre of the Sea is located at Mile Marker 84.5 on US 1, 84721 Overseas Hwy., Islamorada.

From Robby's Marina on US 1, you can take boat tours of both Lignumvitae Key and Indian Key. Boat tours leave for *Indian Key Historic State Park* at 8:30 a.m. and 12:30 p.m. and for *Lignumvitae Key Botanical State Park* at 9:30 a.m. and 1:30 p.m. Closed Tues and Wed. Lignumvitae was named for a type of hardwood tree with healing properties found growing here, and tours of the Botanical State Park reveal many other unusual plants. You'll be fascinated to learn how early Keys residents adapted the fruits, barks, and leaves of the forest to meet their needs. Rangers say this nature preserve "is the last place that truly represents the Keys as they were." For information on Lignumvitae Key Botanical State Park and Indian Key State Park or to arrange a tour to either location, call (305) 664-2540; www.floridastateparks.org.

A once-thriving settlement at Indian Key (a state historic site) was completely destroyed during the Seminole Indian raid in 1840. The tropical foliage here is amazing. Only at the top of the observation tower are you eye level with the tops of towering century plants. A marvelous time to visit is May, when tiny white butterflies are migrating from South America. *Long Key State Park* is noted for great fishing, swimming, snorkeling, boating, and camping. For camping reservations, call (800) 326-3521. For information about the park, contact the Park Manager, PO Box 776, Long Key 33001; (305) 664-4815; www .floridastateparks.org.

San Pedro *Underwater Archaeological Preserve* is a shipwreck that has become, over time, both a dive site and a living museum in the sea. The 287-ton Dutch-built ship, *San Pedro,* carried a cargo of Mexican silver and Chinese porcelain when it went down in 1733 near Indian Key. Today the dive site is attractive with its white-sand seabed surrounded by turtle grass and schools of colorful fish swimming around a large pile of ballast stones. The *San Pedro* is encrusted with more than 10 species of living coral, making this wreck one of Florida's oldest artificial reefs. *San Pedro* is in 18 feet of water, approximately 1.25 nautical miles south from Indian Key at 24° 51.802' north,

Where the Boys Are

Our son Stephen suggested he and his dad celebrate Steve's spring break from college together. They returned home a week later wildly enthusiastic about their adventure in the Keys. What follows is Steve's version of the experience.

Air. We both needed air, but only Dad had it. Moving slowly to conserve oxygen, I gave the out-of-air signal. He took a big breath and passed the regulator to me. I remember his white knuckles and his eyes. Big eyes underwater are the two-second warning signal. Dad's were huge.

I grabbed one quick breath instead of the standard two. We didn't need a problem with 25 feet of water overhead. On my next turn the regulator slipped from our hands and began blowing the precious air out in a great blast of bubbles.

Things were not going smoothly. With some difficulty we managed to get the regulator under control and were able to get a good breathing system going. Then the instructor appeared and turned my air back on. We had passed the buddy breathing test. I inhaled deeply.

For my spring break from my sophomore year in college, I suggested Dad and I chase adventure. I didn't want to look at things from a tour bus. I wanted something physical, something real.

We found it in a one-week scuba-diving course in Key Largo. An impulse stop at a dive center turned out to be a good one. Our first thought had been to do some snorkeling, maybe spear a few fish later on. But the trip we wanted was canceled. That changed our free-flowing, let-it-happen vacation into an intense 5-day Scuba (self-contained underwater breathing apparatus) Certification Course.

I learned a lot, and it wasn't only about diving. The day the class ended we all went out for dinner. The other participants said they envied us, not just because we could have a good time together, but because we cared about each other. They were right. Sharing air in the open ocean gave that caring a new dimension. I knew if things really went wrong, Dad came first.

I figure it's the least I could do. We do go way back.

80° 40.795' west. Please tie up to the mooring buoys to prevent anchor damage to the site. For more information, call the Bureau of Archaeological Research at (850) 245-6400 or visit http://dhr.dos.state.fl.us/archaeology. Locally, contact Windley Key State Geological Site at (305) 664-2540.

The Middle and Lower Keys (from Long Key on to Key West) differ geologically from the Upper Keys, which are the boney skeletons of an ancient coral reef. While all the islands have as a base a thick blanket of limestone, those farther from the mainland are topped with a layer of Miami oolite, egg-shaped particles cemented into rock by the millennia.

Surely you're in need of a dose of old Florida lifestyle. You know—laid-back, take-your-time, what's-your-hurry days where the main activity is cooling off, and the only things that won't wait are tide and sunset. A favorite destination is **Marathon Key,** located in the heart of the Florida Keys. This 10-mile island looks to the sea for recreation as well as sustenance. No wonder this is such an ideal place for a getaway. Well off the beaten path, this family-oriented island community is the place to enjoy fishing, sailing, diving, snorkeling, and Snuba. Snuba is an underwater breathing system developed by combining scuba and snorkeling—easier than scuba, more freeing than snorkeling. Thanks to the convergence of the Atlantic Ocean and the Gulf of Mexico, anglers are drawn to these fertile fishing waters. They fish for billfish and tuna in the winter and dolphin fish in the summer. Sombrero Reef, just a few miles offshore, is a federally protected section of the only living coral barrier reef in the US. The Florida Straits lure divers from around the globe for world-class wreck diving. At Marathon's **Crane Point Museum, Nature Center, and Historic Site,** visitors take special delight in exploring this 64-acre tropical oasis of nature trails, mangrove wetlands, and hardwood trees. The Museum of Natural History serves as the entrance to the elevated piece of land known as hammock. Touring the homestead of George Adderley's family is a real eye-opener. This early 20th-century Bahamian immigrant lived a simple life that required hard work and ingenuity. They survived by selling charcoal and sponges gathered from the transparent waters of the Keys. The home is a popular stop along the 2.5 miles of trails and wooden walkways crisscrossing the hammock. One trail leads to a small footbridge overlooking Florida Bay; another takes you by the Marathon Wild Bird Center, where pelicans, cormorants, egrets, and other wounded birds check in for rehabilitation so they can eventually return to the wild. Crane Point Museum, Nature Center, and Historic Site, 5550 Overseas Hwy., Mile Marker 50.5, Bayside, Marathon; (305) 743-9100.

Each island seems to have a distinct identity, but most activities still center on Key favorites—beachcombing, sun basking, and fishing from bridge, beach, and boat. From Marathon to Key West, spearfishing is permitted 1 mile offshore. Marathon is the starting point for the famous **Seven-Mile Bridge,** the country's longest continuous bridge. Its 65-foot crest is the highest point in the Keys.

Once it was a strip joint; in fact, it was the only topless-dancer bar on Marathon Key. Now Fanny's Bar is—ta da!—the nation's only turtle hospital. Some would call this progress.

Unfortunately, **Hidden Harbor Turtle Hospital** came into being to solve a growing problem: turtles afflicted with multiple tumors. These tumors are symptoms of a debilitating disease known as fibro-papilloma that is now thought to have viral origins. This rapidly spreading epidemic may be affecting as much as 90 percent of the local turtle population and has shown up as far away as Barbados and Hawaii.

Back in 1986 Tina Brown, charter boat captain, and her partner, Richie Moretti, onetime auto mechanic, purchased the Hidden Harbor Motel and converted their saltwater pool for the display of marine life. Soon local anglers began bringing in turtles suffering from grotesque tumors, and it became clear that surgery was needed to save their lives.

Brown and Moretti bartered free fishing and diving trips for the services of a vet until they were able to get a vet on staff who would perform surgery in exchange for a room. They fund their hospital (which needs roughly $100,000 yearly) from proceeds of the Hidden Harbor Motel and give countless hours to the care of their reptilian friends.

They also give educational programs to local schoolchildren and presentations on turtles to the local museum. Currently Brown and Moretti are working with the University of Florida in hopes of finding a cure for a disease that is decimating an already endangered species.

The turtle hospital does not have regular visiting hours for the public, but they give a slide show to motel guests about three times a week as a thank-you, since motel funds operate the hospital. You will be amazed at the modern medical offices—including an x-ray room, necropsy lab, and operating room—and saddened by the sight of so many sick turtles in the saltwater pool behind the hospital. Contact the Hidden Harbor Motel, 2396 Overseas Hwy., Marathon; (305) 743-5711; or you can reach the hospital at (305) 743-8552 or (800) 362-3495; www.turtlehospital.org.

If it's late in the day and you need a place to sleep, why not consider a floating houseboat at dockside or a lighthouse apartment? *Faro Blanco Marine Resort* offers both as well as an assortment of cottages and condos, restaurants, a full-service marina, Olympic-size swimming pool, charter fishing, tours, and dive lessons. The resort has facilities on both Atlantic and Gulf waters.

Faro Blanco is in Marathon, 110 miles southwest of the Florida mainland, 2.5 hours from Miami by car, an hour from Key Largo, or an hour from Key West. The resort is located at Mile Marker 48. Faro Blanco Marine Resort, 1996 Overseas Hwy., Marathon; (305) 743-9018 or (800) 759-3276.

It's easy to whiz right by *Pigeon Key* as you drive across Seven-Mile Bridge. You might look down, see a cluster of old buildings on a tiny palm-sheltered island, and wonder what it's all about. Of course you'd like to take a closer look. Those with a yen to get off the fast track for a little while will be well rewarded by a brief sojourn to Pigeon Key.

This four-acre island, connected to the mainland by a bridge originally built by Henry Flagler for his famous Florida East Coast Railway, has a rich and colorful history. Today its future seems equally promising. Pigeon Key, virtually in the shadow of the Overseas Highway, is a certified historic district listed on the National Register of Historic Places. From 1908 to 1935, this island served as a construction and maintenance camp for the railroad; the Pigeon Key Foundation has carefully restored seven buildings from this era. Since the railroad days, Pigeon Key has been a center for the Road and Toll District, a site for the US Navy, a fishing camp, and a research center for the University of Miami.

The potential for this idyllic island is limitless; it is on its way, gradually but certainly, to becoming a world-class center for environmental education, historical exhibits, and research.

Be sure to sign up for a tour and take the shuttle out to the island. You'll enjoy the ride. The shuttle is an attractive railroad car, modeled after the historic Florida East Coast Railway, that leaves from the Pigeon Key Visitors Center on Knight's Key. This way you'll hear stories of the early railroad as you pass slowly over the Old Seven-Mile Bridge.

Once you reach the island, you'll learn about the heritage of the Florida Keys, the natural environment, and various disastrous hurricanes. Your guide will make memories of onetime residents come alive. And, yes, the island has a ghost—or at least a fairly juicy ghost story.

Be sure to see the museum showing the history of the island, the Overseas Highway, and the overseas railway as well as historical and cultural exhibits, including *Florinda,* a Cuban refugee vessel that carried 24 people to freedom. You'll see the Section Gang's Quarters (1909), a onetime dorm for railway workers (now the Education Center for the Pigeon Key Foundation); the Bridge Tender's House (1909); the Bridge Foreman's House (1916); Negro Quarters (1909); Honeymoon Cottage (1950); and others.

Pigeon Key is a delightful spot for a picnic (you're welcome to use the picnic tables), or you may want to just sit beside the sea and watch the colors shift from aquamarine to cobalt. Artists and photographers return time after time to capture the island's picturesque landscapes and seascapes.

The island's proximity to the Gulf Stream, Florida Bay, coral reefs, sea grass beds, and an abundant variety of marine life makes it an ideal setting for marine research. Mote Marine Laboratory plans to use the island's resources to study such vital concerns as water quality and the biological integrity of tropical marine ecosystems. Mote's Center for Shark Research will continue its study of sharks as an ecologically and economically valuable marine resource.

Approximately 45 miles from Key West, 100 miles southwest of Miami, and 2.2 miles due west of Marathon, Pigeon Key is connected to the mainland by the Old Seven-Mile Bridge.

Sounds interesting, but how do you get to Pigeon Key? Walkers, joggers, cyclists, and skaters are welcome to go out to Pigeon Key via the Old Seven-Mile Bridge at any time during regular hours (9 a.m. to 5 p.m., 7 days a week) for a small admission fee. Access to the island is at Mile Marker 48 at the west end of Marathon.

One thing you can't do is drive your car to Pigeon Key, as regulations prohibit private cars on the old bridge. You may, however, leave your car in the parking lot at the east end of the Old Seven-Mile Bridge.

The best way to experience this historic island (at Mile Marker 47) is to begin and end your trip at the Pigeon Key Visitors Center on the Atlantic side of Knight's Key. Even if you don't have time to meander about Pigeon Key, take a moment to browse the visitor center's intriguing selection of environmental and historical books and gifts.

The shuttle service to Pigeon Key leaves from Knight's Key, with the last shuttle returning to the visitor center at 4 p.m. Why not make a day of it? Pigeon Key Foundation, PO Box 500130, Marathon 33050; (305) 289-0025; www.pigeonkey.net.

Prettiest beach in the Florida Keys? Consider **Bahia Honda State Park,** just south of Marathon's Seven-Mile Bridge. The idyllic, palm-shaded beach at Bahia Honda (Spanish for "deep bay") resembles a tropical island in the South Pacific. Pines, palms, and mangroves frame ocean views that shift from turquoise and violet to milky emerald and navy blue. The water temperature ranges from the low to mid-80s Fahrenheit, and refreshing Caribbean trade winds keep this sunbaked subtropical island comfortable year-round.

This southernmost state park for camping is the perfect place to while away the hours beachcombing, swimming, snorkeling, fishing, exploring, and bird-watching. Be sure to stroll the nature trail to see some of the unusual botanical growth (satinwood trees, spiny catesbaei, and dwarf morning glories) on this unique spit of land, as well as the many beautiful and rare birds (white-crowned pigeons, great white herons, roseate spoonbills, reddish egrets, ospreys, brown pelicans, and least terns) that pass through here.

For a glorious view, climb to the overlook, which includes the first two spans of the original Flagler train trestle and the abandoned narrow span where more than one RV lost an outside mirror in a highway squeeze play. Many of the old bridges in the Upper and Lower Keys, including this one, offer anglers spots to dangle their hooks for mackerel, bluefish, tarpon, snook, grouper, and jewfish. According to a park ranger, tarpon fishing in Bahia Honda rates among the best in the country.

Three campgrounds tempt RVers and tent-campers to linger. Typical of Florida state parks, this one is clean and well maintained. Reservations are suggested, especially around holidays. The campsites are reserved for those who call ahead (reservations are taken up to 11 months in advance). There are six cabins, which also may be reserved in advance. For campsite or cabin reservations, call (800) 326-3521. Bahia Honda State Park, Overseas Highway, Big Pine Key; (305) 872-3210; www.floridastateparks.org.

Dainty Key deer wander through the slash pines and mangrove swamps on Big Pine and a few surrounding keys. This fragile subspecies, thought to have been stranded when the Wisconsin Glacier melted, is the smallest of all whitetail deer. From 26 to 32 inches in height, the deer average 38 inches in length and weigh between 30 and 110 pounds. By 1954 hunting and destruction of habitat had reduced the population of deer to 50. The establishment of the **National Key Deer Refuge** protected the herd, which has stabilized at about 300. These deer, the size of a large dog, are still threatened with extinction, primarily because of loss of habitat and ill-advised feeding by residents and visitors. Feeding can cause the deer to congregate and bring them in contact with such death traps as cars, canals, fences, and dogs. It is now against the law to feed the deer.

National Key Deer Refuge is north of US 1 on Key Deer Boulevard (SR 940). The refuge headquarters is in the Winn-Dixie Big Pine Key Plaza on Key Deer Boulevard, Big Pine Key. Best times to see deer are early morning, late afternoon, and early evening on the north end of Key Deer Boulevard and No Name Key. **Blue Hole,** a rock quarry with an alligator guarding a sign that says PLEASE DON'T FEED THE ALLIGATORS, is nearby. Get information on National Key Deer Refuge at the refuge visitor center in Big Pine Key Shopping Center, or contact the refuge manager at (305) 872-2239; www.fws.gov/nationalkeydeer.

If you don't feel romantic on **Little Palm Island,** you'd better check your pulse. This is the place romantics dream about, a secluded South Seas kind of island abloom with lush tropical foliage including a dense grove of soaring Jamaican coconut palms. And get this: You don't have to jet to the vast reaches of the South Pacific to find this idyllic retreat. It's just 3 miles offshore in the heart of the Florida Keys.

Once upon a time, this five-acre island served as a fishing camp and private getaway for Presidents Roosevelt, Truman, Kennedy, and Nixon, plus a string of other dignitaries and celebrities. Since 1988 it's been a luxury resort for those seeking the ultimate escape from reality.

As you approach the island, you'll catch a glimpse of thatched roofs peeking from beneath luxuriant greenery. These roofs belong to 14 stilted villas scattered throughout the island. Each private abode comes with a secluded, wraparound sundeck, an enticing rope hammock strung between gracefully curved palm trees, and an ocean view.

Inside you'll find a living room, an expansive bedroom with king-size bed draped in gauzy, for-effect-only mosquito netting, and a sitting area. The dressing area and bathroom, complete with whirlpool bath, open directly to a bamboo-fenced, totally private outdoor shower. Go ahead and pinch yourself. Try to remember this is not Fiji—this is Florida.

Every modern comfort is at your disposal, from a minibar to a wet bar with plenty of coffee and tea. However, you will not find the spirit-jarring intrusions of television, telephones, and alarm clocks. They are banned from the island. After all, this is supposed to be a romantic hideaway.

Tropical islands usually unveil their flaws on closer inspection. What Little Palm Island reveals is a heated lagoonlike freshwater pool fringed by palms, a waterfall, flowering shrubs, birds, and a sugar-white-sand beach.

You now have a tough decision. Do you simply relax and enjoy the ambience, or do you take advantage of the resort's many activities? Kayaks, canoes, sailboats, fishing equipment, and snorkeling gear are complimentary. You may want to perk up your appetite with a workout in the exercise room near the Gift Boutique.

Perhaps you'd rather go scuba diving or snorkeling or try your hand at deep-sea fishing. Several offshore and mainland excursions are offered, and guided nature tours by canoe or sailboat are popular. Divers will definitely want to join an excursion to nearby Looe Key to explore the wonders of the last living coral reef in North America.

If your idea of a vacation is simply to relax and be pampered, you'll want to indulge yourself with a spa treatment including a relaxing massage, a facial, and a manicure or pedicure.

Little Palm Island is a delightful spot to enjoy wildlife. Great white herons, little green herons, night herons, frigate birds, white ibises, brown pelicans, ospreys, skimmers, egrets, sandpipers, roseate spoonbills, manatees, dolphins, Key deer, and loggerhead turtles are common sights in the four separate nature preserves near the island and on the surrounding ocean flats.

The island is on the flyway for birds making their spring migratory trip north from the Caribbean basin and Central and South America. Bird migration peaks in early May and continues throughout the month. More than 100 migratory species include blackpoll warblers, palm warblers, falcons, kestrels, orioles, tanagers, bobolinks, cuckoos, ovenbirds, and black-bellied plovers.

OTHER ATTRACTIONS WORTH SEEING IN THE FLORIDA KEYS

Bahama Village, Key West

The Curry Mansion, Key West, www
.currymansion.com

Dolphin Research Center, Grassy Key,
www.dolphins.org

**Florida Keys Wild Bird Rehabilitation
Center,** Tavernier, www.flkwbc.org

Key West Aquarium, Marathon, www
.keywestaquarium.com

**The Maritime Museum of the Florida
Keys,** Key Largo, www.melfisher.org

The water below the resort dock is a favorite hangout for tarpon, bone-fish, angelfish, snapper, lookdown fish, and snook. Sometimes in the evenings hundreds of great tarpon roll around in the deep water at the end of the dock.

You'll notice a sign by the outdoor dining room indicating it is off limits to Key deer. These deer know a good menu when they catch wind of it. These diminutive mammals often swim over to Little Palm from a neighboring island to see what's going on. If they don't show up for dinner, you can commandeer a canoe the next day and paddle to nearby Big Munson Island, home to a herd of about 30 endangered deer.

One thing all resort guests seem to enjoy is eating. The island's gourmet cuisine combines regional cuisine with Caribbean and Asian influences. It's hard to beat an entree of locally caught stone-crab claws, but perhaps the rack of lamb, seared with mustard and served with a Madeira sauce, will do just that. If you're in the mood for a totally decadent dessert, select the bittersweet chocolate soufflé with Guanaja chocolate sauce or the passion fruit crème brûlée.

You may order breakfast served in your room or on your private deck. For lunch and dinner you may dine in the airy dining room, outdoors on a spacious terrace, or a few steps down on the resort's pristine sandy beach. The Tropical Sunday Brunch buffet is an island tradition. You don't need to be a resort guest to take advantage of the superb cuisine on any day, but you do need a reservation. The public may make dining reservations by calling (305) 872-2551.

Little Palm Resort is at the western end of the Newfound Harbor Keys, where the Gulf of Mexico meets the Straits of Florida. The island is a 15-minute launch ride from its Shore Station on Little Torch Key. Little Torch Key is on Overseas Highway (US 1) at Mile Marker 28.5, approximately 28 miles east of

Key West International Airport, 22 miles south of Marathon Airport, and 120 miles southwest of Miami International Airport.

Transfer and van service to the Little Torch Key Shore Station is available from both Key West and Marathon Airports. Limousine service can be arranged from Key West, Marathon, and Miami International Airports. Seaplane service is available from Miami. Advance notice is required for all these services. Contact Little Palm Island, 28500 Overseas Hwy., Little Torch Key; (305) 515-4004 or (800) 343-8567; www.littlepalmisland.com.

Now here's a batty idea: a high-rise for bats. This weather-beaten, 35-foot wooden tower was built to solve a problem. You see, Righter Clyde Perky wanted tourists to enjoy his guest cottages, restaurant, and marina, but they were turned off by hordes of dive-bombing mosquitoes. Perky knew bats had a ravenous appetite for mosquitoes, so he built them the most comfortable lodging he could think of and decorated it with sex-scented bat droppings imported from Texas. Unfortunately, the bats never got wind of the project (although the neighbors certainly did), and the tower remains uninhabited. Modern spraying techniques have largely done away with the mosquito problem, but who can say the tower isn't a success in its own right? After all, it has survived several hurricanes and is listed on the National Register of Historic Places. The **Perky Bat Tower** is near Mile Marker 17 on the Gulf side of US 1 on Sugarloaf Key.

Key West Area

At the end of the Overseas Highway where the Atlantic meets the Gulf of Mexico is Key West, the southernmost city in the continental US. Here the Calusa Indians made a final stand against invading tribes from the north. The Spanish, who came upon the grisly remains of the battle, named it Cayo Hueso, which translates to the "island of bones." Eventually this was anglicized into Key West.

Unruffled by the crosscurrents of its cultural heritage, this exotic community has long been a mecca for writers, artists, and other well-knowns. The claim is that Key West is not really a place but an attitude. The community's freewheeling spirit once led it to secede from the Union, establish the Conch Republic, and demand foreign aid from the US government! On this 5-by-3-mile island, Tennessee Williams spent the final years of his life, Harry Truman had his *Little White House,* and John James Audubon painted tropical birds.

Stop in to visit the six-toed cats (direct descendants of those loved by "Papa" Hemingway) at the Ernest Hemingway Home and Museum. Hemingway bought this Spanish colonial–style house in 1931 and wrote a number of novels here. You'll see memorabilia, original furnishings, and exotic trees and plants from around the world. Open 9 a.m. to 5 p.m. daily 365 days a year.

End of the Road

Key West Cemetery, bordered by Francis, Angela, and Olivia Streets, is a browsable tribute to a truly off-the-beaten-path community. Most of the tombs are aboveground, many identified only by first names or nicknames. You'll want to read the epitaphs, including the infamous "I told you I was sick."

There are separate sections for those of the Jewish and Catholic faiths, and many Cuban crypts are adorned with a statue of a chicken. The chicken usually denotes Santería, a mix of Catholicism and animist beliefs held by descendants of former slaves from Africa.

Find the statue of a tiny Key deer, and you will be in a special section of the cemetery devoted to pets. And don't miss the monument to the crewmen of the battleship USS *Maine* who died in Havana Harbor at the beginning of the Spanish-American War in 1898. The monument is marked by the statue of a single sailor.

The ***Ernest Hemingway Home and Museum*** is located at 907 Whitehead St., Key West. Call (305) 294-1136 or go online at www.hemingwayhome.com for more information.

More Hemingway memorabilia is on tap at ***Sloppy Joe's,*** Papa's favorite bar, at 201 Duval St., Key West.

The ***Audubon House and Tropical Gardens*** contain many of John J. Audubon's original engravings as well as a video about his life. Authentically restored with 18th- and 19th-century furnishings, this early-19th-century house is now a public museum. Once you've seen the incredible bird life on the Keys, it's not hard to understand why this famed naturalist/artist spent so much time here. The Audubon House is open 9:30 a.m. to 5 p.m. daily and is located at 205 Whitehead St., at Greene St., Key West. Call (305) 294-2116 for more information or go to www.audubonhouse.com.

Tennis enthusiasts should head straight for ***Bay View Park*** to experience what must be the most democratic tennis system in the world. Bay View Tennis Club, as it is affectionately dubbed by its many regulars, can be found a few blocks from the cemetery, where Florida Street runs into Truman Avenue. On any given morning, there will be an eclectic mix of locals, snowbirds, and weekly vacationers. To

keywest dreaming

[Key West was] one of the most exhilarating experiences of my life; coming into Key West was like floating into a dream.

—John dos Passos, who rode a train into Key West in the 1920s participate, you simply add your name to the list on the clipboard, and when your name comes up, it's your turn to play a set of doubles. If you want to play another set, you sign up again and will probably play with a different group of people. Play begins early, but until late morning there will almost always be a sizable group socializing in the three-sided "clubhouse" as players wait their turns. Feel free to join them, even if you are not going to play.

An hour's visit to the popular *Key West Butterfly and Nature Conservatory* provides a quiet respite from the bustle of Duval Street. Located 1 block north of the Southernmost Point, the yellow house at 1316 Duval contains a learning center and gift shop that open into a 6,000-square-foot glass mini-paradise where you can wander among more than 1,500 butterflies and hundreds of exotic birds and plants. The butterflies are most active between 9:30 and 2:30, but a late-afternoon visit yields its own reward: The butterflies cluster by species as they settle in for their night's rest. Tickets are sold daily from 9 a.m. to 4:30 p.m. Viewing ends at 5 p.m. 1316 Duval St., Key West; (305) 296-2988; www.keywestbutterfly.com.

Although touristy Duval is Key West's most famous street, there is another perspective just blocks away. Walk or rent a bike to explore the quaint conch architecture and lovely tropical gardens found on the quieter streets of *Old Town.* Start with Caroline, Fleming, Southard, parts of Eaton and Simonton, and the tiny residential streets near the cemetery in an area called the Meadows. If you have time, slip into Nancy Forrester's Secret Garden at the end of Free School Lane (just past 521 Simonton). A private garden for 25 years, it is now open to the public for a small fee. Picnicking is encouraged. Open 10 a.m. to 5 p.m. daily. Self-guided tours. Phone (305) 294-0015.

Those with an interest in Florida's ecological systems should visit the *Florida Keys Eco-Discovery Center.* Conveniently located next to Zachary Taylor Park, the center provides touch-screen interactive exhibits for kids, a replica of the underwater ocean laboratory Aquarius, a gift shop, and a beautiful 20-minute film in its air-conditioned theater. Parking and admission are free. Open Tues through Sat 9 a.m. to 4 p.m. Phone (305) 809-4750; http://floridakeys.noaa.gov/eco_discovery.html.

The *Mel Fisher Maritime Heritage Society Museum* displays treasures recovered from Spanish galleons that have been slumbering on the ocean floor for centuries. Along with more than 150 pounds of gold are silver bullion, emeralds, diamonds, copper, brass cannons, rare antiques, and a wonderful collection of historic artifacts. All told, the treasure, worth more than $40 million, is one of the largest displays of its type anywhere.

Feast your eyes on gold doubloons and discs, more than 50 gold bars, and 35 gold chains—including one measuring 12 feet long and weighing more than six pounds. The prize piece from the recovered collection is a gold poison cup featuring a bezoar stone that changes color when it comes in contact with a toxic substance. You just can't be too careful! Open 9:30 a.m. to 5 p.m. daily. The Mel Fisher Maritime Heritage Society Museum is at 200 Greene St., Key West; open 8:30 a.m. to 5 p.m. Mon through Fri, 9:30 a.m. to 5 p.m. weekends and holidays; (305) 294-2633; www.melfisher.org.

Once shipwrecks were the area's economic mainstay. Settlers from the mainland, the Bahamas, and Europe flocked to the Keys to partake in the rich harvest of the sea. In 1825 Congress legislated that all salvage taken from wrecks in US waters must be taken to a US port for arbitration. Key West, as the islands' first permanent settlement, became the center for the auction of cargoes and repair of ships. By the 1830s wrecking had made Key West the wealthiest city, per capita, in the entire US. The long dreary years of economic drought that followed were not endured in vain. Had the town enjoyed a history of uninterrupted prosperity rather than prolonged recession, its architectural treasure trove might have been leveled to make way for more modern buildings.

The **Wrecker's Museum** in the Oldest House in Key West is actually two houses, typical of 1830s "conch" construction. Browse the displays on the wrecking industry that once made Key West such a wealthy community. Don't miss the elegantly furnished dollhouse, the old kitchen house, and large garden. Guided tours are conducted 10 a.m. to 4 p.m. daily. Maintained by the Old Island Restoration Foundation, 322 Duval St., Key West; (305) 294-9501; www.oirf.org.

A massive restoration effort, centered on **Duval Street,** is currently saving classic buildings that infuse the city with its old-world air. The architecture is a mélange of Bahamian, Spanish, New England, and Southern styles. The Oldest House (circa 1829) in Key West is typical of small residences of that time. Many old homes were built in the 1850s by master ship carpenters who insisted on the best materials and used wooden pegs instead of nails. These handsome homes with wide verandas and gingerbread trim suggest a slower, more gracious era. Some of the most attractive, known as "conch" houses, were built in sections in the Bahamas and shipped over on schooners.

If you can, schedule your visit to coincide with **Old Island Days House Tours and Art Festival,** which begins in December and ends in March. There are four house tours scattered over four weekends, and the art festival is always the last weekend in February. There's even a conch-shell-blowing contest. For information, contact the Key West Tourist Development Council at (800) FLA-KEYS (352-5397) or (305) 296-1552; www.fla-keys.com.

Natives of Key West are called Conchs (pronounced "konks") for the mollusk that thrives in local waters. This favorite local delicacy appears in chowders, fritters, and conch salad and as conch steak. Don't leave the islands without sampling stone crab, Florida lobster, shrimp, and fresh-off-the-boat swordfish, yellowtail, and red snapper. This is the perfect place to indulge in traditional Cuban dishes. Be sure to try a bowl of black-bean soup and some bollos (pronounced "bowyows"), hush puppies made with mashed, shelled black-eyed peas instead of cornmeal. For dessert, key lime pie, made from the piquant key limes that flourish here, wins hands down.

Tourists who take the *Conch Tour Train,* an open-air tram, get a good look at the restoration area as well as the island's major points of interest. This 1.5 tour promises "more than one hundred of the most unusual historical sites you've ever seen." Boarding locations are Mallory Square and Flagler Station. Tours leave approximately every half hour 9 a.m. to 4:30 p.m. daily. Contact Conch Tour Train at 1805 Staples Ave. #101, Key West; (305) 294-5161 or (888) 916-8687; www.conchtourtrain.com.

History buffs will want to visit the *Fort East Martello Museum and Gardens,* part of the 19th-century effort to fortify the country's southern boundary. Ground was broken for East Martello Tower in 1861, but the fort was never involved in a battle. A large collection of artifacts from the Keys (including implements used in cigar making and sponge diving) is housed in the fort's long series of casements, and two permanent art collections are on display. Open 9:30 a.m. to 5 p.m. daily. Fort East Martello Museum and Gardens is adjacent to the airport at 3501 S. Roosevelt Blvd., Key West 33040; (305) 296-3913; www.kwahs.com.

You'll get a commanding view from the 86-foot tower of the lighthouse in the *Key West Lighthouse and Keepers Quarters Museum.* Built in 1847, the museum pays tribute to the unique military history of the Florida Keys and contains many military artifacts. Open 9:30 a.m. to 4:30 p.m. daily. Key West Lighthouse Museum, 938 Whitehead St., Key West; (305) 294-0012; www.kwahs.com.

Key West's newest state park, dedicated on July 4, 1985, is *Fort Zachary Taylor Historic State Park.* This pre–Civil War fortress is a reminder of a time when Union troops occupied Key West during the Civil War. To uncover Fort Taylor's mysteries, Howard England worked alone for more than 10 years with bucket and shovel to uncover the country's largest known collection of Civil War cannons. He assembled a small museum with artifacts, photographs, and a model of the original fort. The park, with one of the finest natural beaches on the island, is an ideal spot to swim and picnic. Open 8 a.m. to sunset every day. Fort Zachary Taylor Historic State Park, 601 Howard England Way, Key West; (305) 292-6713; www.floridastateparks.org.

At Key West arrangements can be made to fly 68 miles west to *Fort Jefferson* and *Dry Tortugas National Park.* The low-flying seaplane passes over shifting sandbars, clearly identifiable sharks, and an old Spanish wreck that has coughed up millions of dollars worth of treasure. Passengers look down on the Marquesas, a ring of islands considered by some to be the only atoll in the Atlantic Ocean.

The Tortugas were considered of great strategic importance to the US. Because the US War Department believed the nation that occupied these islands could protect navigation in the Gulf, it decided to fortify them. Construction began on Fort Jefferson in 1846. Complete with 50-foot-high walls and a water-filled moat, the hexagonal fort covered most of 16-acre Garden Key. It was to be the strongest link in the chain of coastal forts that reached from Maine to Texas during the first half of the 1800s.

drytortugas

Ponce de León discovered the Dry Tortugas in 1513. The islands were named by the Spanish explorer for the abundance of sea turtles (*tortugas* in Spanish) he found there. Later "dry" was added to the name to indicate the lack of freshwater. For most of the next 400 years, the islands were nominally part of the Spanish colonial empire. Spanish patrol vessels frequented the area, as did Spanish ships, especially those laden with treasure passing just offshore en route from Mexico to Havana. Many ships wrecked on these reefs and shoals due to fierce storms and navigation errors.

Federal troops occupied Fort Jefferson throughout the Civil War but saw little action. Although work continued on the fort for 30 years, it was never completed, primarily because the new rifled cannon introduced during the war had already made it obsolete. Used as a military stronghold for captured deserters during the Civil War, Fort Jefferson continued as a prison for almost 10 years after the fighting had ceased.

The fort's most famous prisoner was Dr. Samuel Mudd, the physician who set John Wilkes Booth's broken leg after Booth assassinated Abraham Lincoln (and who was convicted of conspiracy for aiding Booth in the assassination). Brought here in 1865 and sentenced to a lifetime of hard labor, he earned an early pardon by tirelessly tending to the victims of a yellow fever epidemic that swept through the fort. Be sure to see the orientation slide program before taking the self-guided tour.

Snorkeling is especially good off the moat walls of Fort Jefferson. Coral formations and brilliant tropical fish provide fine opportunities for underwater photography. Saltwater fishing is good most of the year, and no fishing license is required.

Fort Jefferson Visitors Center is open 8 a.m. to 5 p.m. daily. Public transportation to the fort is available from Key West by seaplane or boat. Those who want to go by private boat may purchase nautical charts at marinas and boating-supply outlets in Key West. Boaters should be aware of the possibility of extremely rough seas. The Tortugas are isolated, and you must provide for yourself. No housing, water, meals, or supplies are available. Camping is permitted in the grassed picnic area. For information on charter boats and flights, contact the Key West Chamber of Commerce, 402 Wall St., Old Mallory Square, Key West; (305) 294-2587; www.keywestchamber.org. For information on a ferry trip (8 a.m. to 7 p.m.) from Key West to Dry Tortugas National Park, call (877) 243-2378; www.keywestchamber.org. For information on Fort Jefferson and Dry Tortugas National Park, call (305) 242-7700; www.nps.gov/drto.

Frigate birds with 7-foot wingspans soar above the cerulean waters surrounding the *Dry Tortugas.* Sooty terns, which have turned Bush Key into a rookery, lay their eggs in shallow depressions on its warm sandy beaches. The Tortugas also host noddy terns, brown and blue-faced boobies, and a variety of passing songbirds en route from Cuba and South America. During the nesting season from March to October, Bush Key is reserved for birds only. All keys except Garden Key and Loggerhead Key are closed during the turtle-nesting season from May through the end of September.

Visitors should not leave Key West without seeing the ***southernmost point in the continental US.*** (The Big Island of Hawaii claims the honor for the nation.) Chinese immigrant Jim Kee began selling shells here in the late 1930s, and his descendants still cater to tourists' yen for souvenirs.

Some of Key West's appeal is its temperature, which varies only 12 degrees all year and averages a balmy 77 degrees Fahrenheit, and some is its luxuriant palms, hibiscus, oleander, bougainvillea, and fragrant frangipani blooms. But the city's greatest charm is that it is a true original.

Few other communities have the good sense to celebrate such a daily marvel as the sunset. The crowd starts to gather at *Mallory Square* about half an hour before the main event. The Cookie Lady, when she comes, arrives on her bicycle and does a bustling business selling warm brownies and cookies. Locals show off their parrots and pet iguanas. Some juggle, dance, sing, or swallow flaming swords. All the entertainment is free (although the entertainers do pass a hat). After the sun's final farewell, everyone heartily applauds the performance. For those who have purposely strayed far from the beaten path, it is an entirely appropriate celebration—a fine way to end a day or, for that matter, a book.

State Parks in the Keys

State park information: (850) 245-2157 or www .floridastateparks.org. For camping reservations in any state park, call (800) 326-3521.

Bahia Honda State Park, (305) 872-2353

Curry Hammock State Park, (305) 289-2690

Fort Zachary Taylor Historic State Park, (305) 292-6713

Indian Key Historic State Park, (305) 664-2540

John Pennekamp Coral Reef State Park, (305) 451-1202

Lignumvitae Key Botanical State Park, (305) 664-2540

Long Key State Park, (305) 664-4815

Windley Key Fossil Reef Geological State Park, (305) 664-2540

Places to Stay in the Keys

ISLAMORADA

Cheeca Lodge
81801 Overseas Hwy.
(305) 664-4651
www.cheeca.com

Kon-Tiki Resort
81200 Overseas Hwy.
(305) 664-4702
www.kontiki-resort.com

Pelican Cove
84457 Old Overseas Hwy.
(305) 664-4435
www.pcove.com

KEY LARGO

Marriott's Key Largo Bay Beach Resort
103800 Overseas Hwy.
(305) 453-0000
www.marriottkeylargo.com

Ramada Limited Resort & Marina
99751 Overseas Hwy.
(305) 451-3939
www.ramadakeylargo.com

Hilton Key Largo Resort
97000 S. Overseas Hwy.
(305) 852-5553 or
(888) 871-3437
www.keylargoresort.com

KEY WEST

Galleon Resort & Marina
617 Front St.
(305) 296-7711
www.galleonresort.com

DoubleTree Grand Key Resort
3990 S. Roosevelt Blvd.
(305) 293-1818
www.doubletree1.hilton .com

VISITOR INFORMATION FOR THE FLORIDA KEYS

Key Largo Chamber of Commerce, 106000 Overseas Hwy., Key Largo; (800) 822-1088; www.floridakeys.org

Key West Chamber of Commerce, 510 Greene St., 1st floor, Key West; (305) 294-2587 or (800) LAST-KEY (527-8539); www.keywestchamber.org

Key West Information Center, 201 Front St., Ste. 108, Key West; (305) 292-5000 or (888) 222-5590; www .keywestinfo.com

Monroe County Tourist Development Council—Florida Keys and Key West, 1201 White St., Ste. 102, Key West; (800) FLA-KEYS (352-5397) or (305) 296-1552; www.fla-keys.com

Pier House
1 Duval St.
(305) 296-4600 or
(800) 723-2791
www.pierhouse.com

MARATHON
Hawks Cay
61 Hawk's Cay Blvd.
Overseas Highway at Mile
Marker 61
Duck Key
(305) 743-7000 or
(888) 395-5539
www.hawkscay.com

Holiday Inn and Marina
13201 Overseas Hwy. at
Mile Marker 54
(305) 289-0222 or
(800) 449-1460
www.holidayinn.com

Places to Eat in the Keys

ISLAMORADA
Marker 88
Mile Marker 88, Overseas
Highway
(305) 852-9315
www.marker88.info

KEY LARGO
Mrs. Mac's Kitchen
Mile Marker 99.4
99336 Overseas Hwy.
(305) 451-3722
www.mrsmacskitchen.com

KEY WEST
Louie's Backyard
700 Waddell Ave.
(305) 294-1061
www.louiesbackyard.com

The Restaurant at
La-Te-Da
1125 Duval St.
(305) 296-6706 or
(877) 528-3320
www.lateda.com

Pisces (seafood)
1007 Simonton St.
(305) 294-7100
www.pisceskeywest.com

Florida State Parks

Florida State Parks are divided into five districts:

DISTRICT 1 (D1): NORTHEAST FLORIDA STATE PARKS

State parks located on the upper panhandle from the Gulf of Mexico to the east coast mainly between Tallahassee and Jacksonville.

DISTRICT 2 (D2): NORTHWEST FLORIDA STATE PARKS

State parks in the Florida panhandle mainly from Pensacola to Tallahassee.

DISTRICT 3 (D3): CENTRAL FLORIDA STATE PARKS

State parks located on the north side of Florida's east coast mainly from Jacksonville to Vero Beach.

DISTRICT 4 (D4): SOUTHWEST FLORIDA STATE PARKS

State parks located on the west coast of the Gulf of Mexico mainly from Homosassa Springs to Naples.

DISTRICT 5 (D5): SOUTHEAST FLORIDA STATE PARKS

State parks located on the east coast of Florida's southern tip mainly from Vero Beach to Key West.

We have listed the parks by first by name followed by the District in parenthesis.

For More Information:

Florida State Parks Information Center, Florida Division of Recreation and Parks, 900 Commonwealth Blvd., Tallahassee; (850) 245-2157; www.floridastateparks.org.

Reservation system for campsites and cabins: (800) 326-3521 (8 a.m. to 8 p.m.); (888) 433-0287 (TDD).

Listing of Parks by Name

Addison Blockhouse Historic State Park (D3)
2099 N. Beach St., Ormond Beach; (386) 676-4050

Alafia River State Park (D4)
14326 S. CR 39, South Lithia; (813) 672-5320

Alfred B. Maclay Gardens State Park (D2)
3540 Thomasville Rd., Tallahassee; (850) 487-4556

Amelia Island State Park (D1)
12157 Heckscher Dr., Jacksonville; (904) 251-2320

Anastasia State Park (D1)
1340A SR A1A, South Street, St. Augustine; (904) 461-2033

Anclote Key Preserve State Park (D3)
#1 Causeway Blvd., Dunedin; (727) 469-5942

Avalon State Park (D5)
See Fort Pierce Inlet State Park

Bahia Honda State Park (D5)
36850 Overseas Hwy., Big Pine Key; (305) 872-2353

Bald Point State Park (D2)
146 Box Cut, Alligator; (850) 349-9146

Barnacle Historic State Park (D5)
3485 Main Hwy., Coconut Grove; (305) 442-6866

Big Lagoon State Park (D2)
12301 Gulf Beach Hwy., Pensacola; (850) 492-1595

Big Shoals State Park (D1)
PO Drawer G, White Springs 32096; (386) 397-4331

Big Talbot Island State Park (D1)
12157 Heckscher Dr., Jacksonville; (904) 251-2320

Bill Baggs Cape Florida State Park (D5)
1200 S. Crandon Blvd., Key Biscayne; (305) 361-5811

Blackwater Heritage Trail State Park (D2)
7720 Deaton Bridge Rd., Holt; (850) 983-5363

Blackwater River State Park (D2)
7720 Deaton Bridge Rd., Holt; (850) 983-5363

Blue Spring State Park (D3)
2100 W. French Ave., Orange City; (386) 775-3663

Bulow Creek State Park (D1) (D3)
2099 N. Beach St., Ormond Beach; (386) 676-4040

Bulow Plantation Ruins Historic State Park (D1) (D3)
PO Box 655, Bunnel 32110; (386) 517-4050

Caladesi Island State Park (D3)
#1 Causeway Blvd., Dunedin; (727) 469-5918

Camp Helen State Park (D2)
23937 Panama City Beach Pkwy., Panama City Beach; (850) 233-5059

Cayo Costa State Park (D4)
PO Box 1150, Boca Grande, 33921; (941) 964-0375

Cedar Key Museum State Park (D2)
12231 SW 166 Ct., Cedar Key; (352) 543-5350

Cedar Key Scrub State Reserve (D2)
PO Box 187, Cedar Key 32625; (352) 543-5567

Charlotte Harbor State Park (D4)
12301 Burnt Store Rd., Punta Gorda; (941) 575-5861

Collier-Seminole State Park (D4)
20200 E. Tamiami Trail, Naples; (239) 394-3397

Constitution Convention Museum State Park (D2)
200 Allen Memorial Way, Port St. Joe; (850) 229-8029

Crystal River Archaeological State Park (D3)
3400 N. Museum Point, Crystal River; (352) 795-3817

Curry Hammock State Park (D5)
56200 Overseas Hwy., Marathon; (305) 289-2690

Dade Battlefield Historic State Park (D3)
7200 CR 603, S. Battlefield Drive, Bushnell; (352) 793-4781

Dagny Johnson Key Largo Hammock Botanical State Park (D5)
PO Box 487, Key Largo 33037; (305) 451-1202

Deer Lake State Park (D2)
357 Main Park Rd., Santa Rosa Beach; (850) 267-8300

DeLeon Springs State Park (D3)
601 Ponce DeLeon Blvd., DeLeon Springs; (386) 985-4212

Delnor–Wiggins Pass State Park (D4)
11100 Gulfshore Dr., Naples; (239) 597-6196

DeSoto Site (D2)
1022 DeSoto Park Dr., Tallahassee; (850) 922-6007

Devil's Millhopper Geological State Park (D1)
4732 Millhopper Rd., Gainesville; (352) 955-2008

Don Pedro Island State Park (D4)
PO Box 1150, Boca Grande 33921; (941) 964-0375

Dr. Julian G. Bruce (St. George Island) State Park (D2)
1900 E. Gulf Beach Dr., St. George Island; (850) 927-2111

Dudley Farm Historic State Park (D1)
18730 W. Newberry Rd., Newberry; (352) 472-1142

Econfina River State Park (D2)
4384 Econfina River Rd., Lamont; (850) 922-6007

Eden Gardens State Park (D2)
PO Box 26, Point Washington 32454; (850) 267-8320

Edward Ball Wakulla Springs State Park (D2)
550 Wakulla Park Dr., Wakulla Springs; (850) 926-0700

Egmont Key (D4)
4905 34th St. South, #5000, St. Petersburg; (727) 893-2627

Estero Bay Preserve (D4)
PO Box 7, Estero 33928; (239) 992-0311

Fakahatchee Strand Preserve State Park (D4)
PO Box 548, Copeland 33926; (941) 695-4593

Falling Waters State Park (D2)
1130 State Park Rd., Chipley; (850) 638-6130

Fanning Springs State Park (D1)
18020 NW US 19, Fanning Springs; (352) 463-3420

Faver-Dykes State Park (D1)
1000 Faver Dykes Rd., St. Augustine; (904) 794-0997

Fernandina Plaza Historic State Park (D1)
See Fort Clinch State Park

Florida Caverns State Park (D2)
3345 Caverns Rd., Marianna; (850) 482-9598

Forest Capital Museum State Park (D2)
204 Forest Park Dr., Perry; (850)
584-3227

Fort Clinch State Park (D1)
2601 Atlantic Ave., Fernandina Beach;
(904) 277-7274

Fort Cooper State Park (D3)
3100 S. Old Floral City Rd., Inverness;
(352) 726-0315

**Fort George Island Cultural State Park
(D1)** .
12157 Heckscher Dr., Jacksonville; (904)
251-2320

Fort Pierce Inlet State Park (D3)
905 Shorewinds Dr., Fort Pierce; (772)
468-3985

**Fort Zachary Taylor Historic State Park
(D5)**
PO Box 6560, Key West 33041; (305)
292-6713

**Fred Gannon Rocky Bayou State Park
(D2)**
4281 SR 20, Niceville; (850) 833-9144

Gainesville-Hawthorne State Trail (D1)
Region 2 Administration, 4801 Camp
Ranch Rd., Gainesville; (352) 466-3397

**Gamble Plantation State Historic Site
(D4)**
3708 Patten Ave., Ellenton; (941)
723-4536

**Gamble Rogers Memorial State
Recreation Area at Flagler Beach (D1)**
3100 S. SR A1A, Flagler Beach; (386)
517-2086

Gasparilla Island State Park (D4)
PO Box 1150, Boca Grande 33921; (941)
964-0375

**George Crady Bridge Fishing Pier
State Park (D1)**
12157 Heckscher Dr., Jacksonville; (904)
251-2320

Grayton Beach State Park (D2)
357 Main Park Rd., Santa Rosa Beach;
(850) 231-4210

Guana River State Park (D1)
2690 S. Ponte Vedra Blvd., Ponte Vedra
Beach; (904) 823-4500

Henderson Beach State Park (D2)
17000 Emerald Coast Pkwy., Destin;
(850) 837-7550

Highlands Hammock State Park (D3)
5931 Hammock Rd., Sebring; (863)
386-6094

Hillsborough River State Park (D3)
15402 US 301 North, Thonotosassa;
(813) 987-6771

**Homosassa Springs Wildlife State Park
(D3)**
4150 S. Suncoast Blvd., Homosassa;
(352) 628-5343

Honeymoon Island State Park (D3)
#1 Causeway Blvd., Dunedin; (727)
469-5942

Hontoon Island State Park (D3)
2309 River Ridge Rd., DeLand; (386)
736-5309

Hugh Taylor Birch State Park (D5)
3109 E. Sunrise Blvd., Fort Lauderdale;
(954) 564-4521

Ichetucknee Springs State Park (D1)
12087 SW US 27, Fort White; (386)
497-4690

Indian Key Historic State Park (D5)
PO Box 1052, Islamorada 33036; (305)
664-2540

**John D. MacArthur Beach State Park
(D5)**
10900 SR A1A, North Palm Beach; (561)
624-6950

John Gorrie Museum State Park (D2)
PO Box 267, Apalachicola 32329; (850)
653-9347

John Pennekamp Coral Reef State Park (D5)
PO Box 487, Key Largo, 33037; (305) 451-1202

John U. Lloyd Beach State Park (D5)
6503 N. Ocean Dr., Dania; (954) 923-2833

Jonathan Dickinson State Park (D5)
16450 SE Federal Hwy., Hobe Sound; (561) 546-2771

Judah P. Benjamin Confederate Memorial at Gamble Plantation State Historic Site (D4)
3708 Patten Ave., Ellenton; (941) 723-4536

Key Largo Hammocks Botanical State Park (D5)
PO Box 487, Key Largo 33037; (305) 451-1202

Kissimmee Prairie Preserve State Park (D3)
33104 NW 192 Ave., Okeechobee; (863) 462-5360

Koreshan State Historic Site (D4)
PO Box 7, Estero 33928; (239) 992-0311

Lafayette Blue Springs State Park (D1)
799 NW Blue Springs Rd., Mayo; (386) 294-3667

Lake Griffin State Park (D3)
3089 US 441-27, Fruitland Park; (352) 360-6760

Lake Jackson Mounds Archaeological State Park (D2)
3600 Indian Mounds Rd., Tallahassee; (850) 922-6007

Lake June-in-Winter Scrub State Park (D4)
See Highlands Hammock State Park

Lake Kissimmee State Park (D3)
14248 Camp Mack Rd., Lake Wales; (863) 696-1112

Lake Louisa State Park (D3)
7305 US 27, Clermont; (352) 394-3969

Lake Manatee State Park (D3)
20007 SR 64 East, Bradenton; (941) 741-3028

Lake Talquin State Park (D2)
1022 DeSoto Park Dr., Tallahassee; (850) 922-6007

Letchworth Mounds (D2)
4500 Sunray Rd. South, Monticello; (850) 922-6007

Lignumvitae Key Botanical State Park (D5)
PO Box 1052, Islamorada 33036; (305) 664-2540

Little Manatee River State Park (D3)
215 Lightfoot Rd., Wimauma; (813) 671-5005

Little Talbot Island State Park (D1)
12157 Heckscher Dr., Jacksonville; (904) 251-2320

Long Key State Park (D5)
PO Box 776, Long Key, 33001; (305) 664-4815

Lovers Key State Park (D4)
8700 Estero Blvd., Fort Myers Beach; (239) 463-4588

Lower Wekiva River Preserve State Park (D3)
1800 Wekiwa Circle, Apopka; (407) 884-2008

Manatee Springs State Park (D2)
11650 NW 115th St., Chiefland; (352) 493-6072

Marjorie Kinnan Rawlings Historic State Park (D1)
18700 S. CR 325, Cross Creek; (352) 466-3672

Mike Roess Gold Head Branch State Park (D1)
6239 SR 21, Keystone Heights; (352) 473-4701

Myakka River State Park (D4)
13207 SR 72, Sarasota; (941) 361-6511

Natural Bridge Battlefield Historic State Park (D2)
7052 Natural Bridge Rd., Tallahassee; (850) 922-6007

Ochlockonee River State Park (D2)
PO Box 5, Sopchoppy 32358; (850) 962-2771

O'Leno State Park (D1)
410 SE Olena Park Rd., High Springs; (386) 454-1853

Oleta River State Park (D5)
3400 NE 163rd St., North Miami; (305) 919-1844

Olustee Battlefield Historic State Park (D1)
PO Box 40, Olustee 32072; (386) 758-0400

Oscar Scherer State Park (D4)
1843 S. Tamiami Trail, Osprey; (941) 483-5956

Payne's Creek Historic State Park (D3)
888 Lake Branch Rd., Bowling Green; (863) 375-4717

Paynes Prairie Preserve State Park (D1)
100 Savannah Blvd., Micanopy; (352) 466-3397

Peacock Springs State Park (D2)
18081 185th Rd., Live Oak; (386) 776-2194

Perdido Key State Park (D2)
12301 Gulf Beach Hwy., Pensacola; (850) 492-1595

Ponce de Leon Springs State Park (D2)
2860 Ponce de Leon Springs Rd., Ponce de Leon; (850) 836-4281

Pumpkin Hill Creek Preserve State Park (D1)
13802 Pumpkin Hill Rd., Jacksonville; (904) 696-5980

Rainbow Springs State Park (D1)
19158 SW 81st Place Rd., Dunnellon; (352) 465-8550

Ravine Gardens State Park (D1)
1600 Twigg St., Palatka; (386) 329-3721

River Rise Preserve State Park (D1)
410 SE Olena Park Rd., High Springs; (386) 454-1853

Rock Springs Run State Reserve (D3)
See Wekiwa Springs State Park

Rocky Bayou State Park (D2)
4281 SR 20, Niceville; (850) 833-9144

St. Andrews State Park (D2)
4607 State Park Ln., Panama City; (850) 233-5140

St. George Island State Park (D2)
1900 E. Gulf Beach Dr., St. George Island; (850) 927-2111

St. Lucie Inlet Preserve State Park (D5)
4810 SE Cove Rd., Stuart; (772) 219-1880

San Felasco Hammock Preserve State Park (D1)
12720 NW 109 Ln., Aluchua; (386) 462-7905

San Marcos de Apalache Historic State Park (D2)
148 Old Fort Rd., St. Marks; (850) 925-6216

San Pedro Underwater Archaeological Preserve State Park (D5)
PO Box 1052, Islamorada 33036; (305) 664-2540

Savannas Preserve State Park (D3)
9551 Gumbo Limbo Ln., Jansen Beach; (772) 398-2779

Seabranch Preserve State Park (D5)
4810 SE Cove Rd., Stuart; (772) 219-1880

Sebastian Inlet State Park (D5)
9700 S. SR A1A, Melbourne Beach; (321) 984-4852

Silver River State Park (D3)
1425 NE 58th Ave., Ocala; (352) 236-7148

Skyway Fishing Pier State Park (D4)
4905 34th St. South #5000, St. Petersburg; (727) 865-0668

Stephen Foster Folk Culture Center State Park (D2)
PO Drawer G, White Springs 32096; (386) 397-2733

Stump Pass Beach State Park (D4)
PO Box 1150, Boca Grande 33921; (914) 964-0375

Suwannee River State Park (D1)
20185 CR 132, Live Oak; (386) 362-2746

T. H. Stone Memorial (St. Joseph Peninsula) State Park (D2)
8899 Cape San Blas Rd., Port St. Joe; (850) 227-1327

Tallahassee–St. Marks Historic Railroad Trail State Park (D2)
3900 Commonwealth Blvd., MS 795, Tallahassee; (850) 245-2052

Tarklin Bayou Preserve State Park (D2)
See Big Lagoon State Park

Three Rivers State Park (D2)
7908 Three Rivers Park Rd., Sneads; (850) 482-9006

Tomoka State Park (D3)
2099 N. Beach St., Ormond Beach; (386) 676-4050

Topsail Hill Preserve State Park (D2)
7525 W. Scenic Highway 30A, Santa Rosa Beach; (850) 267-0299

Torreya State Park (D2)
2576 NW Torreya Park Rd., Bristol; (850) 643-2674

Troy Spring State Park (D1)
674 NE Troy Springs Rd., Banford; (386) 935-4835

Waccasassa Bay Preserve State Park (D3)
PO Box 187, Cedar Key 32625; (352) 543-5567

Washington Oaks Gardens State Park (D3)
6400 N. Oceanshore Blvd., Palm Coast; (386) 446-6780

Wekiwa Springs State Park (D3)
1800 Wekiwa Circle, Apopka; (407) 884-2008

Werner–Boyce Salt Springs State Park (D4)
PO Box 490, Port Richey 34673; (727) 816-1890

Windley Key Fossil Reef Geological State Park (D5)
PO Box 1052, Islamorada 33036; (305) 664-2540

Withlacoochee Trail State Park (D1)
315 N. Apopka Ave., Inverness; (352) 726-2251

Ybor City Museum State Park (D3)
1818 9th Ave., Tampa; (813) 247-6323

Yellow Bluff Fort Historic State Park (D1)
12157 Heckscher Dr., Jacksonville; (904) 251-2320

Yulee Sugar Mill Ruins Historic State Park (D3)
3400 N. Museum Point, Crystal River; (352) 795-3817

Index

Already "Been There, Done That"?
Then Get Off the Beaten Path!

"For the traveler who enjoys the special, the unusual,
and the unexpected."—*The Traveler* newsletter

Alabama	Kansas	Nevada	Quebec
Alaska	Kentucky	New Hampshire	Rhode Island
Arizona	Louisiana	New Jersey	South Carolina
Arkansas	Maine	New Mexico	Southern California
British Columbia	Maritime Provinces	Metro New York	Tennessee
Colorado	Maryland &	Upstate New York	Texas
Connecticut	Delaware	North Carolina	Utah
Dakotas	Massachusetts	Northern California	Vermont
Florida	Michigan	Ohio	Virginia
Georgia	Minnesota	Oklahoma	Washington, D.C.
Hawaii	Mississippi	Oregon	West Virginia
Idaho	Missouri	Pennsylvania	Wisconsin
Indiana	Montana	Philadelphia	Wyoming
Iowa	Nebraska	Puerto Rico	

**To order call 800-243-0495
or visit www.GlobePequot.com**